DEPRESSION
AND
DICTATORSHIP

DEPRESSION
AND
DICTATORSHIP

INTRODUCTION BY

ASA BRIGGS

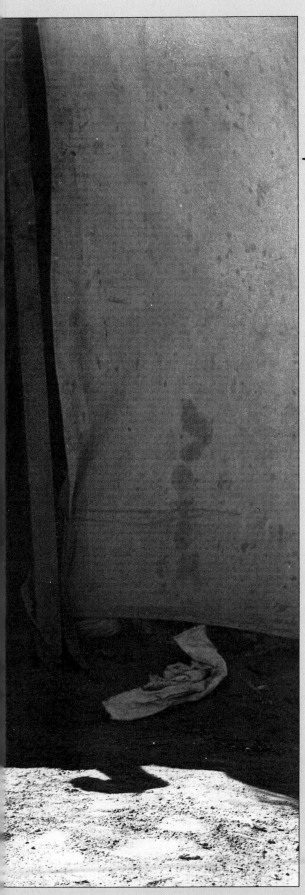

HAMLYN

Project editor Peter Furtado

Project art editor Ayala Kingsley

Text editors Robert Peberdy, Mike March, Sue Martin

Cartographic manager Olive Pearson

Cartographic editor Zoë Goodwin

Designers Frankie Wood, Janet McCallum, Wolfgang Mezger, Gill Mouqué, Niki Overy, Linda Reed, Nicholas Rous, Tony de Saulles, Dave Sumner, Rita Wütrych

Picture research manager Alison Renney

Picture research Jan Croot, Diane Hamilton, Rebecca Hirsh, Angela Murphy, Diana Phillips, Linda Proud, Christine Vincent, Charlotte Ward-Perkins

Editorial assistants Elaine Welsh, Monica Byles

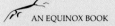

AN EQUINOX BOOK

© Andromeda Oxford Ltd 1993

Devised and produced by
Andromeda Oxford Ltd
11–15 The Vineyard
Abingdon Oxfordshire OX14 3PX
England

This edition published by
Hamlyn, part of Reed
Consumer Books Ltd,
Michelin House,
81 Fulham Road,
London SW3 6RB

ISBN 0-600-57992-1

Printed in Germany by
Mohndruck Graphische Betriebe
GmbH. Gutersloh.

ADVISORY EDITORS

Alan Borg
Imperial War Museum,
London

Asa Briggs
Worcester College, Oxford

Carlo Cipolla
University of California,
Berkeley, USA

Sir Napier Crookenden
Formerly Lieutenant of Her
Majesty's Tower of London

Andrew J. Goodpaster
US Army (retired)

Wolfgang Krieger
Ebenhausen, Germany

David Landes
Harvard University, USA

William McNeill
University of Chicago, USA

Peter Pulzer
All Souls College, Oxford

**Hartmut Pogge von
Strandmann**
University College, Oxford

Philip Waller
Merton College, Oxford

Geoffrey Warner
Open University

M.L.H.L. Weaver
Linacre College, Oxford

Charles Webster
All Souls College, Oxford

EDITORS

John Campbell
Freelance writer, London

John Harriss
London School of
Economics

Richard Maltby
University of Exeter

C. S. Nicholls
St Antony's College, Oxford

Sidney Pollard
Formerly of University of
Bielefeld, Germany

J. M. Winter
Pembroke College,
Cambridge

CONTRIBUTORS

Gerold Ambrosius
University of Bremen,
Germany

Duncan Anderson
Royal Military Academy,
Sandhurst

Ian Beckett
Royal Military Academy,
Sandhurst

Geoffrey Best
Formerly of University of
Sussex

Robert Bideleux
University of Swansea

Simon Boughey
Corpus Christi College,
Cambridge

Gail Braybon
Freelance writer

Sir Julian Bullard
All Souls College, Oxford

Kathleen Burk
Imperial College, London

Angus Calder
Open University

Peter Carey
Trinity College, Oxford

Jane Carmichael
Imperial War Museum,
London

Malcolm Cooper
Formerly of Newfoundland
University, Canada

P. L. Cottrell
University of Leicester

Robert Dare
University of Adelaide,
Australia

Martin Dean
Formerly of University of
Cambridge

Anne Deighton
University of Reading

John Erickson
University of Edinburgh

David Fletcher
The Tank Museum,
Wareham

CONTENTS

James Foreman-Peck
University of Hull
Brian Foss
Freelance writer
Michael Geyer
University of Chicago, USA
Robert Gildea
Merton College, Oxford
Anthony Glees
Brunel University
Roger Griffin
Oxford Polytechnic
Jennifer Hargreaves
Roehampton Institute,
London
Nathaniel Harris
Freelance writer
Nigel Harris
University College, London
Gundi Harriss
Birkbeck College, London
David Horn
University of Liverpool

Julian Jackson
University College of
Swansea
Keith Jeffrey
University of Ulster
Matthew Jones
St Antony's College, Oxford
Paul Kennedy
Yale University, USA
Ghislaine Lawrence
National Museum of Science
and Industry, London
Peter Lowe
University of Manchester
Keith Lyons
London School of
Economics
Dermott MacCann
Brunel University
Peter Martland
Corpus Christi College,
Cambridge
Roger Morgan
London School of
Economics

Lucy Newton
Leicester University
A. J. Nicholls
St Antony's College, Oxford
David Penn
Imperial War Museum,
London
Brian Holden Reid
King's College, London
Catherine Reilly
Freelance writer
Denis Ridgeway
Formerly of Royal Navy
Scientific Service
Gowher Rizvi
University of Warwick
Keith Sainsbury
University of Reading
Harry Shukman
St Antony's College, Oxford
Penny Sparke
Royal College of Art,
London
Jill Stephenson
University of Edinburgh

Stanley Trapido
Lincoln College, Oxford
T.H.E. Travers
University of Calgary,
Canada
S.B. Whitmore
Formerly British Army of
the Rhine, Germany
Paul Wilkinson
University of Aberdeen
Elizabeth Wilson
North London Polytechnic
Roger Zetter
Oxford Polytechnic

CARTOGRAPHIC
ADVISORS
Colin Bruce
Imperial College, London
John Pimlott
Royal Military Academy,
Sandhurst

INTRODUCTION

The adjective "great", once applied to World War I, a "war to end wars", was soon applied to the unprecedented international economic depression that began in 1929. It was a depression with implications that were political, cultural and ultimately military, as well as economic; for in retrospect it served as the prelude to World War II, which began in the Far East with the invasion of China by Japan in 1937, and in Europe in September 1939. Recovery from the depression was in many countries strictly limited and owed more to expenditure on rearmament than to any other factor. National Socialist Germany eliminated unemployment, the greatest human problem of the Great Depression, but at an intolerable cost; for mass employment was secured by the preparation for war, and war would bring desolation and holocaust.

One of the most familiar words of the 1930s was "crisis", and this was a label which was used first in relation to the economic crisis, triggered off by an unprecedented financial crash on New York's Wall Street financial district. On "Black Thursday", 24 October 1929, nearly thirteen million shares were sold on the American Stock Exchange and prices fell faster than on any other day in history. The ramifications were widespread, both national and international. In the United States industrial output fell sharply, farming languished, and unemployment rose to a figure of nearly five million in 1930. By 1933 13 million people were unemployed. What had begun with a run on the banks ended with bread lines in the streets.

The world divided by crisis

The financial crisis led immediately to demands for the repayment of American loans overseas, and this in turn produced credit crises in other countries and a sharp decline in the volume of international trade. Between 1929 and 1933 world output of goods fell by an estimated thirty-eight percent.

International depression spread to rich and poor countries alike. Britain, which had not been as prosperous as the United States had when the Wall Street financial crash hit the headlines, went into a slump worse than any that the country had ever experienced before. Desperate measures were tried to deal with the crisis: in 1931 it abandoned the gold standard and the following year it set aside the long-cherished gospel of free trade. In the winter of 1932–33 almost three million people in Britain were unemployed, a quarter of the insured population.

In Germany unemployment was even more serious. In the grim winter of 1931–32 it reached a record figure of more than six million. The size of such figures was bound to lead to demands for government action, usually national action. Economics and politics could not be kept apart.

International agreement on a policy for recovery was impossible, and in an increasingly divided world the political responses varied significantly from country to country. So, too, did the ideological reactions, for experience of depression reinforced strongly held opinions. The left, divided between communists and socialists, regarded capitalism as doomed. The right, divided between conservatives and fascists, sought to strengthen national feeling and the interests that sustained it against the dangers of revolutionary insurrection. The Germans talked of *Blut und Boden*, blood and soil. Yet the ideologies were not concerned solely with economics and politics: they encompassed literature and the arts. Works of art, music, paintings and sculpture, were judged in terms of political commitment. There was a pressure everywhere to take sides, a pressure felt most strongly during the Spanish Civil War which began in July 1936 and ended on April 1939 with a fascist victory, less than six months before a European war began. Germans, Italians, Russians, Frenchmen and Britons – artists, intellectuals, soldiers and common men alike – went to Spain to fight on one side or the other.

In the United States the Democratic candidate, Franklin D. Roosevelt, who was elected president in 1932 with a landslide majority, offered a New Deal which incorporated public works, power development and farm betterment programs as well as unemployment relief. The New Deal was designed not to destroy capitalism but to save it through government effort and investment, and it too had a cultural side. Artists and photographers were commissioned *en masse* to celebrate and decorate their nation. Roosevelt took office for the second time in 1936 with an even greater majority than that of 1932. In Britain the second Labour government was elected in 1929, a minority government like the first Labour administration of 1924. It fell in August 1931, although the new "National Government" retained the same prime minister, Ramsay MacDonald. The new government also won a landslide victory at the general election later that year, but it had no program comparable to the New Deal. By 1935 there were signs of recovery (from *Bleak House* to *Great Expectations*, as Neville Chamberlain, the chancellor of the exchequer, put it) and in that year the government won a new general election with a reduced majority and a different prime minister, Stanley Baldwin, a man who disliked totalitarian regimes of all kinds. In 1938 he was succeeded by Neville Chamberlain who was willing to appease the dictators, as they were usually called, Hitler and Mussolini.

The Soviet Union, because of its economic and political system, did not acknowledge the existence of unemployment, nor did it acknowledge that Stalin was as much of a dictator as Hitler or Mussolini. Its first two Five-Year Plans, each of which achieved a doubling of industrial output, were ruthlessly implemented, but were held up for world approval and attracted much favorable attention in Britain and in France. In the United States business critics of Roosevelt complained that the New Deal bore "a Soviet seal endorsed by a Moscow hand", though Roosevelt himself did not look to Russia for his model for economic recovery by state intervention.

Conflict between left and right

Stalin's political maneuvers inside the Soviet Union were as devious as ever, and the 1930s was a decade of mysterious purges and much publicized state trials. Critics of the regime were dispatched either to Siberia or to death. Stalin proved that he could maneuver in his foreign policy also. In 1934 the Soviet Union joined the League of Nations. In 1936 it was backing "popular fronts" to resist fascism wherever they could be formed. No other European country copied a Stalinist Five-Year Plan, but in 1936 a Popular Front government, headed by the socialist Léon Blum, took office in France and embarked

▶ **Building the Grand Coulee Dam, USA, 1937.**

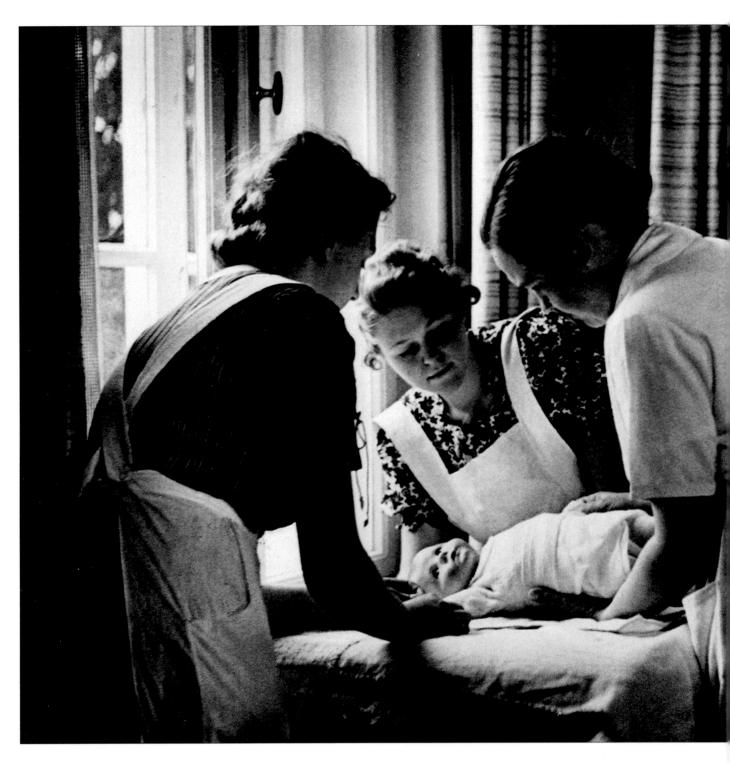

upon public works schemes, devalued the franc, raised money wages and introduced a 40–hour week. It met with increasing business opposition and fell from office after nine months of bitter controversy.

Germany's fortunes were very different during the 1930s, and all other countries had to take account of them. Faced with the problems of the Great Depression in 1929 and 1930, the German Chancellor, Heinrich Brüning, had lost the support of parliament and had governed by emergency decrees and exchange control; and when Hitler became chancellor in January 1933 it was as a result of political maneuvering on the part of other parliamentary parties. A corporal during World War I, Hitler was handed the chancellorship by Germany's president, the most famous of its World War I heroes, Field Marshal von Hindenburg. The National Socialist party by then had won 196 seats in parliament, but they were only 196 out of 584. New elections were held, and during the run-up to them the Reichstag, the parliament building, was burnt down. Hitler alleged a Communist plot and a man was charged. The National Socialists now won 288 seas out of 647 in the subsequent elections.

The Communist party, still bitterly divided from the leftist Social Democrats, was now declared illegal, and an Enabling Bill was passed which gave Hitler dictatorial powers which he retained until his death in 1945. Soon all other parties disappeared too, and the leadership even of the National Soocialist (Nazi) party was drastically purged in June 1934. The pre-Hitler government bureaucracy remained and supported him. So too for the most part did the army. Freedom was lost,

both from the transformed League of Nations and from the World Disarmament Conference which had first met in February 1932. In October 1935, however, Mussolini, the Fascist dictator of Italy, prepared the stage for the naked militarism of the late 1930s, when his troops invaded Abyssinia. The League of Nations tried to apply economic sanctions, but the attempt to restrain Italy failed (the sanctions were withdrawn in July 1936) and the main effect of the crisis was to draw more closely together National Socialist Germany and Fascist Italy in what came to be called the Berlin–Rome axis.

In March 1936 German troops entered the Rhineland, a demilitarized zone under the terms of the World War I settlement, thereby in one move repudiating both the treaties of Versailles and Locarno. Then in March 1938 Austria was annexed. German troops could now mass along the borders of Czechoslovakia, economically and politically the most successful of all the new nation states created at Versailles in 1919. There was a large German minority in the Sudetenland, the northwestern part of Czechoslovakia, and their interests could provide a pretext for intervention.

In case of a German attack, France and the Soviet Union, who had entered into alliance in May 1935, were pledged to go to the aid of the Czechs, but the alliance did not prove effective and in September 1938 under pressure from Britain and France, the Czechs were forced to yield to German territorial demands. Hitler promised Neville Chamberlain that these were his last territorial demands in Europe. Czechoslovakia was divided and weakened, while Chamberlain, cheered by London crowds when he flew back to London from a second visit to meet Hitler, claimed that he had brought back "peace in our time". He even carried with him a document to prove it. There was opposition in both France and Germany to the so-called policies of appeasing the dictators, but there was a greater public sense of relief than of foreboding when war was avoided. The relief did not last, however, for in March 1939 the Czech provinces of Bohemia and Moravia were also occupied, and Hitler turned his attention to Poland, where he provoked the final interwar crisis centering on Danzig (Gdansk) in the summer of 1939.

Not all the crises of the 1930s were in Europe. Abyssinia was an African kingdom which suddenly hit the headlines. Further away from Europe, in the "Far East", as it was still usually called, Japan had attacked northern China in 1931 and in 1932 had set up a puppet state in Manchuria called Manzhouguo, reinstating the deposed Manchu emperor of China. A year later, branded an aggressor, Japan left the League of Nations. In 1936 it signed an anti-Comintern Pact with Germany, and in 1937 once more attacked China, capturing Nanjing, then the capital Beijing and, later, Canton. Its declared aim was to create a "greater East Asia Coprosperity Sphere", though in practise this was an empire solely of benefit to the Japanese. The Berlin–Rome–Tokyo axis survived Hitler's pact with Stalin in 1939, even though the pact was to be broken when Hitler invaded Russia on 22 June 1941 and the Japanese bombed the American fleet at Pearl Harbor on 7 December, propelling the United States into what thereby became a world war.

In retrospect, though, the 20th-century revolution in physics was even more decisive than diplomacy or ideology. The 1930s saw the key advances in nuclear physics that were to unlock the power of the atom, a development that would shape world history for decades to come. The race to unravel the secret of the atom involved all the countries that would take a leading role in World War II.

propaganda reigned. An ideology of race, unscientific in argument and content, was expounded which proclaimed Aryan superiority. It involved the total elimination of Jews from national life and as its final, tacit objective their extermination. One of the most distinguished Jews to join in a great exodus from Germany and later from Austria was the scientist, Albert Einstein, whose theory of relativity was a triumph of 20th-century physics. Another was Sigmund Freud, whose new psychology had created what the English poet Auden called a completely new "climate of opinion".

The approach of war

Most of the international crises of the 1930s involved Hitler's Germany, which in October 1933 withdrew at the same time

THE
TOTALITARIAN
THREAT

Time Chart

	1930	1931	1932	1933	1934	1935	1936	1937
Europe/Mediterranean	• Jan: End of Primo de Rivera's dictatorship in Spain • 1 Jul: Last Allied troops withdrew from German Rhineland	• 14 Apr: King Alfonso XIII left Spain, in face of rising Republicanism • Sep: Yugoslavia adopted new constitution, ending King Alexander's royal dictatorship • Dec: Spain became a republic, with Alcalá Zamora as its 1st president, Manuel Azaña as prime minister	• Feb: Protective tariffs introduced in UK, ending free trade • May: Assassination of French president, Paul Doumer • Jul: Elections made Nazi Party largest in German Reichstag (parliament) • 5 Jul: António de Oliveira Salazar made Portuguese prime minister, with virtual dictatorial powers	• Spanish Fascist party, Falange, founded by Jose Antonio Primo de Rivera (son of former dictator) • 30 Jan: Hitler became German chancellor, at request of President von Hindenburg • Mar: Parliamentary government suspended in Austria, by Chancellor Engelbert Dollfuss • 14 Jul: Germany became 1-party state	• Feb: Signature of Balkan Pact • 17 Mar: Rome Protocols signed • 29–30 Jun: Night of the Long Knives (Ger) • 25 Jul: Assassination of Chancellor Dollfuss by Austrian Nazis • Aug: Adopting title of Führer, Hitler abolished German presidency • Dec: Start of Stalinist purges in USSR	• Mar: Saar Basin returned to Germany; Hitler announced German rearmament, repudiating disarmament clauses of Treaty of Versailles • 15 Sep: Nuremberg Laws in Germany, legitimizing anti-semitism • Nov: Restoration of Greek monarchy by plebiscite (King George II)	• Mar: Germany reoccupied Rhineland • Jun: 1st Popular Front government (Fr) • 18 Jul: Start of Spanish Civil War. Oct: General Francisco Franco led provisional Nationalist government • Aug: Gen. Joannis Metaxas, dictator of Greece (to Jan 1941) • October: Berlin–Rome Axis established • 10 Dec: Abdication of King Edward VIII (UK)	• 1 Jan: Public Order Act came into force in UK, banning political uniforms and private armies • 27 Apr: Undefended Basque capital of Guernica destroyed by Nazi aerial bombing (Sp) • Jun: Irish Free State renamed Eire, when new constitution as dominion within Commonwealth came into force
The Middle East	• Mar: Beginning of active civil disobedience campaign by Gandhi in India, with breaking of salt tax laws • May: Syria granted constitution by France	• Universal suffrage introduced in UK colony of Ceylon • Sep–Dec: 2nd Round Table talks on India held in UK, attended by Gandhi • Dec: Conference in Jerusalem (Pal) attended by 22 Muslim nations; warning against Zionism issued	• Sep: Imprisoned in India, Gandhi fasted to improve political status of Harijans (untouchables) • 20 Sep: King Ibn Saud created Saudi Arabia from his lands of Nejd and Hejaz • Oct: Iraq achieved full independence from UK on entry to League of Nations	• First Saudi Arabian oil concession made to Standard Oil Co. of California (US) • Murder of Afghan king, Nadir Khan, succeeded by son, Mohammed Zahir	• Mohammed Ali Jinnah returned to India, to lead new Muslim League Party • Jan: Libya formed by union of Cyrenaica and Tripolitania, with Fezza • Nov: French rejected Young Moroccan nationalists' reforms • Dec: Turkish women granted vote	• Persia officially renamed Iran • 2 Aug: UK Government of India Act proposed federation and provincial autonomy • Nov: Arab parties in Palestine demanded end to Jewish immigration (from 30,000 in 1933 to 61,000 in 1935)	• Apr: King Farouk succeeded his father to Egyptian throne • Apr: Start of Arab rebellion in Palestine (to 1939); formation of secret Jewish force, Haganah • Aug: Anglo-Egyptian Treaty agreed withdrawal of UK forces, except from Suez Canal Zone	• Jan–Feb: 1st general elections in India • 7 Jul: Peel Report in UK recommended partition of Palestine into Arab and Jewish states • 9 Jul: Pact of Saadabad (Tur, Irq, Irn, Afg) for nonaggression
Africa	• May: White women given vote in S Africa • 2 Nov: Makonnen Tafari crowned Emperor Haile Selassie of Ethiopia			• Coalition government formed in S Africa by Hertzog's segregationalist Nationalist Party and Smuts' S African Party	• DF Malan formed Purified Nationalist Party (S Afr) • 5 Dec: Clashes on borders of Ethiopia and Italian Somaliland	• 3 Oct: Ethiopia invaded by Italian troops	• Segregation extended (S Afr) • May: Addis Ababa captured; Ethiopia merged with Italian Somaliland and Eritrea to form Italian E Africa	
The Americas	• Getúlio Vargas came to power after revolt in Brazil (to 1945) • Feb: General Rafael Trujillo began 31-year dictatorship, Dominican Republic • Jul: Richard Bennett became prime minister of Conservative government in Canada • Dec: US President Hoover presented unemployment relief program to Congress		• Jul: War broke out between Paraguay and Bolivia over Chaco Boreal	• US marines withdrawn from Nicaragua (since 1917) • Mar–Jun: New Deal program: Creation of numerous welfare and unemployment agencies by Franklin D Roosevelt, following his inauguration as 32nd US president • Nov: US–USSR diplomatic and trade relations resumed, after 14 years	• General Lázaro Cárdenas became president of Mexico, instituting program of social reform (to 1940) • Jun: Reciprocal Tariff Act improved US overseas trade relations • Jun: US–Cuban treaty abrogated enforcement of Platt Amendment	• Start of Roosevelt's 2nd New Deal program • Jun: Armistice ended Chaco War between Bolivia and Paraguay • Oct: Liberal Party reelected in Canada • 17 Dec: Death of General Gómez in Venezuela, ending 26-year dictatorship	• 1–23 Dec: Inter-American Conference for Maintenance of Peace	• 1 Jan: General Anastazio García became president of Nicaragua; start of family's dictatorship
Asia and Pacific	• Nov: Assassination of Japanese prime minister, Hamaguchi • Dec: Launch of 1st Kuomintang campaign against Chinese communist bases (Soviets)	• New Zealand National Party formed, from United and Reform parties • 18 Sep: Start of Japanese occupation of Manchuria (NE China) • Oct: Chinese Soviet republic proclaimed by Mao Zedong, in Kiangsi province	• 18 Feb: Japanese puppet state of Manchukuo established in Manchuria • May: End to party government in Japan after assassination of Prime Minister Inukai • Jun: Coup in Siam led to constitutional government	• Feb: League of Nations' censureship over Manchukuo led to Japan's withdrawal from organization • Apr: Western Australians voted 2:1 to secede from Commonwealth; move rejected by UK government	• Mar: Philippines granted autonomy and president by US Tydings–McDuffie Act with US high commissioner retaining some rights • Oct: Long March began, as Communists broke through Nationalist encirclement of Kiangsi Soviet (China)	• 1st New Zealand Labor government elected • Oct: End of Long March, as Communists reached Yenan, N Shensi (China) • Nov: Manuel Quezon became 1st president of Commonwealth of Philippines	• Feb: Failure of coup by military extremists in Japan; power of central faction consolidated • Dec: In China, Jiang Jieshi kidnapped by communists to force nationalist–communist front against Japan	• China signed nonaggression pact with USSR • 7 Jul–23 Nov: Japanese occupation of NE and E China
World	• Worldwide unemployment as Depression took effect • 21 Jan–22 Apr: London Naval Conference; treaty limited size and number of warships and submarines (UK, US, Jap)	• 11 Dec: Statute of Westminster: Dominions (Can, Aus, NZ, S Afr, Irish Free State, Newfoundland) defined as autonomous and equal in status within Commonwealth of Nations	• Feb: League of Nations disarmament talks, Geneva (Sui); no agreement reached • 21 Jul–20 Aug: Imperial Economic Conference in Ottawa (Can)	• Jun–Jul: World Monetary and Economic Conference held in UK; no consensus reached • Oct: Germany withdrew from Geneva disarmament talks and League of Nations	• Sep: USSR joined League of Nations	• 18 Nov: League of Nations imposed economic sanctions on Italy following its invasion of Ethiopia	• Jul: League's sanctions against Italy suspended, despite its annexation of Ethiopia • 25 Nov: German–Japanese Anti-Comintern Pact against international communism	• Nov: Italy joined Anti-Comintern Pact • 11 Nov: Italy withdrew from League of Nations

12

1938	1939
• 1–13 Mar: German military occupation of Austria; *Anschluss* (union) proclaimed • 30 Sep: Munich Agreement (UK, Ger, Fr, Ita); led to German annexation of Sudeten region (Tch) • 9–10 Nov: *Kristallnacht* pogrom in Germany	• Mar: End of Spanish civil war • 6 Apr: Mutual assistance pact (Pol, Fr, UK) • 22 May: Italo–German Pact of Steel • 24 Aug: Non-aggression pact between USSR and Germany • 1 Sep: German invasion of Poland. • 3 Sep: UK and France declared war on Germany; start of World War II
• Wafd government of Nahas Pasha ousted by King Farouk (Egy) • Nov: Death of Mustafa Kemal (Atatürk); Ismet Inönü succeeded him as president of Turkey	• Oct: Turkey signed mutual assistance pact with UK and France
• Popular Front government in Chile established by President Aguirre Cerda (to 1941), led to social reform • Mar: In Mexico, expropriation of US and UK oil companies in dispute over wages and conditions • 9–27 Dec: Declaration of Lima; 8th Pan-American Conference confirmed North–South solidarity	• 5 Sep: US neutrality announced at outbreak of WWII
• In New Zealand Social Security Act provided state medical service	• National conscription ordinance in Japan • Jun: Siam officially renamed Prathet Thai, 'land of the free' • 3 Sep: Australia and New Zealand declared war on Germany
• 30 Apr: Switzerland requested unconditional neutrality at League of Nations	

"*...the well-being of our people is obviously in firm hands!*"

NIKITA KHRUSHCHEV on Stalin, 1930

"*Never forget this, comrades, and repeat it a hundred times a day so that you will say it in your dreams: 'The Jews are to blame. They will never escape the judgment they deserve.'* "

JOSEPH GOEBBELS, 1932

"*JEWISH FAMILIES SEEK SAFETY IN CONCENTRATION CAMPS*"

BRITISH NEWSPAPER HEADLINE, 1933

"*We have no territorial demands to make in Europe. We are aware, above all, that all the causes of tension which arise as a result either of faulty territorial provisions or of a disproportion between the size of populations and their living space cannot be solved by means of war in Europe.*"

ADOLF HITLER, 1936

"*Although we must discount the exuberant petulance of Mussolini's language, it is evident that he is determined in the end to secure the triumph of 'Might against right'.*"

HAROLD NICHOLSON, 1937

"*Nothing is more dangerous than an idea, when a man has only one idea.*"

ALAIN, 1938

"*...behind political problems, there are always psychological problems , and these are always more difficult to handle.*"

J. NEHRU, 1939

"*Germany is controlled by one man, Herr Hitler, whose will is supreme and who is a blend of fanatic madman and clear visioned realist and who regards Germany's supremacy in Europe as a step towards world supremacy....all our sources are at one in declaring that he is barely sane...*"

GLADWYN JEBB, 1939

"*I would...say that...he (Hitler) would be as likely to keep it [his word] as any other foreign statesman – under certain conditions probably more so.*"

N. HENDERSON (British ambassador in Berlin), 1939

Datafile

The Great Depression was at once a product of the dislocation of the world economy caused by World War I and a major contribution to the destabilization of world politics which caused World War II. The Great War had broken networks of international trade, forced industrial economies down dangerous corners of change, and artificially altered the balance between victor and vanquished. Recovery was an unstable process, attended by hot-house growth and massive speculation, and by the late 1920s the entire international economy was in a state of volatile disequilibrium, which required only the collapse of the US stock market to push it into longterm depression. The Depression, attended by mass unemployment and material shortages, inevitably produced political change. As traditional forms of government grappled ineffectually with huge problems, electors turned increasingly to advocates of strong government and radical political solutions. By the time the world economy began to recover, preparations for war were already well underway.

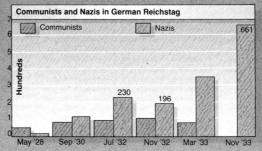
Communists and Nazis in German Reichstag

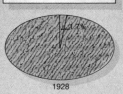
Jewish immigration into Palestine

◄ In Germany, the Communist and National Socialist (Nazi) parties presented rival solutions to the nation's problems. Although the Communists began with the political advantage, their rigid adherance to Moscow left them vulnerable to the popular nationalism that was being preached by Hitler.

▼ ▼ Between 1928 and 1940 the state-imposed policy of collectivization changed the face of Soviet agriculture, replacing small individual peasant holdings with large communal farms. The economic results were impressive but the human cost was high as a traditional way of life was destroyed and opposition ruthlessly suppressed.

▼ US domination of the world industrial scene was damaged by the Great Depression (which hit the American economy more heavily than many of its competitors) and by renewed competition. Particularly significant in the latter regard were Germany, reasserting its strength under new leadership, and the USSR.

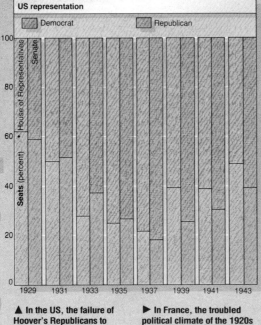
US representation

▲ Jewish immigration into Palestine rose dramatically in the 1930s as political persecution and economic difficulties drove many out of Europe in search of a fresh start in a new national homeland. The war rudely interrupted the migration, but with the return of peace those fortunate enough to survive genocide flooded towards Palestine.

Soviet collectives

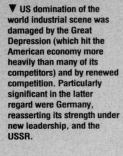
Manufacturing output

1928

1938

 USA
 Germany
UK
France
USSR
Italy
Others

▲ In the US, the failure of Hoover's Republicans to provide solutions to economic crisis, the Democrats under the banner of Roosevelt's "New Deal", produced a transformation of the political balance.

US Presidents
1929 H Hoover R
1933 FD Roosevelt D
1937 FD Roosevelt D
1941 FD Roosevelt D

▶ In France, the troubled political climate of the 1920s produced heavy polarization, with the traditional radical, socialist and republican parties losing ground to Communist and rightwing extremists. The resulting governments were neither stable nor effective and France entered World War II in a state of political division and low morale.

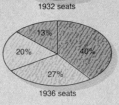
French elections

1932 seats

1936 seats

Radical Socialist
Socialist
Republican
Left Republican
Radical independent
Center party/Right Wing
Communist

Soviet collectivization

1928

1932

1940

Households collectivized
Other farm households

POLITICS OF THE DEPRESSION

At the beginning of 1929 the world seemed to be dominated by democratic states with political systems that were liberal in character. The only major exceptions were Italy and the Soviet Union. Among the democracies, the United States was by far the most powerful and the wealthiest. In March 1929 the new US president Herbert Hoover promised a "new day" that would bring more progress towards prosperity. Seven months later, on 24 October, the Wall Street stock market collapsed and a catastrophic slump led to widespread bankruptcy and unemployment both at home and abroad. Yet, despite widespread impoverishment and insecurity, the American people continued to support the traditional Republican and Democratic parties.

Franklin Delano Roosevelt, a Democrat who succeeded Hoover as president in 1933, had been an energetic governor of New York state, introducing social reforms and state relief for victims of the slump. Roosevelt demanded from Congress the same powers to deal with the economic emergency as would be granted to him in a war against a foreign invader. Inaugurated on 4 March, he at once closed all banks and sum-

moned an emergency sitting of Congress to enact new banking legislation. In the following months, Roosevelt rushed through a mass of relief measures for agriculture and the unemployed, including the establishment of a Civilian Conservation Corps for environmental protection and a Federal Emergency Relief Administration. His National Recovery Act, passed on 16 June 1933, enabled federal agencies to regulate pricing arrangements and conditions of work in order to halt the deflationary spiral and increase employment. By 1934 unemployment was falling, bank reserves were rising and bankruptcies were in decline.

However, despite Roosevelt's New Deal, as he called it, the US economy remained depressed compared with how it had been in 1928. In 1935 Roosevelt secured an Emergency Relief Appropriation of nearly five billion dollars, which was channeled through a new agency, the Works Progress Administration, to create more work. The Social Security Act of June 1935 provided federal funds for the handicapped and the poor, and a system for unemployment insurance.

In his foreign policy, Roosevelt was an isola-

▼ **A world out of work.** The financial crisis of 1929 produced a massive business slump, condemning millions to unemployment. The bewildered workforce supported any leader who promised to restore pride and prosperity. In the United States this produced Roosevelt and the New Deal, but in Germany it brought in Hitler.

tionist. Although he recognized the threat to peace posed by Nazi Germany, he refused to allow the United States to become entangled in European affairs, preferring to concentrate on solving the domestic crisis. In August 1935 Congress passed the Neutrality Act, forbidding the United States to supply arms to belligerent countries. Roosevelt himself publicly boasted of American non-involvement in European conflicts.

The end of German democracy

By 1928, Adolf Hitler was the undisputed leader of racialist, intransigent anti-republicanism in Germany. However, in the elections to the Reichstag (German parliament) held in that year, his Nazi party gained only 12 seats. On 9 July 1929 the leader of the German National People's party, Hugenberg, set up a committee to oppose the Young Plan, a revised reparations payments scheme, by organizing a plebiscite to condemn as traitors politicians who accepted such a scheme. Hitler's participation in the campaign gave the Nazis good publicity through Hugenberg's syn-

dicated newspapers. Although the campaign failed, the Nazis benefited from it and lost none of their independence.

After the US stock-market crash had crippled the German economy, the republican coalition government faced a crisis over unemployment benefit, forcing socialist chancellor Hermann Müller to resign his office. His successor, Heinrich Brüning, invoked emergency powers to rule without a parliamentary majority, but was forced to dissolve the Reichstag and hold fresh elections. These gave Hitler's Nazis a gain of 107 seats, second only to the Social Democrats. The Nazi party appealed to nearly all sections of society, except for Roman Catholics and unionized industrial workers. In particular, the vote of smaller middle-class parties collapsed, as their supporters deserted to the Nazis.

To meet Germany's deepening economic crisis Brüning imposed austerity measures that forced many firms to close. As unemployment rose to five million in February 1931 and six million in February 1932, support for the Nazis grew. On 10 April 1932 Hitler stood as presidential candidate against Hindenburg, and though he was defeated, he gained over thirteen million votes. At the Reichstag elections held on 31 July of that year the Nazis received 37.4 per cent of the votes cast and became the largest party with 230 seats. Apart from the Communists and Social Democrats, most parties were willing to compromise with the Nazis if Hitler would accept a subordinate role. However, he refused, even after further elections in November showed a drop in Nazi support. By this time the official and propertied classes in Germany, who had hoped to use Hitler but contain him within a government of the right, were seriously alarmed. Franz von Papen, who had succeeded Brüning, was replaced by the army leader General Kurt von Schleicher, but he too failed to resolve the crisis and came under pressure from his military colleagues, who disliked the army becoming involved in politics.

▶ The pageantry of power. Hitler, like other rightwing dictators, made extensive use of paramilitary displays, uniforms and banners to underpin his grasp on power. To the dispirited people of Germany the Nazis promised the rebirth of a nation.

◀▶ The political parties of the 1930s made extensive use of the cartoon to attack their opponents and put across their own message. Some cartoons were grim and austere in their approach, others were flippant and amusing. To German Communists Hitler was an oppressor of the working class, enslaving it in the service of capitalism and militarism (left) – a view not always shared by the millions who regained employment, prosperity and a sense of national worth under the Nazi regime. European governments were too easily deluded by Hitler's love of display and histrionics, and even perceptive British cartoonists portrayed him as a bloated demagog with no firm grasp on his people's loyalties (right).

Conflict in Palestine

British colonialism faced intractable problems in Palestine, where tensions were growing between Arab inhabitants and an increasing number of Jewish settlers fleeing from persecution in Europe. In 1935 there were 65,000 new arrivals – double the figure for 1933. In December 1935 the British proposed a mixed legislative council for Palestine, but this was rejected by the Zionists because Jews would have considerably fewer representatives than Arabs. The Palestinian Arabs reacted strongly. Led by the Mufti of Jerusalem, Amin al-Husaini, they organized a strike which lasted from April to October 1936 and was accompanied by serious violence. With no prospect of a compromise settlement, the intensification of racialist pressure on Jewish communities in Europe and the ever-growing numbers of Jewish immigrants from Europe meant that the situation was bound to grow worse.

▶ A visionary Jewish settlement of the 1920s.

ALL BLOWN UP AND NOWHERE TO GO

Hitler

Hitler's Third Reich

To fill the political vacuum, Hitler was called to office as chancellor on 30 January 1933. Hindenburg and his advisers still believed that Hitler could be controlled by experienced cabinet colleagues like von Papen and Hugenberg.

On 28 February 1933 Hitler accused the Communists of setting fire to the Reichstag building and obtained a presidential decree giving the government emergency powers to deal with subversion. This decree remained in force throughout the Third Reich, as the Nazi dictatorship was known, and enabled the Nazis to arrest or silence countless political opponents.

On 5 March, at a further Reichstag election, which was marked by officially sanctioned intimidation, Hitler gained less than forty–four percent of the vote. However, thanks to his nationalist allies and the arrest of Communist deputies before parliament assembled, on 24 March he succeeded in passing an enabling law giving the government the power to rule by decree. Germany's reign of democracy was at an end. On 2 May 1933 the Nazis abolished trade unions and on 14 July declared Germany a one-party state. They reduced the Reichstag to a rubber stamp and on 30 January 1934 abolished individual state (*Land*) parliaments.

Political opponents were held without trial, in concentration camps, tortured and sometimes murdered. The police were under Nazi control. The army was acquiescent, especially since Hitler promised large-scale rearmament. Ernst Röhm, the leader of the Nazi militia, the SA (*Sturm-Abteilung* or "stormtroops"), had himself hoped to take over the armed forces. However, the SA's unruly behavior had made them unpopular and on 30 June 1934 Hitler ordered Röhm's murder, a purge of the SA leadership and the liquidation of other political opponents. The SS (*Schutz Staffel*, or "defense squadron"), a Nazi elite force, carried out the killings on what became known as the "night of the long knives". To the German public, the eclipse of the SA seemed to herald a return to a more orderly method of government.

When President Hindenburg died on 2 August 1934 Hitler abolished the presidency and assumed dictatorial powers as Führer (leader). The army took an oath of allegiance to him on the same day. Hitler appointed Heinrich Himmler, who was head of the SS, to be in charge of the political police (Gestapo) in Germany and made the SS responsible for the concentration camps. The Hitler Youth movement and Dr Joseph Goebbels' Propaganda Ministry became increasingly important in preparing the German people for military struggle. In the autumn of 1936 a new four-year plan was announced under Hermann Göring's leadership, ostensibly to maximize economic self-sufficiency, but in reality to equip Germany for war by 1940.

Hitler's dictatorship was fascist and viciously antisemitic. It destroyed freedom of expression and denied parliamentary government and individual rights under the law. However, the Nazis did not threaten private property, except that belonging to Jews and political opponents,

▲ The 1930s saw massive construction activity in the Soviet Union, as Stalin attempted to provide the country with the necessary economic infrastructure for a modern power. The Ferghana canal, in the southeast of the country, was built after 1935 with no large earthmoving equipment.

The question is sometimes asked, whether it is not possible to reduce the tempo, to hold back the movement. No, it is not possible, comrades!... On the contrary, it is necessary to increase the tempo, our obligations to the workers and peasants of the USSR demand this of us.

JOSEPH STALIN 1929

and business profited under National Socialism (Nazism), especially since trade unions were abolished. Civil servants and army officers, too, welcomed the end of parliamentary democracy, some of them under the delusion that Germany was returning to the kind of authoritarian society it had been under the kaiser.

Stalin's "socialism in one country"

By 1928 the Comintern (Communist International) had become an instrument of Stalin's foreign policy rather than an organization to promote worldwide revolution. At its meeting in Moscow in the summer of that year, the Third Communist International decided that fascism was just a symptom of the last throes of capitalism, and that it was therefore not fascism that was now the main enemy, but the Western Social Democrats and Liberals who tried to prop up parliamentary regimes. However, by 1935, Stalin had changed the party line to call for anti-fascist coalitions of Communists, Socialists and Liberals.

Throughout this period Stalin's main preoccupation was his domestic policy—the building of "socialism in one country"—and, in particular, securing his own personal rule. Having already ousted Trotsky, he next isolated and eliminated his former rightwing allies, Bukharin, Rykov and Tomsky.

From 1928, Stalin began to press for radical measures to industrialize the Soviet Union, introducing strict, centralized controls and encouraging the development of grandiose invest-

ment schemes. His Five-Year Plan, which was presented to the 16th Communist party Conference in April 1929 but had already been in operation for six months, was designed to revolutionize the Russian economy.

By the end of 1932, when it was claimed that the plan had been fulfilled, industrial production had increased dramatically. Electricity output had more than doubled, coal production had risen from 34.5 million tons to 64.3 million, and pig iron from 3.3 million tons to 6.2 million. There were huge new industrial plants in the Urals, the Volga region and Soviet Central Asia. However, the rapid pace of industrialization led to much waste and confusion, and certain industries, such as textiles or craft industries, as well as the consumer, suffered badly. By 1933 there was a sharp decline in the growth of industrial production, which had officially been rising at 20 percent per annum since 1928, and it was clear that the original targets had been optimistic and counterproductive. The second Five-Year Plan, adopted in February 1934, was less ambitious, but it still envisaged more than doubling Soviet industrial production by 1937. Once again the greatest successes were in heavy industry and armaments and the biggest losers were the consumers.

The shortage of consumer goods discouraged the peasants from delivering grain to the towns, since the money they received for it could buy little of value. Often they preferred to hoard their grain or feed it to their animals, so that confiscation and forced deliveries became the main ways of obtaining food for the urban

The Popular Front in France

Until 1933, the Comintern had denounced socialists (after then Communist party members) everywhere as "social fascists", but by 1934 the French socialists had overcome their deep resentment of the Communists and joined them in a "popular front" against "fascism and war". After the Franco-Soviet pact of 1935 the "radical" middle-class party in France, led by Herriot and Daladier, offered their support to the front and agreed on a joint program with the socialists and Communists. The seventh Comintern congress, held in the summer of 1935, praised this union of left-wing parties as a model for antifascist action everywhere.

In 1936 the front won a majority in parliament. The socialist leader Léon Blum formed a new government, which the Communists supported but did not join. Indeed they continued to organize strikes against the government and attacked it for not intervening in the Spanish Civil War. Blum banned fascist organizations and introduced important reforms. These included a 40-hour working week, paid annual vacations and the nationalization of the armaments industries and the Bank of France. Measures such as devaluing the franc made little impression on unemployment, however, and the Popular Front government fell in April 1938, unable to win the parliamentary support needed to pay for its social reforms.

▶ Socialist leader Léon Blum in the 1930s.

population. The government accused the *kulaks* (literally "fists"), the richer peasants, of deliberately creating shortages by speculating and hoarding. In fact, the number of *kulaks* was much smaller than the propaganda suggested.

To overcome the problem of food shortages the government decided to rationalize production by collectivizing agriculture. In 1928 only 2.7 percent of arable land in the Soviet Union was controlled by collective or state farms. The other 97.3 per cent was tilled by individual peasants. On 5 January 1930 the Politburo decreed a program for the collectivization of most of the Soviet Union by 1933. Party cadres were sent into the countryside to implement the plan, which included the collectivization even of peasants' tools and domestic animals.

Many party activists believed in the Leninist concept of class war between the richer and poorer peasantry and that the latter would support collectivization. In fact, only the use of brutal repression could induce the peasantry to collectivize. The collectives themselves were chaotically organized. Peasants resisted by destroying their livestock. Between 1928 and 1932, the number of cattle in the Soviet Union fell by nearly 45 percent, and sheep, goats and pigs by about 60 percent. Even grain production, at which collectivization had been primarily aimed, fell sharply and did not regain the already poor levels of 1928 until 1935.

Collectivization, however, succeeded in its objective of bringing grain production under government control. In 1933 agricultural produce was exported to finance the five-year plans despite widespread famine at home. By 1934 over 70 percent of peasant households had been collectivized, and 87 percent of the crop area was in collective farms. But this had been achieved only by the use of brutality and repression.

To consolidate his own position after the fiasco of collectivization, Stalin used the murder of S. M. Kirov, a Communist-party leader in Leningrad, on 1 December 1934, as the pretext for a massive purge of his former rivals, together with any other functionaries whose loyalty was questionable. (In fact, Stalin himself probably engineered the killing of Kirov.) Terror, once only a weapon used against "class enemies", became commonplace. The purges unleashed a wave of denunciations, mass arrests and forced "confessions" which spread fear and mistrust throughout the country. By December 1936, with the worst of the purges still to come, some five million people had been seized by the security police and many were never seen again.

Outside the Soviet Union, the horrors of collectivization and the purges attracted less attention than they might otherwise have done, because of the world economic depression. To those in the West who were disillusioned with capitalism, the five-year plans seemed a great achievement, and a major step forward at a time when Communism had seemed to be in retreat. To some leftwing intellectuals the Soviet Union presented the only alternative to fascism.

▼ First among equals. Stalin (left) in amicable discussion with associates at the sixth Communist party Congress of 1931. While Stalin was consolidating his grip on power, he paid lip service to the tradition of consultative government, cooperating with old comrades from the days of the revolution. Three years later, Stalin began a ruthless purge of the party leadership in pursuit of one-man dictatorship. Of 139 members and candidates of the Central Committee, 98 were arrested and shot along with 1,108 of the 1,966 delegates: and over one-fifth of the Red Army's officer corps was executed.

THE CULT OF THE DICTATORS

It was generally assumed in 19th-century Europe that all forms of despotism would gradually be replaced by representative government, but the 20th century proved to be as much the age of dictatorship as the age of democracy. The hallmarks of modern dictatorship is that it avails itself of the fruits of the technological revolution, especially where instruments of terror are concerned, and involves the exercise of autocratic powers for an indefinite period. In this latter respect it is the antithesis of dictatorship as it was known to Republican Rome, where it was considered an exceptional and strictly temporary expedient for the preservation of the state in a time of state crisis. Instead, it resembles more closely the type of rule instituted by Julius Caesar, who was granted autocratic powers for life, though modern tyrannies can just as well be associated with the relatively impersonal despotism of a political party or a military junta as with charismatic leadership.

Most dictatorships of the ultra-right are at least reminiscent of the Republican model in that they justify themselves as necessary to crush the enemies of law and order to resolve a state crisis. In the interwar period Admiral Horthy in Hungary, Miguel Primo de Rivera in Spain, Pilsudski in Poland, King Alexander in Yugoslavia and General Antonescu in Romania all claimed to have rescued the nation from risk of anarchy or a Bolshevik takeover. Military governments throughout the world since 1960 can be said to perpetuate this form of dictatorship in the sense that they took over power in *coups* against democratically elected governments.

Other forms of modern autocracy attached greater importance to mobilizing the masses in their support through elaborate structural transformation and propaganda, as was the case of Salazar in Portugal, Franco in Spain, Perón in Argentina, and Qaddhafi in contemporary Libya. The most sophisticated forms of dictatorship in this respect were those instituted by Mussolini and Hitler, in which the systematic eradication of liberal freedoms was accompanied by extensive structural change and propaganda designed to present the leader as the incarnation of the national will, so that the single-party state was allegedly more democratic than the liberal party-political system.

Dictatorships have also been instituted in all countries whose regimes are based on Marxist-Leninist theory. Though Lenin envisaged a transitional phase of the "dictatorship of the proletariat" before the state would "wither away", the result in practice was an extraordinary concentration of power within the hands either of a single leader (Mao Zedong in China, Fidel Castro in Cuba, Enver Hoxha in Albania, Tito in Yugoslavia, Ceauşescu in Romania) or small ruling factions. The potential for abuse of such concentrations of power whatever their theoretical democratic function was realized most gruesomely in the mass atrocities committed by the orders of Stalin in the Soviet Union and Pol Pot in Cambodia.

▶ The crowd's adulation of Hitler whenever he appeared in public constitutes an outstanding expression of the force of "plebiscitary" democracy on which modern dictatorships depend for their legitimacy and survival. Autocratic power needed to call on popular consensus, cynically manufactured if "charisma" is lacking or should start to wane.

▲ In the public burning of "unGerman" or "decadent" literature, the Third Reich created a ritualistic expression of the totalitarian drive for mind control in the name of a "higher freedom".

◀ In ancient Rome the emperor was considered divine. A personality cult is no less central to the power of the new Caesars, as can be seen from this portrait of Franco. In it symbols of medieval chivalry, monasticism, and modern militarism are interwoven into a composition in the baroque style associated with Spain's 16th century Golden Age. The result is an iconic representation of the *Caudillo* as a contemporary incarnation of Charles VI synthesizing past and present, tradition and modernity, the religious and the secular, monarch and savior.

▲ Iranian women in purdah display their enthusiasm (or conformism) at a political rally. When the Ayatollah ousted the Shah in Iran in 1979 a new permutation of charismatic dictatorship had arrived, one based on fundamentalist religion.

◀ Mass rallies, ritual and propaganda are not sufficient to ensure the survival of modern dictatorships. They must be reinforced by a climate of fear maintained by the ruthless use of paramilitary violence and torture. These two victims of El Salvador's government death squads stand for untold thousands who have "disappeared" for resisting autocratic law in the 20th century.

◀◀ Hitler and Mussolini, the archetypical new Caesars, celebrated the imminent appearance of a heroic race of "new men" born out of the ashes of the old order.

Datafile

In Western Europe democratic governments remained wedded to doctrines of appeasement and disarmament: internationally they were prepared to make concessions to avoid embroilment in another costly continental war; domestically they were largely concerned with economic retrenchment and hesitant to authorize increased public expenditure on armaments. Elsewhere, however, the escape from economic stagnation went hand in hand with an expansionist foreign policy and a reallocation of resources to arms production. The drift to war was accelerated by great-power involvement in local war: the League of Nations proved incapable of stopping the Italian conquest of Ethiopia; the USSR on one side and Germany and Italy on the other became heavily involved in the bloody civil war in Spain; and in the Far East the Japanese occupation of Manchuria in 1931 led directly to the invasion of China itself six year later. As the expansionist ambitions of the military dictatorships became clearer, so the democrats turned to rearmament themselves.

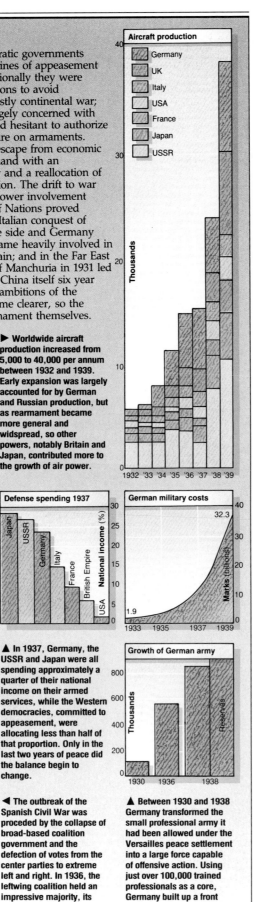

Spanish elections

1931 seats

- Socialist
- Radical
- Radical Socialist
- Right parties
- Catalan Esquerra
- ARAP
- Progressive
- CQGN

1933 seats

- Right parties
- Radical
- Socialist
- Others pro-government
- Acción Republicana

1936 seats

- Left
- Right
- Center

▶ Worldwide aircraft production increased from 5,000 to 40,000 per annum between 1932 and 1939. Early expansion was largely accounted for by German and Russian production, but as rearmament became more general and widspread, so other powers, notably Britain and Japan, contributed more to the growth of air power.

Aircraft production

- Germany
- UK
- Italy
- USA
- France
- Japan
- USSR

Thousands

1932 '33 '34 '35 '36 '37 '38 '39

Defense spending 1937

Japan, USSR, Germany, Italy, France, British Empire, USA

National income (%)

▲ In 1937, Germany, the USSR and Japan were all spending approximately a quarter of their national income on their armed services, while the Western democracies, committed to appeasement, were allocating less than half of that proportion. Only in the last two years of peace did the balance begin to change.

◀ The outbreak of the Spanish Civil War was proceded by the collapse of broad-based coalition government and the defection of votes from the center parties to extreme left and right. In 1936, the leftwing coalition held an impressive majority, its rightwing opponents looked to military action to reverse the situation.

German military costs

Marks (billions)

1.9 ... 32.3

1933 1935 1937 1939

Growth of German army

Thousands

Reserves

1930 1936 1938

▲ Between 1930 and 1938 Germany transformed the small professional army it had been allowed under the Versailles peace settlement into a large force capable of offensive action. Using just over 100,000 trained professionals as a core, Germany built up a front line force eight times that size, backed up by even larger reserves.

The diplomatic counterpart of the national and democratically organized parliamentary regimes that dominated the world by the late 1920s was the League of Nations at Geneva. After a shaky start, it had established itself, with leading statesmen from all over the world playing a role. Economically, the world had also become more liberal. Commercial restraints imposed during and after World War I were relaxed, and currencies had become more stable.

On 24 October 1929 this stability was shattered by the US stock-market crash, producing the worst world depression in modern history. In the ten years that followed, the concept of collective security embodied in the Paris peace treaties of 1919 and the League of Nations Covenant gave way to national egoism as governments tried desperately to protect themselves from the effects of the slump.

Armaments and reparations

The first casualty of the new international environment was an agreement over German reparations payments for World War I, which had been imposed under the Paris peace treaty of 1918. On 7 June 1929, a new reparations scheme, the Young Plan, was announced to supersede the earlier Dawes Plan. It restored financial sovereignty to Germany but forced the country to pay larger annuities than before. The plan came into effect on 17 May 1930 but by that time the world's economic situation had deteriorated. The German chancellor, Heinrich Brüning, instead of seeking to reschedule the payments, or raise a loan, decided to force the issue by imposing harsh economic measures at home in the hope that the contraction in world trade would force Germany's creditors to seek a mutually acceptable solution. A credit crisis in Europe followed, and President Hoover announced a moratorium on war debts from France and Britain if they would suspend reparations demands from Germany. This arrangement, intended as a temporary measure, became permanent at the Lausanne Conference in June 1932.

Another aim of German foreign policy was to achieve equality of armaments and, above all, the right to restore conscription, or some form of short-term service, without which there would be no prospect of creating a powerful field army. The French, who feared a resurgence of German militarism, opposed any such move, especially after Hitler's Nazis became a political force. The British government, however, headed by the Labour leader Ramsay MacDonald, sought a general agreement on disarmament and was prepared to override French concerns. MacDonald's National Government, which was formed on 24 August 1931 and included Conser-

THE DRIFT TO WAR

vatives, wanted to keep Britain out of continental entanglements. The Treasury even refused requests by British army chiefs in March 1932 to increase resources to meet Britain's obligations under the League Covenant and the Locarno treaties.

The international disarmament conference at Geneva, which lasted from 2 February 1932 until October 1933, ended inconclusively. The British and Americans were eager for an agreement, but the French refused to reduce their land forces by as much as Britain requested, and the Germans looked for excuses to expand their own. Eventually, Hitler, acting under pressure from his generals, and backed by a plebiscite, left the disarmament conference and on 14 October 1933 announced Germany's withdrawal from the League of Nations.

Japanese aggression in China

After 1929 Japan was crippled by the world de-

▼ A Popular Front demonstration in Paris against the Nationalist uprising in Spain. The Spanish Civil War became a focus for left-wing opposition to the rise of fascism.

pression and morale was low. Its silk trade suffered a catastrophic decline and pressures for tariff protection against Japanese imports were mounting in the United States and the British Empire. At the same time, the military in Japan were alarmed at the prospect of an increasingly confident nationalist China, headed by Jiang Jieshi's Guomindang forces. In 1931, tension grew in Manchuria, an area where the Japanese controlled and policed parts of the railroad system, after the Chinese warlord Marshal Chang Hsueh-liang, aligned himself with the nationalists to initiate a railroad-building program that would reduce the province's dependence on the Japanese.

On 18 September 1931 the Japanese forces in Manchuria suddenly seized Mukden and captured other major cities. The Japanese cabinet had not sanctioned the action, but was too weak to countermand it. By the end of 1931 most of Manchuria had fallen to the Japanese army. The

▲ Cartoon attacking Japanese aggression in China.

◄ Chinese nationalist soldiers holding out against the Japanese.

▼ In 1931–32 the Japanese occupied Manchuria and installed the former Qing emperor Pu Yi (seated next to the emperor Hirohito) as a Japanese puppet.

following February the Japanese created a puppet republic of Manzhouguo, an action that they justified by claiming to restore order in a region torn by anarchy. After the Chinese had appealed to the League of Nations, a commission of inquiry was set up under Lord Lytton to investigate the events in Manchuria. The commission reported its findings on 2 October 1932 and on 24 February 1933 the League's assembly condemned Japan's aggression and called on the Japanese to withdraw. They refused, pressed farther into northern China and announced their withdrawal from the League. The Sino-Japanese conflict continued to smoulder, interspersed with periods of truce, until it burst forth again in 1937, with greater ferocity.

The Polish-German treaty

Although the European powers were concerned at the danger presented by a resurgent Germany, and by Japanese aggression, they could not agree on how best to deal with the situation. On 18 March 1933 Mussolini proposed to the British a four-Power pact between Britain, Italy, France and Germany to revise the terms of the Paris peace treaty of 1918, which had so offended Germany. However, the proposal was abandoned after protests from the Little Entente (Romania, Czechoslovakia and Yugoslavia), who feared its consequences, and by France. The Poles also became suspicious that their western border might be regarded as negotiable by the other powers and decided to look after their own interests by making a nonaggression pact with Germany. This agreement, which was signed on 26 January 1934, turned out to be worthless to the Poles, but greatly benefited Hitler by removing the danger of a Polish preemptive strike while Germany was rearming.

The pact also weakened the French security system in Europe. Louis Barthou, the French foreign minister, tried to rally former Entente countries, and the assassination of the Austrian Chancellor, Engelbert Dolfuss, by German-

backed Nazis, on 25 July 1934, drew Mussolini once more towards France. However, Italy was on bad terms with Yugoslavia, and once again splits appeared in the allied camp. On 9 October 1934, Barthou met King Alexander of Yugoslavia in Marseilles to discuss the situation in Central Europe, but both were murdered by a Croatian dissident.

Franco-Soviet treaty
During 1931 and 1932 the Soviet Union, increasingly worried about Japan's power in the Far East, signed nonaggression pacts with many of its neighbors, including Poland, Finland and Latvia, and with France. In September 1934 the Soviet Union was admitted to the League of Nations, sponsored by Britain, France and Italy.

Hitler's fierce anti-Bolshevism and his rapprochement with Poland further encouraged Stalin to mend fences with the West. On 2 May 1935 the Soviet Union and France signed a treaty of mutual assistance, which later that month was extended to include Czechoslovakia.

The change in Stalin's foreign policy was reflected in the Comintern, which now urged Communist parties everywhere to form a "popular front" with democratic forces against fascism, as the French had done. In his determination to create a European security system against Hitler, Stalin was pursuing Soviet interests, but at the time these coincided with the needs of the Western European democracies.

Britain, however, was most concerned about the Franco-Soviet alignment, both because it regarded the Soviet Union as an enemy of the British Empire, and because many Britons deplored the division of Europe into armed camps.

French attempts to buttress the security of Europe gave Hitler excuses for further breaches of Germany's treaty obligations. On 9 March 1935 the Germans announced that they had created an air force, and on 16 March Hitler reintroduced conscription, which was in clear breach of the Treaty of Versailles.

One month before, Britain and France had agreed not to release Germany from its obligations under the Versailles treaty without the consent of the other. Yet, on 18 June 1935 Britain, without referring to France, concluded a naval treaty with Germany allowing the Germans to build up to just over one third of the British naval strength. The British also tried—unsuccessfully—to make an air pact with the Germans to guarantee the security of their island by limiting offensive aerial forces.

German reoccupation of the Rhineland
Using as a pretext the ratification of the Franco-Soviet treaty that was in process in Paris, Hitler marched his troops into the demilitarized zone of the German Rhineland on 7 March 1936. This action violated not only the Versailles treaty but also the Locarno pact. The British, consistent in their policy of noncommitment, refused to mobilize forces against Germany in response to this provocation, and the French government under Pierre-Étienne Flandrin was too weak to take action unilaterally. Hitler's bold action, having gone

The Chinese Civil War

Torn by warlordism since the collapse of the Qing dynasty in 1912, China was pushed into full-scale civil war when in 1927 Jiang Jieshi, leader of the nationalist Guomindang party, purged the Communists from the ranks of his army. After a series of abortive urban uprisings, the Communists finally established themselves in the countryside, using peasant guerrilla forces to neutralize superior Guomindang military strength. There followed a hard-fought three-year siege, with Jiang finally destroying the Communist mini-state in the east of the country, the Jiangxi soviet. However, Mao Zedong successfully led survivors on the Long March of 1934–35 to establish a secure base in Yenan province in the north. The Japanese invasion of 1937 led to an uneasy truce between the two sides. Guomindang forces recovered from early defeats, while the Communists fought an increasingly well-supported guerrilla war. In 1945 hostilities flared up again, developing into full-scale warfare a year later, after the failure of a US-sponsored compromise settlement. By the end of 1947 a massive Communist counteroffensive was in full swing and in 1949 the Communists emerged as victors. The People's Republic of China was proclaimed and Jiang fled to Taiwan.

▲ Mao Zedong leads his followers on the Long March of 1934–35, rescuing Chinese Communism from military defeat and securing his own position as party leader. Arguably the most influential political figure of the 20th century, he developed the ideological and political systems that welded millions of Chinese together as a Communist nation. He was also one of the major theorists of guerrilla warfare.

▼ Jiang Jieshi with the Indian leader Gandhi. Jiang was a curious blend of military dictator and populist leader. He rid China of its warlords and kept his forces together for years in the face of a fierce battering from the Japanese. But his administration was corrupt and inefficient and his failure to develop a coherent ideology led to his defeat by Mao's Communists.

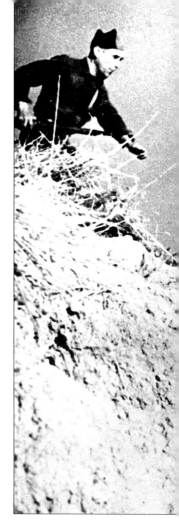

unchallenged, further undermined the collective security of Europe.

Already on 6 March 1936 the threatening state of Franco-German relations and a distaste for the Franco-Soviet alliance had led the Belgians to renounce a military agreement with France that had existed since 1920. The Nazi reoccupation of the Rhineland increased their nervousness, and on 14 October 1936 King Leopold publicly stated that Belgian foreign policy would concern itself solely with Belgian interests. Strategically, this decision left the French with a vulnerable open flank that was not covered by their sophisticated defensive system, the Maginot Line, which had been under construction since 1929. At the same

time, Germany had created a "western wall" to prevent French incursions into Germany while Hitler's rearmament program, which surged into top gear in 1936, could continue unchecked.

Italian aggression in Ethiopia

Abyssinia (or Ethiopia as it is today) was one of the few remaining independent African states, having resisted colonization and repulsed an Italian invasion in 1896. In 1934 Mussolini, to enhance his own and Italian prestige, began preparing to attack the country, whose temperate highlands were long regarded as suitable for European settlement. From his colonies in Eritrea and Somaliland, on 5 December 1934 he provoked a clash between Italian and Ethiopian troops at Wal Wal in Somaliland, causing the Ethiopian government to appeal to the League of Nations to make peace. Determined on conquest, Mussolini rejected the League's peace proposal, and on 3 October 1935 Italian forces invaded Ethiopia. The Ethiopian army was defeated by aerial bombardment, using poison gas, banned by an international convention that had been signed by Italy.

Public opinion in democratic countries was outraged by Mussolini's aggression and supported the economic sanctions imposed by the League on Italy, on 11 October 1935. However, the governments of France and Britain, themselves colonial powers, were not wholly unsympathetic to Mussolini's aims in Africa. Furthermore, Italy was a former ally whose power might be needed to check Hitler in the future.

The Spanish Civil War

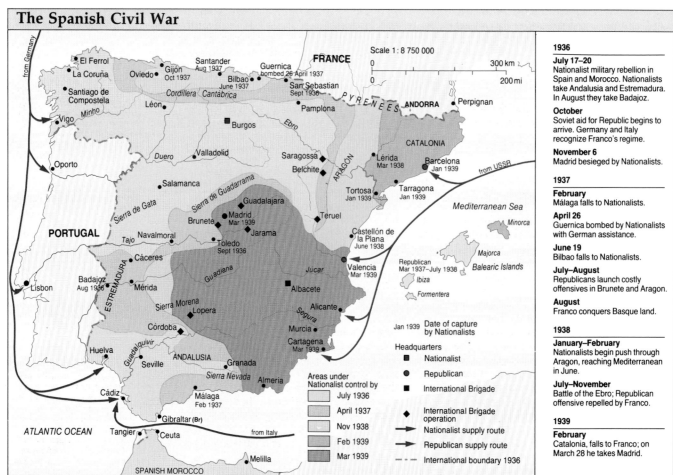

Scale 1 : 8 750 000

1936

July 17–20
Nationalist military rebellion in Spain and Morocco. Nationalists take Andalusia and Estremadura. In August they take Badajoz.

October
Soviet aid for Republic begins to arrive. Germany and Italy recognize Franco's regime.

November 6
Madrid besieged by Nationalists.

1937

February
Málaga falls to Nationalists.

April 26
Guernica bombed by Nationalists with German assistance.

June 19
Bilbao falls to Nationalists.

July–August
Republicans launch costly offensives in Brunete and Aragon.

August
Franco conquers Basque land.

1938

January–February
Nationalists begin push through Aragon, reaching Mediterranean in June.

July–November
Battle of the Ebro; Republican offensive repelled by Franco.

1939

February
Catalonia, falls to Franco; on March 28 he takes Madrid.

Areas under Nationalist control by
- July 1936
- April 1937
- Nov 1938
- Feb 1939
- Mar 1939

Jan 1939 Date of capture by Nationalists

Headquarters
- ■ Nationalist
- ● Republican
- ■ International Brigade
- ◆ International Brigade operation
- → Nationalist supply route
- → Republican supply route
- --- International boundary 1936

◀ A Spanish Civil War poster above satirizing the Nationalists. Republican forces counterattack against advancing Nationalists. The disunited leftist forces of the Spanish republic fought with great spirit (left), but Italian and German military assistance decided the issue in Franco's favor.

◀ The image of Mussolini in Ethiopia. The refusal of Western democracies to use force to oppose military aggression gave the fascist dictators a free hand in the imperial adventures.

Together, the French foreign minister, Pierre Laval, and his British colleague, Sir Samuel Hoare, secretly drew up a compromise arrangement to give Mussolini important trade routes and frontier areas, while formally preserving Ethiopian independence. When this scheme leaked out in Britain in December 1935, Hoare was forced to resign in a storm of public indignation. His successor, Anthony Eden, fully supported sanctions and loathed Mussolini. However, the League's sanctions proved useless, not least because they did not apply to oil traffic. Mussolini was angry with the democracies for trying to thwart him, and contemptuous of their failure. He pressed on with his invasion and by spring 1936 Ethiopia was overrun. On 2 May 1936 the Emperor, Haile Selassie, left his country and did not return until 1941. In July 1936 sanctions against Mussolini were lifted, having proved a failure.

The Spanish Civil War
On 17 July 1936 a group of disaffected army officers staged a coup to replace the democratic, if somewhat chaotic, Spanish republic with an authoritarian, nationalistic regime. The coup failed, in that only part of the country fell to the rebels, while the Republican government in Madrid rallied and appealed for help from abroad.

The rising, which sparked off a civil war, was led by Generals Sanjurjo and Mola, and—most importantly—Francisco Franco, who commanded the elite Spanish Foreign Legion in Morocco. From early on, Franco was aided by Hitler and Mussolini, who airlifted his crack military unit

from North Africa to Spain, and who continued to support the Nationalists throughout the three-year conflict. The Republicans, who were aided by volunteers of the International Brigade, eventually succumbed to Franco's military might when Barcelona and Madrid in 1939.

Franco, having seized power, took the title of *Caudillo* (leader), rejecting parliamentary democracy in favor of a fascist corporate state. Unlike Hitler or Mussolini, who had a mass party behind them, from which they built up paramilitary forces, Franco had the backing of the regular army from the outset.

Hitler and Mussolini had political and strategic, as well as ideological, reasons for becoming involved in the Spanish Civil War. The Italians had hoped to extend their influence in the western Mediterranean. The Germans benefited from valuable battle experience, especially the deployment of the German air force's Condor legion. The Germans also secured a supply of strategic minerals such as iron ore from Spain. At first, the German foreign office had been concerned about Germany's involvement in Spain, but Hitler realized that the war would serve as a distraction to other powers while Germany was busy rearming. The war also helped to cement the relationship between Hitler and Mussolini. In the early 1930s Mussolini had regarded Hitler with contempt, deriding his antisemitism and rejecting any increase in German power in the Danube basin. By the end of 1936 his own commitments in Ethiopia and Spain had made him Hitler's natural ally.

▲ A child tries to shelter from the Nationalist bombs during the Spanish Civil War.

◀ The war began in the west and spread to the north and the east. As the war entered its second year, Franco's grip on the war tightened, with massive German and Italian military assistance. The Republicans, supported by the Soviet Union and European volunteers finally succumbed to superior military might.

Datafile

During the 1930s and early 1940s, which were dominated by the fascist governments, European artists and intellectuals took on a defensive role. Institutions such as the Bauhaus were closed down. Many artists fled to the United States: during World War II almost all the major Surrealists could be found in New York. Picasso's decision to remain in occupied Paris made him the cultural representative of a world struggling for its freedom.

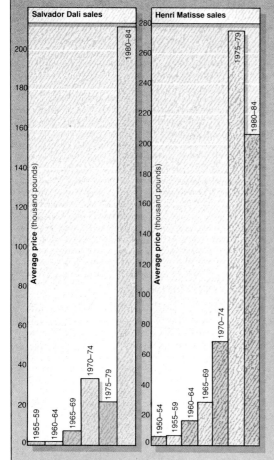

▲ The Spanish painter Salvador Dalí became famous as much for his appearance and behavior as for his extraordinary, highly skilled but essentially formulaic painting. In this respect he was the perfect Surrealist, setting out to shock and disconcert as much of the civilized world as would grant him a platform.

▶ The Venice Film Festival was an indication that the medium had acquired the status of high art. Certainly it reflected the greater seriousness with which Europe viewed cinema, with several literary adaptations among its winners, including *Anna Karenina* and Olivier's *Hamlet*. The award system was dropped in 1968.

"Degenerate Art" exhibition
A. Archipenko (Ukraine)
Ernst Barlach (Germany)
Willi Baumeister (Germany)
Max Beckmann (Germany)
Marc Chagall (Russia)
Otto Dix (Germany)
Christof Drexel (Germany)
Max Ernst (Germany)
Lyonel Feininger (USA)
George Grosz (Germany)
Erich Heckel (Germany)
Wassily Kandinsky (Russia)
Ernst Ludwig Kirchner (Ger)
Paul Klee (Switzerland)
Oskar Kokoschka (Austria)
El Lissitzky (USSR)
Franz Marc (Germany)
Jean Metzinger (France)
Laszlo Moholy-Nagy (Hun)
Piet Mondrian (Netherlands)
Emil Nolde (Germany)
Pablo Picasso (Spain)
Hans Richter (USA)
Oskar Schlemmer (Germany)
Karl Schmidt-Rottluff (Ger)
Kurt Schwitters (Germany)

▲ The Nazis sent an exhibition of "Degenerate Art" on tour round Germany in 1937. This was intended to show that modern art, both in style and subject-matter, was perverting normal human values. In fact, it was a quite exciting gathering (if rather badly hung) of more than 100 painters from Germany and elsewhere in Europe.

◀ Henri Matisse, a generation older than many of his "contemporaries" in the avant-garde, had little of the flamboyance of Dalí. But his genius for color made him one of the most sought-after modern masters. These figures are compiled from the averages of his three highest prices per year, converted into sterling at current rates.

Venice Film Festival – best foreign film award		
1934	*Man of Aran*	Robert Flaherty (UK)
1935	*Anna Karenina*	Clarence Brown (USA)
1936	*Der Kaiser von Kalifornien*	Luis Trenker (Germany)
1937	*Un Carnet de Bal*	Julien Duvivier (France)
1938	*Olympia*	Leni Riefenstahl (Germany)
1940	*Der Postmeister*	Gustav Ucicky (Germany)
1941	*Ohm Kruger*	Hans Steinhoff (Germany)
1942	*Der grosse König*	Veit Harlan (Germany)
1946	*The Southerner*	Jean Renoir (France-USA)
1947	*Sirena*	Karel Stekly (Czechoslovakia)
1948	*Hamlet*	Laurence Olivier (UK)
1949	*Manon*	H.G. Clouzot (France)
1950	*Justice is Done*	André Cayatte (France)
1951	*Rashomon*	Akira Kurosawa (Japan)
1952	*Forbidden Games*	René Clement (France)
1954	*Romeo and Juliet*	Renato Castellani (Italy-UK)
1955	*Ordet*	Carl Dreyer (Denmark)
1957	*Aparajito*	Satyajit Ray (India)
1958	*Muhomatsu no Issho*	Hiroshi Inagaki (Japan)
1959	*Il Generale della Rovere*	Roberto Rossellini (Italy)
1960	*Le Passage du Rhin*	André Cayatte (France)
1961	*Last Year at Marienbad*	Alain Resnais (France)
1962	*Childhood of Ivan*	Andrei Tarkovsky (USSR)
1963	*Le Mani sulla Città*	Francesco Rosi (Italy)
1964	*Red Desert*	Michelangelo Antonioni (Italy)
1965	*Of a Thousand Delights*	Luchino Visconti (Italy)
1966	*Battle of Algiers*	Gillo Pontecorvo (Italy)
1967	*Belle de Jour*	Luis Buñuel (France)
1968	*Artists of the Big Top*	Alexander Kluge (Germany)

The term "International Style" first became current through the publication in 1932 in New York of a book of the same title, written by the critic and historian, Henry Russell Hitchcock, in collaboration with the architect Philip Johnson. Thirty years later, Hitchcock still maintained that the style was the "dominant architectural development" of the second quarter of the 20th century.

Architects of the 19th century had sought long and hard for a new "modern" style. This quest can be seen to have produced the *fin de siècle* Art Nouveau style and the subsequent revolt against excessive ornament had prompted the Viennese architect Adolf Loos to declare in 1908: "Ornament is crime."

While the English Arts and Crafts Movement had been influential in Germany before World War I, the Deutscher Werkbund, formed in 1907 by Hermann Muthesius, was more concerned to involve architects and designers in the possibilities of modern manufacturing processes. Connnections between the Werkbund and the Bauhaus, and later with the Congrès Internationaux d'Architecture Moderne, produced a heady mixture of ideas concerned not only with the potential of modern materials and methods of construction, but with variants of a social program that veered from revolutionary socialist to humanist egalitarian or even elitist meritocratic. Following a prewar exhibition in Cologne in 1914, which had displayed a number of proto-modern buildings in glass, concrete and steel, Ludwig Mies van der Rohe, the vice-president of the Werkbund, directed an exhibition primarily of modern housing prototypes in the Stuttgart suburb of Weissenhof in 1927. The houses, which were all required to have flat roofs, were designed by a glittering array of avant-garde architects, including Mies himself, Walter Gropius of the Bauhaus, the Dutch architect J.J.P. Oud and the Swiss-born French architect, Le Corbusier. Every form of modern construction was used and the architecture was consistently recognizable as belonging to what is now usually known as the "International Style".

At one level, the style is easy to define: loosely, it is what we still call "modern" architecture. At another level, though, it is an illusion, for the superficial stylistic consistencies of architecture gathered together by the term conceal a wide range of variations of approach by individual architects. Apart from a concern with new materials and rational forms of building construction, the quality which marks the style most clearly in the minds of theorists is the promotion of spatial organization as the overriding concern. To non-architects, the chief distinguishing features tend to be flat roofs, a lack of color and ornamentation,

RESPONSES TO TOTALITARIANISM

and the dominance of areas of rectilinear plain glazing – or "white architecture", as some critics have called it.

In 1928, following the Weissenhof exhibition, Hélène de Mandrot, a Swiss patron of architecture, aided by an academic, Siegfried Giedion, and by Le Corbusier, set up a cycle of "Congrès Internationaux d'Architecture Moderne" (CIAM) that was to continue into the 1950s. It attracted wide support from "modern" architects. The thematic meetings resulted in manifestos and more serious reports: CIAM II, held in Frankfurt in 1929, resulted in a report on low-cost housing, *Die Wohnung für das Existenzminimum*. By 1933, when CIAM IV was held on the steamship *Patras* between Athens and Marseilles, the focus had moved to "The Functional City" and town planning issues. The resulting Athens Charter was an influential manifesto for modernist city development, and typical of the way in which the conferences promoted international debate on architecture in an ambience of general agreement about the appropriateness of modern construction techniques and architectural forms.

The Lovell Health House in Los Angeles (1927–29), designed by the expatriate Austrian architect Richard Neutra, and much influenced by Loos, is an early and enduring icon of the International Style, with its steel frame structure and light cladding. But it is probably the work of Le Corbusier and Mies van der Rohe which

broadly encompasses the range of the style. The flowing space of Mies's German Pavilion at the 1929 Barcelona Exhibition, with its sheer planes and refined columns, was hugely influential. He spent the rest of his life refining the design elements employed: column, articulating plane and glass curtain. Le Corbusier's range was broader, and his work, both hypothetical and actual, ranged across the globe from Europe to North Africa and India, and in scale from single dwellings to plans for whole cities. Despite the variety of his work, the quality of complex flowing space manipulation was constant. Two houses, Maison Stein at Garches (1929) and Villa Savoye (1930), Poissy, France, perhaps most embody the common qualities of the International Style.

In many countries of the world, more International Style architecture was built after World War II than before. The prewar avant-garde had often become the postwar establishment, and recovery from global war gave rise to more social programs and the need for rapid construction, both apparently well served by modern architecture.

A "New Deal" for the arts

In the United States, the stockmarket crash of October 1929 brought an end to the expansionist years of the 1920s. For the next three years, one in four of the American labor force was out of work. The knock-on effect on European economies was, if anything, even more disastrous. In Germany,

▼ Villa Savoye, designed by Le Corbusier (1930). He did a series of designs in the 1920s to illustrate his architectural theory. In 1914 he had patented "Dom-ino", a skeletal frame for mass-produced housing. In doing so he was following a central principle of the International Style, established in 1895 by Otto Wagner. Modernist architects favored the reinforced concrete frame and larger areas of glazing made possible by industrial advances.

the National Socialists gathered support as the government failed to contain the economic crisis, and Hitler became Chancellor in 1933. Everywhere hardship fostered extremism. Ironically, full employment returned only when World War II created a demand for men, munitions and food that reached far beyond Europe itself.

As a response to the economic state of the nation, President Franklin D. Roosevelt, elected in 1932, inaugurated in 1933 his New Deal, a wide range of funded initiatives to stimulate growth and relieve suffering. As part of this, the Works Progress Administration set up various programs to provide employment in the arts. The best-known was the Federal Arts Project, begun in 1935. There were similar programs for theater workers and writers. In the same year the Farm Security Administration (FSA) began to document the appalling conditions in some of the depressed agricultural regions of the country such as the Oklahoma Dustbowl (also commemorated in John Steinbeck's novel *The Grapes of Wrath*). The Administration employed a team of photographers including Walker Evans, Dorothea Lange, Margaret Bourke-White and Arthur Rothstein. Photography has always had a clear documentary function, but now between Lange's direct, warm and compassionate work and Walker Evans's strict "defining of observation", with its almost Cubist passion for pictorial organization, the possible range of documentary photographic art was brilliantly extended. Indeed, much of the impulse behind the Federal Projects in the various arts was documentary. The writers produced guidebooks to America, the ac-

tors developed Living Newspapers, pungent clips of acted news following one another like film newsreel. Nearly ten thousand painters, sculptors and other artists were employed in the eight years the Federal Arts Project (FAP) was running. Between them they produced well over four hundred thousand works – murals, paintings, sculptures, prints, posters, designs – much of which recorded the regions and social conditions of America. The projects were in the hands of enlightened administrators, notably Roy E. Stryker, who ran the FSA photographic program, and Holger Cahill, who directed the Federal Arts Project. The governing philosophy was not so much to do with producing masterpieces as with providing the means for as many artists as possible to create in comparative freedom and to bring about a "naturalization" of art throughout the whole country, rather than merely "an effervescence along the Atlantic Seaboard".

While there was a definite emphasis on expressing social and regional awareness, there was no enforcement of a particular line or style, and among the major beneficiaries of the scheme were young abstract artists. They tended to gather in New York, where the group known as American Abstract Artists was formed in 1936. A number of artists who were to become prominent on the international painting scene in the next wave of American painting, such as William Baziotes, Willem de Kooning, Jackson Pollock and Mark Rothko, were all supported by the scheme. Another artist who was to become central to American abstract art, Arshile Gorky, an Armenian who had emigrated to the United

[Lange's] photographs, as well as those of other FSA photographers, were dramatic evidence of the tragedy of displacement but they included moments of hope, laughter and tranquility as well. All who photographed for the FSA maintained an abiding respect for human nature and constant consideration for the feelings of the people they portrayed. When the office was closed in 1943, the FSA photographers had created a mirror of America and established definitive procedures for implementing the attitudes and intentions that were now known as documentary photography

MINOR WHITE, 1974

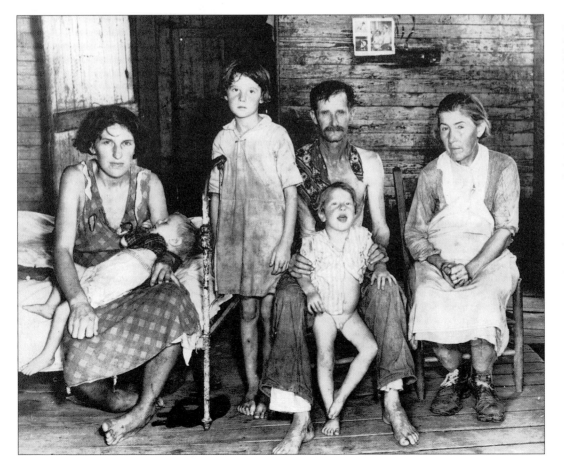

◄ In 1935, under the "New Deal", the US Farm Security Administration commissioned a number of photographers to document the appalling conditions in the Dust Bowl at the height of the Depression. The starkness of the results appalled America. A ramshackle dreariness was recorded with compassionate but uncomprising attention to detail. Dorothea Lange portrayed familes of "white trash" on the move, at their wits' end, searching for work, investing her subjects with a moving grandeur and a sense of spiritual resourcefulness. Walker Evans, who took this photograph of a family in Alabama, was described, famously, as having put "the physiognomy of the nation on your table".

▲ *The Changing West I*, by T.H. Benton, from a series of murals painted in the early 1930s with the Mexican artist Orozco for the new School of Social Research, New York. Benton adhered to the sentimental Regionalist movement. However, these twisting figures owe something to European Modernism. This might have influenced one of the models Benton used, his young pupil Jackson Pollock.

States in 1920, painted a mural on aviation under FAP auspices at Newark airport.

An earlier emigrant, Ben Shahn, who had come to the United States from Lithuania in 1906, also worked with the FAP, both as a photographer and a muralist. In 1933 he worked on murals at the Rockefeller Center in New York, helping Diego Rivera, who, like fellow Mexicans José Clemente Orozco and David Alfaro Siqueiros, carried out mural projects in the United States in the 1930s. Shahn was a key social realist painter. In 1931–32 he painted a superb series documenting the murder trial in Massachusetts of Nicolà Sacco and Bartolomeo Vanzetti, immigrant Italian anarchists who were executed on 28 August 1927 after a manifestly unjust trial that aroused international condemnation. It was these

paintings that led Rivera to take on Shahn. In many ways Shahn's impassioned directness and humanity summed up FAP aims. Fittingly, one of his most moving paintings was *The Blind Accordion Player*, showing the accordionist who played as Roosevelt's funeral cortège passed after his sudden death in 1945. It was Shahn's tribute to the New Deal President and to the simple dignities of human feeling.

During the later 1920s Edward Hopper, a pupil of Robert Henri of the prewar Ashcan School, had been as concerned with portraying American subjects as they had been, though in a more Romantic mood. Hopper painted the loneliness of American urban life – deserted suburban streets in the early morning, hotels, a corner drugstore at night – but in such a way as to extol

▲ The catalog for an exhibition of "Degenerate Art," selected by the Nazis in 1937. Hitler, who twice failed the entrance exam to the Viennese Academy of Fine Arts, wished to persuade the German people that art should be subservient to the state.

its poignant beauty. By the 1930s, concentration on purely American concerns resulted in the flowering of the work of the Regionalist painters led by Thomas Hart Benton. Benton and Grant Wood both used Realist styles, and Benton also painted murals. Here too a preoccupation with the documentary was evident. In *City Scenes*, at the New School for Social Research in New York, in order to get as many aspects of the city into view as possible, he divided up the painted area with heavy irregular frames, a photomontage device used in newspapers of the time. Grant Wood's style was clean and precise. His landscapes have an idyllic air, but in his portrayal of crabbed mid-Western faces something seems to have dried up in the American pioneer soul.

The dangers of looking only within the United States at a time of international ferment, or of looking only to Europe, were partly answered by Gorky and Shahn but most emphatically of all by the Cubist painter Stuart Davis. Davis held executive posts in both the Artists' Union and in the Artists' Congress, edited the campaigning journal *Art Front*, worked in the FAP and was generally militant in the 1930s. But while he saw his art as a response to "the dynamic American scene", tak-

ing its energies from neon signs, gas stations, chainstore fronts, jazz music and the hard, strident colors of the street, he used techniques derived from French Synthetic Cubism which he felt had "universal validity". He was immensely dedicated to his art. For a full year, 1927–28, he painted his "Egg-Beater" series, based on the multiple optical suggestions he derived from an egg-beater, an electric fan and a rubber glove he nailed to his table. He was wryly witty and agile enough as a painter to bring together, in an entirely personal style, his response to the drab streets of the social realists, to the America of the Regionalists and to the abstract sense of picturemaking possessed by the young artists of the New York school.

The Nazis and "degenerate art"

While the United States looked inwards, Europe was rapidly reaching a state of turmoil that would only be resolved by war. The Spanish Civil War broke out in 1936, commanding active support from both Hitler in Germany and Mussolini in Italy. In the Soviet Union, Stalin began a reign of terror in which no one was safe. In Germany, Nazi power became supreme. All other political

The Harlem Renaissance

A number of black writers came to prominence in the United States during the 1920s. Their center was Harlem, New York's black ghetto, and the movement included historians, musicians and artists as well as writers. They dispersed with the Depression in the 1930s, but this did not stop their work. That of Langston Hughes (1902–67), in particular, developed strongly through the 1930s and 1940s. Their ideas and examples influenced both the American black protest tradition and the "Negritude" movement of French-speaking black writers in Africa, Madagascar and the French West Indies. Another important black American writer of the time, not so deeply associated with New York but, in retrospect, one of the most impressive figures, was Jean Toomer (1894–1967), whose book *Cane* (1923) mingled poetry, prose and drama in a startling and very modern way.

Various themes were given prominence by Harlem Renaissance writers. They celebrated a distinctive African heritage, soulful and beautiful, which linked different phases of the history of African peoples. "My soul has grown deep as rivers", wrote Hughes and he recalled equally the Euphrates, the Congo, the Nile and the Mississippi. The writers of the Harlem Renaissance showed both a love and a fear of the American South, particularly strong in the work of Jean Toomer. They affirmed the black contribution to the United States. Some looked for a spiritual fusion of the various elements in American society, while showing clearly the problems posed by the actions of white society. Countee Cullen (1903–46), who was the most influenced by the English poetic tradition, wondered ironically why God should make a poet black and "bid him sing". There was a wide response in these writers to black music. It was strongest in Langston Hughes, who spoke of jazz as "honey mixed with liquid fire".

◄ Paul Robeson in *All God's Chillun Got Wings* (1924).

Sie hatten vier Jahre Zeit

▲ At the exhibition of "Degenerate Art", the slogan over the door reads "They have had four years" – referring to the period elapsed since the Nazi accession to power in 1933. This appeal to the lowest common denominator of the public taste was typical of the Nazis' strategy of slow corruption. In the place of such "Decadent Expressionism" they would institute the allegorical nude and the Aryan family. "Classical" standards had become as distorted as any figure by Picasso.

sented, as well as a number of international giants such as Picasso and Chagall – a total of 730 works by over a hundred artists. It toured to huge crowds. Between July and November it was visited by over two million people.

The day before the exhibition of "Degenerate Art" opened, Hitler inaugurated a companion "Great Exhibition of German Art", also in Munich, directly opposite. Some of the things that he said were not unlike the things said by advocates of the Federal Arts Project in America: "The artist does not create for the artist but just like everyone else he creates for the people." He looked in painting for "the good" and "the decent". However, he opposed this to the "insane" and the "criminal", which could be seen across the way at the Degenerate Art Exhibition. In fact, most of his speech was not about the exhibition he was opening but about "degenerate" art, especially that of the German Expressionists, whose own aim, ironically enough, had been precisely to create a "German art". (In the case of the unfortunate Emil Nolde, whose pictures naturally graced the "Degenerate" exhibition, he had actually derived his manner from the art of the people.) Hitler denounced all the Expressionist phrases – "inner experience", "original primitivism" – and the Futurist slogans – "emotions pregnant with the future", "forceful will" – as so much "jabbering". Curiously, the posters advertising the Degenerate Art Exhibition used Expressionist and even Cubist techniques, presumably recognizing that they worked as art. The Exhibition itself, with its careless display and its use of wall captions, which were quotations from "degenerate" critics praising the work, had much of the air of a Dadaist show.

Elsewhere in his speech, Hitler laid great stress on "cultural" values. Germany's defeat in World War I had led to the release of a "flood of slime and ordure", and international art was the main sign of the country's "inner decomposition", having no necessary relationship to an "ethnic group". Cut off from such origins and defined only by its period as "modern", it became modish, not essential. He wished to replace such "modern" art with "true and everlasting" German art. Such modern canvases dirtied "with color droppings" would no longer be available to the German people.

It was a terrifying performance. Many artists, including Wassily Kandinsky, Paul Klee and Kurt Schwitters, had already left the country when the Nazis first came to power in 1933, but now more fled, Max Beckmann the very day after the opening. Many were to settle in the United States and to help broaden the base of American painting. Since Hitler's view of modern art was shared by Stalin in Russia, except that he called it fascist art, the United States received Russians as well, some directly, some by way of other European countries. Marc Chagall, Pavel Tchelitchew and Ossip Zadkine all spent time there.

The recourse of artists who stayed in Germany, if they survived, was to enter into an exile of the mind. Otto Dix and Ernst Heckel retreated close to Switzerland and painted noncontroversial pictures. Käthe Kollwitz defiantly sculpted sturdy

parties were outlawed, trade unions abolished, and the civil service and judiciary brought under Nazi control. Heavy censorship was imposed on the press and radio, and on all forms of art and literature.

Hitler, himself a painter of sorts, held strong views on the place of art in the German state. Works of art that did not meet with Nazi approval were confiscated, later to be sold at auction in Switzerland, destroyed, or siphoned off on the quiet by Nazi collectors such as Josef Goebbels, Hitler's minister for propaganda. In 1937 an exhibition totally unlike any other this century opened in Munich. It was billed by the Nazis as an exhibition of "Degenerate Art", the decadent work of "Bolsheviks and Jews", and drawn from a collection of some twenty thousand such pictures confiscated from German museums. Nearly all Germany's leading modern artists were repre-

expressive figures of grieving solidarity. And in various secret ways artists painted on, at night after approved daytime jobs or in the army in occupied territories far from Germany. This enforced privacy was to lead inevitably, after World War II, to the rehabilitation of abstract art among German artists, as an art which answered only to the demands of the artist's mind. In Italy Benito Mussolini had taken dictatorial powers in 1925, but his view of art, though also based on the premise that what was needed was a "pure Italian art", was far less coercive than Hitler's. Various

styles coexisted, many claiming to interpret the ideals of the state. Futurists, Realist painters, Geometrical Abstractionists and impressionistic naturalists could all claim to represent or at least not to be in conflict with some aspects of the Fascist program, populist, ordered and technological as it sought to be. The Novecento style, with its modernist simplification of classical styles most powerfully represented by the work of Mario Sironi, bid fair to be recognized as a state style for some time during the 1930s, but eventually its own sentimentality and provincial eclecticism

▼ The entrance to the New Chancellery, Berlin, built by Albert Speer, the mastermind of architectural theory in the Third Reich. He used classical theory to create overblown monuments to the principles of fascism. This led to the bizarre postwar spectacle of Allied troops demolishing buildings because of their underlying ideological principles.

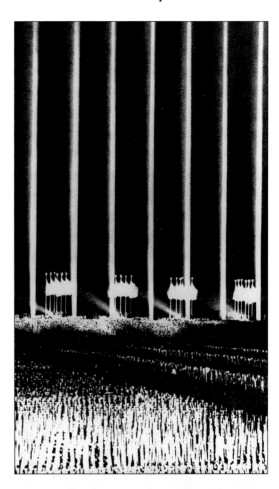

▶ A nighttime rally at Nuremberg. These elaborately organized events marked the highpoint of the Nazi year. Between 1927 and 1938 the average attendance was half a million. These dazzling military displays of searchlights and marching amounted to a national delusion. The theme of the 1939 rally, abruptly cancelled, was "Peace".

If today I could go back 31 years and choose whether to lead a peaceful, settled life in Augsburg or Göttingen ... this, then; or instead everything over again as it was, the glory and the guilt, the capital of the world and Spandau, as well as the sense of a miscarried life: how would I decide? Would I be ready to pay the price again? I am dizzy with these questions. I hardly dare to ask them. I cannot answer them.

ALBERT SPEER, 1964

▲ *Head of Mussolini* by R.A. Bertelli, 1933. Il Duce's attitude towards modern art was an embarrassment for the Nazis. He had stated: "A new state, a new people, can prosper only if the whole of art is revolutionized." The Futurists, fascistic in temperament, were eager to comply.

undermined its credibility. The perennial question of the relationship between art and the state is only obscured by the manic attitude of a Hitler or Stalin. The case of Italy perhaps shows a more realistic picture of the unending and shifting relationship between the independence of the artist, the power of the state, and the assumed needs of the public, into which both state and artist claim insight.

Architectural intimidation

There is little doubt that the stripped monumental classicism of the major public buildings of the Nazi era was deliberately chosen for its power to overawe and intimidate, as well as for its obvious reference to previous imperial rule. In the country or the provinces, Aryan culture was represented by the crude pseudo-vernacular *Heimatschutzstil* ("protected home style") that linked international military might to the national *Blut und Boden* (blood and soil) of the "master race".

Following his seizure of power, Hitler moved swiftly to take a controlling interest in the architecture of the Third Reich. The force of the stylistic preference of the new government was not immediately perceived. In 1933 a competition was held for the first major Nazi building in Berlin, and a broad range of architects submitted entries, including the Bauhaus architects Ludwig Mies van der Rohe and Walter Gropius. The winning design by Heinrich Wolff was, however, selected personally by Hitler, overruling the views of the juries.

The style favored by Hitler was not in fact exclusive to Nazi architecture. The starkly colonnaded House of German Art (1933–37) in Munich, designed by the first architect of Nazi Germany, Paul Troost, is similar in style to Paul Cret's American Battle Monument at Château Thierry (1928) and his Federal Reserve Board Building in Washington DC (1935).

It is with the work of Albert Speer, the architect of the Nuremberg Arena (1935) and the New Chancellery in Berlin (1938–40), that Nazi architecture is most closely associated. Speer was Hitler's protégé, and in 1936 was charged by him to produce a redevelopment plan for Berlin, for his personal approval. The most striking feature of the plan was a new north–south axis for the city. This was to culminate in the colossal Great Hall at one end and a vast station square at the other. The square was to be entered through a triumphal arch 120 meters (400 feet) high, designed by Speer directly from a detailed sketch made by Hitler in 1925. The Hall, which dwarfed the Reichstag, was to be 320 meters (over 1000 feet) high; it would hold 180,000 people and was to be mirrored in a huge reflecting pool.

In Italy Fascism produced a similar architecture, largely influenced by the work of Marcello Piacentini, whose Senate Building for the University City in Rome (1935) is strikingly similar to the work of Cret. A remarkably different building was designed by Giuseppe Terragni for the Fascists of Como (1932–36). Although demonstrably classical in conception and proportion, this is a rare example of an undeniably modernist building accepted to serve the Fascist cause.

Bayreuth under the Nazis

The Bayreuth Festival inaugurated by Wagner in 1876 continued after his death under the watchful direction of his widow Cosima and his son Siegfried. Cosima's death in 1930 was shortly followed by that of her son, and when the young Hungarian composer Miklós Rózsa revisited Bayreuth in 1934 after a gap of four years, he found it totally changed: "The old Bayreuth of Toscanini had gone, and had become the Bavarian arsenal for the National Socialists." Instead of rapturous applause for the performers, Rósza recounts how at the end of each act the audience would turn to face Hitler's box and raise their arms in the "Heil Hitler" salute.

Ironically, Bayreuth was facing decay when Hitler turned it, at the warm invitation of Siegfried Wagner's English widow Winifred, into his private court theater. The Festival suddenly found itself in receipt of generous subventions from the Reich Chancellery as well as from Hitler's private funds. In Nazi ideology, all acts, however atrocious, were elevated in the cause of a supposed higher good. Hitler and his colleagues found in the operas of Wagner the perfect expression of such spurious "noble and sacred" ideals. His new acquisition allowed Hitler to indulge to the full his belief in himself as Nietzschean superman and Wagnerian hero. Unfortunately for him, he did not foresee his own *Twilight of the Gods*. Bayreuth survived to become once more a festival where Wagner's music could be appreciated, not used.

The Spanish Civil War

The Spanish Civil War of 1936–39 was a human disaster: a million dead, a catalog of appalling atrocities, a bitter ravaged land and hundreds of the best minds in exile for the next thirty years. And yet it stood as a rallying cry for many people from all parts of the world, holding out for both right and left elusive hopes of a better tomorrow and a more united world. And in that spirit many were drawn to the battle lines, including in their numbers an astonishing array of artists and writers.

Spain had suffered from political instability for many years, and in 1931, in reaction against military dictatorship, had become a republic with a parliament elected by universal suffrage. But by 1936 the government – now composed of socialists, republicans and Communists – had lost control. In July 1936 a military revolt was started by General Franco, with support from the Falange, the Spanish Fascist party. They had expected little resistance, but the people were against them and civil war was inevitable. Military and economic intervention on the part of Hitler and Mussolini to help Franco, and of the Soviet Union on behalf of the Republicans, escalated the conflict, which rapidly took on the nature of a struggle to the death between Fascism and Communism – or between faith and godlessness. As World War I had been "the war to end all wars", the Spanish Civil War became for many "the last great cause". Writers, poets, painters from all over the world rallied to the Republican cause as members of the International Brigades, coordinated in Paris by the Soviet Communist party. Robert Jordan, the fictional hero of Ernest Hemingway's novel *For Whom the Bell Tolls* (1940), spoke for them all when he said: "If we win here we will win everywhere." The French novelist Georges Bernanos was in Majorca at the time. In *A Diary of My Times* (1938), his outraged account of the atrocities committed there, he described the war as the "pretext and alibi" for the war that was to come in Europe, a "foretaste of the tragedy of the Universe".

◀ A scene from the film *L'Espoir*, by André Malraux, 1939. At the outbreak of the Spanish Civil War, the French novelist organized a squadron to fight on the Republican side, and himself became a bomber-pilot in the International Brigade. In this scene a pilot being shot down brought out the entire local community in a display of solidarity which, Malraux stated, stretched from mountain-top to valley. Malraux survived the war and went on to work for the French Resistance during World War II.

▼ *Guernica* by Picasso, 1937. On 26 April, the German Condor Legion, testing its ability to destroy civilian targets, bombed this Basque town; 1600 people were killed. Picasso's painting universalized the horror of the event.

English poets who went to Spain included Stephen Spender, W.H. Auden and C. Day Lewis. They all supported the Republic, but Roy Campbell, poet, bullfighter and author of the long pro-Fascist poem *Flowering Rifle* (1939), fought for the rebels. The French novelist André Malraux was in the Republican Air Force; his novel *Days of Hope* (1938) graphically recorded the defense of Madrid. The great Chilian poet Pablo Neruda was ambassador to the Republic during the Civil War, when he wrote *Spain in the Heart* (1937). The Peruvian César Vallejo raised money for the Republic and wrote a sequence of poems that was printed behind the Republican lines, *Spain, Take Thou This Chalice From Me* (1938).

The English writer George Orwell, who was wounded in the war, documented the confusions of the left, their complex allegiances and "organized disorder", in the classic *Homage to Catalonia* (1938). His experiences in Spain also shaped his later *Animal Farm* (1945), a chilling fable of the perversion of dreams and decency by political force. The most brazen use of such force in Spain came from Hitler. It included the operations of the Condor Legion, Germany's crack aviation unit, which was to blast civilian targets to pieces in bombing raids. On 26 April 1937 it destroyed the Basque town of Guernica. Pablo Picasso commemorated the bombing in one of his most famous paintings, simply called *Guernica*. He had earlier that year illustrated a pamphlet he wrote,

The Dream and the Lie of Franco, with a series of horrific engravings of destruction and suffering. *Guernica* maintained that searing visual pressure. It was as stark and impassioned a response to inhumanity as anything this century, full of passion and inhumanity, has produced. And it was appropriate that it should come from the hand of a Spaniard, rather than from one of the many strangers drawn into the conflict.

As with the poets, so with the painters: the best of them were for the Republic. Like Picasso, the Spanish Surrealist Joan Miró supported the Republican cause, and produced work whose horror derived directly from the war. There was a spectacular output of posters, both educational and propagandist, from both sides, but again the more impressive examples, in a lively Socialist Realist style, were from the artists of the Republic. But when the war ended on 1 April 1939 and the count of dead, exiled and imprisoned was there for all to see, Spain was the heaviest loser. The death at the hands of the rebels of Federico García Lorca, one of Spain's finest poets ever, was the most grievous loss, but many other major writers were driven into exile, imprisoned or had their work banned. The immensely promising poet Miguel Hernandez died in prison in 1942. The list was enormous and the loss intellectually impoverishing – though by the same token the life of Latin America in particular was enriched.

Voices of the thirties
The decade was marked by the activity of some fine poets in the British Isles. T.S. Eliot still provided a critical focus, and a model for other poets; although his rightwing politics diminished his popularity. "Ash Wednesday" (1930) and *Four Quartets* which he embarked on in 1935, show the signs of his conversion (in 1927) to Anglo-Catholicism: "Ash Wednesday" includes repeated fragments of the liturgy; the main strand of the poem is a swelling paean to Mary, Queen of heaven and earth; the "rose garden" with its echoes of the mystic consummation of saints and

▲ The British novelist, George Orwell, on the Aragon Front in Huesca, March 1937. Many artists and liberal intellectuals joined the Communist-organized International Brigade. Orwell ended up in the POUM, a smaller organization.

The Spanish struggle is the fight of reaction against the people, against freedom. My whole life as an artist has been nothing more than a continuous struggle against reaction and the death of art. How could anybody think for a moment that I could be in agreement with reaction and death? When the rebellion began, the legally elected and democratic republican government of Spain appointed me director of the Prado Museum, a post which I immediately accepted. In the panel on which I am working which I shall call Guernica, and in all my recent works of art, I clearly express my abhorrence of the military caste which has sunk Spain in an ocean of pain and death.

PABLO PICASSO, 1937

◄ The Egyptian desert, photographed by Lee Miller, the American photographer and companion of Man Ray. The window on a desolate landscape, combining claustrophobia with emptiness, expressed the Existentialist vision.

of alchemists is her domain. *Four Quartets* was a tour de force in which Eliot took universal philosophical ideas and symbols and created a Christian mystical work of substance and exaltation. Even so, the difficulty he had in experiencing Christ in his fellows is noticeable even here.

The poetic and literary ascendancy in 1930s Britain was taken by a poet who seemed to see more closely into the human hearts. W.H. Auden spearheaded the four poets (the others were C. Day Lewis, Louis MacNeice and Stephen Spender) collectively labeled the "New Country" poets (after a 1933 anthology in which their work appeared), more tellingly the "pylon poets" for their celebration of the postindustrial world and later simply the "thirties poets".

Auden, who has been called the first poet writing in English to feel at home in the 20th century, drew initially on the work of Eliot, as well as Wilfred Owen and Thomas Hardy. His Anglo Catholic upbringing and Nordic ancestry also provided him with raw material. He had digested Marx and Freud; and his work shows a concern with social injustices, and with the tendency for emotional suppression and starvation to result in physical disease. "Miss Gee", written in the

French Cinema in the 1930s

At the end of the 1920s the focus of imaginative filmmaking shifted from Germany to France, where it entered the 1930s in a blaze of Surrealism, encouraged by René Clair's inventive *Entr'acte* of 1924 (a work that involved Erik Satie, Marcel Duchamp and Man Ray) and by Jean Epstein's atmospheric *The Fall of the House of Usher* (1928). A galaxy of great French directors included Jean Renoir, son of the great Impressionist artist, Jean Vigo, Marcel Carné and Clair himself. The Spanish director Luis Buñuel was also working in Paris at the time. His films *Un Chien andalou* (1928; made in association with Salvador Dalí) and *L'Age d'or* (1930) challenged familiar notions of time and space. Bizarre images were presented as a form of assault upon the viewer. Those of a razor slashing an eye and of two dead donkeys draped over two grand pianos became justly famous. Among the central themes of his work were attacks on the Catholic church and middle-class values; these images recurred in his films up to the late 1970s. Interesting experimental work followed, notably in Jean Cocteau's *Blood of a Poet* (1930). This was the multi-talented artist's first film, and it was greeted with incomprehension at the time. Many of its themes reappeared in his later works such as *Beauty and the Beast* (1946) and *Orphée* (1950).

In the 1930s French tended to settle into a smoother and more conventional representation of contemporary life – too smooth and conventional, later directors were to feel. Nevertheless, there was much wit and fantasy in Clair's *A nous la liberté* (1931), and evidence of a memorable personal vision in Jean Vigo's *Zéro de conduite* (1933) and *L'Atalante* (1934). The decade produced one undisputed master in Jean Renoir, whose *La Grande Illusion* (1937) and *La Régle du jeu* (1939) are classics by any standards. The former is set in a World War I prison camp in Germany, the latter in a French country house, but both explore the ways in which men and women manage to keep or break their promises,

and point out the dangerous charm, even the necessity, of maintaining fictions and lies from the past. Renoir's other notable films from the late 1930s were *La Bête humaine* (1938) and *Une Partie de campagne* (1936).

During the German occupation of France many of the French directors, including Renoir, and Clair, went to Hollywood, returning to France after the war. In the 1960s, the so-called New Wave of French film directors – Claude Chabrol, Jean-Luc Godard, Louis Malle, François Truffaut – were to reject both the gloss and the sentiment they found in the national cinema that had developed following this period. Instead, they sought to return to Renoir's concern for human subjects, though investing them with the new energies they found in the blossoming Hollywood genres.

▼ *La Grande Illusion*, by Jean Renoir, 1937. An anti-war film set in a German prison camp for officers in 1917, often considered one of the greatest films of all time. Renoir claimed the story was true, and certainly drew on his experience in the French air force in World War I. In this scene the prisoners perform a vaudeville routine in women's clothing.

▲ Jean Cocteau in his studio. As well as poet and painter, Jean Cocteau played social gadfly to prewar Paris. In the 1920s he worked on ballets, including *Antigone* (1922), on which he collaborated with Picasso and Coco Chanel. In the 1930s he turned to film, including the experimental *Blood of a Poet* (1930) and *Beauty and the Beast* (1946), possibly his masterpiece.

The chestnut tree's root plunged into the ground, just under my seat. I no longer remembered that it was a root. Words had disappeared, and with them the meaning of things, their modes of use, the faint landmarks men have traced on their surface. I was sitting, a little hunched, head down, alone before this black knotty mass, wholly insensate, and which frightened me. And then this enlightenment. Never, up to the last few days, had I guessed what "to exist" meant.

JEAN-PAUL SARTRE, *NAUSEA* (1938)

ballad form which he employed for a time, is the succinctly told tale of a woman who, convention-bound to the point of total emotional negation until "the days and nights went by her/Like waves round a Cornish wreck" dies of cancer and becomes a physical object of interest for medical students.

This preoccupation echoes his attitude to the land, which he wrote about often. As the human body for Auden plainly showed forth the human psyche, so, conversely, the depth of feeling evoked in him by the landscape told him that the land also was a living and spiritual entity.

Like the other "thirties poets", Auden, a self-diagnosed "pink liberal", saw as his the role of truthful witness in the Depression years, darkened further as they were by the growing shadow of Fascism. Hardly surprising that such observers as these should turn to Marxism as the proper antidote; but by 1939 Day Lewis, Spender and Auden had been disillusioned by the reality of Soviet communism.

The consistency of Auden's work is in his effort at truth, which espouses different styles, from the comic or the chatty to lovely lyrics like "On This Island" (1935) or soul-searching as in "The Question" (1930). In "Consider" (1930) he pointed to the difficulty of the innocent pursuit of private happiness in a plainly tormented world, and warned, "It is later than you think." He shared with Eliot a mystical concern with finding the invisible and indescribable core of experience.

Day Lewis and Spender share a more anxious earnestness about the world of economic and moral constriction; their commentary also bore witness – Day Lewis' "Magnetic Mountain" (1933) is a solid work – but they lacked the scope and playfulness of Auden. MacNeice took no political stance, but "The Sunlight on the Garden" (1937) and *Autumn Journal* (1938) show the depth of his awareness of the coming horror.

Another Irishman, the literary giant W.B. Yeats, was still active during the 1930s. Politically rightwing, like Eliot, he was concerned with internal Irish politics; and was most inclined to deal in his poetry with the eternal; as in "Byzantium" (1930): "A starlit or a moonlit dome disdains/All that man is". During his last years Yeats concerned himself habitually with death, as in "Under Ben Bulben".

A quest for meaning: Existentialist writers

In a century in which individual freedom had been so curtailed, so many cherished assumptions declared suspect, so many agonizing choices presented to men and women, and in which life itself had come to seem so overwhelming as to be without meaning, it was not surprising that a major philosophy should be built around exactly those conditions. Existentialism concerned itself with the reality of human freedom, the nature of what can be said to be "given" and the necessity of choice, however impossible that choice might seem.

Existentialist ideas were not new. In the 17th century, the French mathematician Blaise Pascal

meaning beyond itself in a meaningless world. The condition of the world is absurd and human beings are alienated from it, in a condition of "nausea" – the title of his major novel of 1938. In fact, just because it was concerned precisely with how people act or should act in a harrowing world, Existentialism lent itself readily to the concerns of fiction: the determination of human character by human choices, and the consequences of human action. Novels and plays were therefore as valid ways of examining such questions as philosophical treatises. It was heroic dedication to useful action in a meaningless world that characterized the philosophy, and these novels and plays emerged as actions in themselves. *Nausea* demonstrated the otherness of the world as Sartre's hero Roquentin confronted it. Sartre's plays, such as *The Flies* and *No Exit*, come across as vivid action even though they turn on ideas.

The outbreak of war made questions of human responsibility even more crucial. Simone de Beauvoir prefaced her novel of the French Resistance, *The Blood of Others* (1945), with a quotation from the Russian novelist Dostoyevski: "Each of us is responsible for everything and to every human being." Sartre, who worked with the French Resistance during the war, declared in his major philosophical work, *Being and Nothingness* (1943): "I am as profoundly responsible for the war as if I had myself declared it." In the novel *The Outsider* (1942), by the Algerian-born Albert Camus, the unemotional Meursault shoots an Arab and is condemned to death. In the uncannily clear and objective world of the novel, the whole world seems to come to a standstill under the Algerian sun, and it crosses Meursault's mind that "one might fire or not fire – and it would

▲ Henry Moore sketching in the London Underground. The terrible conditions which prevailed in London during the Blitz gave rise to his extraordinary series of drawings of sleepers, in which Londoners were portrayed as if caught up in a collective nightmare. The experience of recording the impact of the war on ordinary people had a subtle influence on Moore's work. Like the work of other artists caught up in documentation, his sculpture acquired a more popular basis in the postwar period.

had argued that religious faith involved unavoidable decisions taken in the face of unavoidable doubt: "God is or He is not: which side should we come down on?" The Danish 19th-century thinker Søren Kierkegaard saw the answer to that, beyond a reasoned balance of probabilities, as a "leap" of commitment. The German Martin Heidegger, who held a professorial chair of philosophy at Freiburg right through the Nazi period, saw people as "thrown" into existence, a "given" state beyond which decisions had to be made which either merged individuals into the crowd or led them to self-realization. It was from such ideas that Existentialism developed, and it became especially important in France during the 1930s and 1940s, when its leading ideas were propounded by Jean-Paul Sartre, who had studied under Heidegger. Albert Camus and Simone de Beauvoir were also major French Existentialist writers. Although Paris was the acknowledged center for Existentialist thought during these years, it was developed outside France too by writers such as Miguel de Unamuno in Spain, Nikolay Berdyayev in the Soviet Union and by the Germans Martin Buber and Karl Jaspers.

Sartre's view was that we are "given" our existential state and that our subsequent actions are the measure of our authenticity, of our being in good or bad faith, as he put it. Action has no

▲ *Behind Barbed Wire*, by Henri Pieck, drawn in Buchenwald concentration camp. Despite the risks and the insurmountable difficulties of getting materials, art persisted, and with it, the morale of the victims.

▼ *Europe after the Rain II* (1940–42) by Max Ernst. The painting was begun in Europe, then, with typical Surrealist nonchalance, wrapped in a parcel and posted to America. Ernst, by this time in exile, then completed the image. This muddy world, strewn with fragments of bodies and presided over by half-human soldiery, was a disconcertingly realistic portrait of Europe in the early 1940s.

come to absolutely the same thing." This is the existential world, to live and die with the absurd or to wrench it into meaning by right action. In the real world of the 1930s and 1940s, with the specters of depression, repression and war never far away, it was a philosophy that held much intellectual appeal.

Politics in the cabaret

Cabaret culture had flourished in Europe's major cities, particularly in Paris, Berlin and Vienna, since the turn of the century. Cabaret – a sophisticated nightclub with singers and review artists – offered a sympathetic social setting to young artists at odds with Establishment culture, and evolved its own style, a curious blend of the sentimental and the satirical. Singers (or rather *diseuses*) such as Yvette Guilbert, angular and unconventionally attractive, ruled the small stages of the smoky clubs, singing sweet-sounding ballads with emotional sourness or political bite. Debussy, Milhaud, Satie and Schoenberg were all at one time attracted to the cabaret, and as the changing political environment inexorably limited freedom of expression, the "underground" nature of cabaret could give – at times not without risk – a home to the freethinking and the experimental.

The cabaret was one of the genres informing the work of the German playwright Bertolt Brecht, particularly in his collaborations with two fellow-Germans, composers Hanns Eisler and Kurt Weill. Brecht's ideas for an epic (ie objective) theater were both political and esthetic. His first collaboration with Weill had been the *Mahagonny Songspiel* (1927), a setting of five related poems. Three years later, after working together on *The Threepenny Opera*, *The Lindberg Flight* and *Happy End*, Brecht and Weill expanded the *Songspiel* into

a full-scale opera, *Rise and Fall of the City of Mahagonny*. Mahagonny itself is a capitalist symbol, in which pleasure is strictly related to the ability to pay. The various dubious characters who people the city are given music that is often both lyrical and catchy. Brecht was ambivalent about its effectiveness, however, feeling that he and Weill had not moved far enough from the attitudes of conventional opera, where the members of the audience are allowed the luxury of not following the implications of the stage action for their own lives.

One of Weill's most successful scores was for a later collaboration with Brecht. The Jewish composer had fled to Paris with little more than he stood up in after a Nazi-inspired campaign to have all his work banned in state-subsidized theaters. *The Seven Deadly Sins* (1933) is both song sequence and ballet score. The character of Anna is split into two: the hard-headed "good" Anna (who sings) has constantly to keep in check her soft-hearted "bad" sister (who dances). Conventional morality is stood on its head as the virtues are shown to be wasteful and uneconomic. Brecht's irony acquired a pungent, touching wistfulness as well as an occasional jokiness in Weill's realization.

Hanns Eisler had studied with Schoenberg and Webern, but he joined the German Communist party and broke with Schoenberg. When he met Brecht he was already seeking a way to use music to serve and change society. Between 1926 and 1933 he wrote many marching songs for leftwing groups, which were used throughout Europe. His tunes were straightforward and often in minor keys, which Eisler believed to be more threatening than the major. His first collaboration with Brecht was *The Measures Taken*, followed in

their art into the service of the state. Music was no exception. If it was to be acceptable to the authorities it had to ignore all the developments in compositional techniques that had happened since the turn of the century. Socialism under Stalin demanded optimism and aspiration. In creative terms this meant diatonic tonality and hummable soaring tunes.

In the 1920s, Dmitri Shostakovich had been closely allied with the experimental principles of composers such as Webern, Berg and Hindemith. By the time of the 1932 decree that brought music under state control, he had already completed a number of works including his satirical opera *The Nose* (1930), and was nearing completion of his second opera, *The Lady Macbeth of the Mtensk District*. *Lady Macbeth* did not fit Stalin's scheme

◀ **Kurt Weill rehearsing in America. Weill and his fellow German Bertolt Brecht were only two among a mass exodus of artists, writers, musicians who flooded America and New York in particular. As the situation in Europe became clear, more socialist and Jewish intellectuals arrived, galvanizing American culture. The exiles included Piet Mondrian, André Breton, and Salvador Dalí.**

1931 by the Gorky adaptation, *The Mother*, which Brecht undertook in memory of Rosa Luxemburg. When Hitler came to power in 1933, Eisler's music was banned. There followed 15 years in exile and a series of highly political, anti-fascist works. Eisler collaborated with Brecht on *Round Heads and Pointed Heads*, and later, in the United States in 1945, on the montage of eyewitness accounts of Nazi persecution, *Fear and Misery in the Third Reich*.

Another German composer, Paul Hindemith, was also an early Brecht collaborator. He approached the pressures on the artist in a time of political repression in a different way. His opera *Mathis der Maler*, set at the time of the Peasants' Revolt in Germany, follows the inner debate of the German painter Matthias Grünewald as he decides to abandon his art and devote himself to political action, and his discovery of the futility of such a course. The opera is clearly personal; Hindemith wrote that Grünewald's experiences had "shattered his very soul". He too proved a target for the Nazis. His membership of an "international" group of atonal composers, the "immorality" of his operas and his "parody" of a favourite Nazi Bavarian military march inspired a personal attack by Goebbels at a 1934 rally. He lost his teaching position and his music was boycotted. In 1937 he left for Switzerland and in 1940 went to New York.

Writing to order: Russian music under Stalin
In parallel with Nazi persecution of artists whose views did not support those of the party, in the Soviet Union throughout the 1930s Stalin increased the pressure on artists of all kinds to put

of things. Although it was well received at its première in 1934, in 1936 Stalin saw a performance, and almost immediately afterwards it was denounced in a famous article in *Pravda* entitled "Chaos instead of Music" as being "fidgety, screaming, neurotic, coarse, primitive and vulgar". As a result of this officially sanctioned outburst, the Union of Soviet Composers convened a meeting to discuss the "correct" future for Soviet music. Composer after composer denounced Shostakovich.

He could have turned out some bombastic celebratory work to regain his position. Indeed his next major work, the Fifth Symphony, did restore his political fortunes, but.it did so without artistic compromise. He had been pondering the question of tragedy in a socialist environment

(part of the complaint about *Lady Macbeth* was that it portrayed tragedy, which was of necessity pessimistic). Shostakovich saw this as a false connection: "I think Soviet tragedy has every right to exist. But the contents must be suffused with a positive inspiration, like, for instance, the life-affirming pathos of Shakespeare's tragedies." It was a wise analogy. The lyricism and final optimism of the symphony bore out his words, and probably saved him from one of Stalin's camps.

In June 1941 Hitler invaded the Soviet Union and Shostakovich was trapped in the siege of Leningrad, where he joined a firefighting squad. His Seventh Symphony, the "Leningrad", was the musical result of that 900 days. A microfilm score was flown to the United States and immediately taken up by the conductor Arturo

▼ A still from *Alexander Nevsky*, an epic film dealing with Russian national glory, made by Eisenstein in 1938. Prokofiev collaborated on the score. The partnership was resumed on the even larger-scale production *Ivan the Terrible*, released in two parts (1942 and 1945). Eisenstein's presentation of Russian history fulfilled a Soviet need for nationalistic solidarity in the face of Germany's aggression.

Writers under Totalitarianism

The relative freedom enjoyed by Soviet writers in the 1920s came to an abrupt end in 1929, when Stalin decided to bring both the peasantry and the intelligentsia under the total control of the Communist party. Through the militant Russian Association of Proletarian Writers (RAPP), a campaign of terror was unleashed aimed at breaking the will of those who opposed such control. Vladimir Mayakovsky was put under great pressure to join RAPP, and finally capitulated in February 1930, only to shoot himself in despair two months later. Evgeny Zamyatin, marked down as a scapegoat, managed to leave the country. His emigration together with Mayakovsky's suicide marked the end of creative freedom. In 1932 RAPP was replaced by an organization called the Union of Soviet Writers, membership of which was essential for anyone who wished to write professionally. At the First Congress of Soviet Writers in 1934, Andrey Zhdanov, Stalin's spokesman on cultural matters, announced a new policy of "Socialist Realism": literature was to be easily intelligible to ordinary people, to present positive heroes and happy endings, in order to affirm the existing order. By the late 1930s all Soviet literature was also required to contain glorification of Stalin. Not surprisingly, most writers of any stature gradually disappeared from the scene. Many hundreds were imprisoned, executed or exiled in the purges of 1936–38, among them Isaac Babel, Osip Mandelstam and the theater director Vsevolod Meyerhold. Only a few writers were fortunate enough to return from exile. Stalin himself affected a great interest in the arts, asserting that writers should be "engineers of human souls", and apparently chose to spare the lives of Boris Pasternak and Mikhail Bulgakov – though Bulgakov's masterpiece *The Master and Margarita*, written in the 1930s, was not published until 1966–67. Others too, such as Andrey Platonov and Anna Akhmatova, produced "underground" literature that was only published after Stalin's death.

World War II brought some relief, but in 1946 the expulsion of Akhmatova and Mikhail Zoshchenko from the Writers' Union signaled the bleak period known as the "Zhdanov era". The years from 1946 to Stalin's death in 1953 were to be the most sterile of all.

Toscanini. Its celebration of the Russian struggle against Nazism proved an ideal symbol of heroic resistance for the American public. His Eighth Symphony (1944) was more successful as an evocation of the horrors of war. The unavoidability of pain and the eternal desire for peace run through the work, and if the optimism called for by the authorities is present, then it is there in a very dark but also very truthful form.

Shostakovich's compatriot Sergey Prokofiev had spent much of his early life in Paris, with visits to the United States. Although he knew what the situation was like for composers in the Soviet Union, he decided in the early 1930s to return home. He was not a natural diplomat, and although he subscribed to the party line of making music appeal to everyone and including some didactic content, his work frequently did not meet with approval. His Sixth Symphony (1945–

47), much influenced by the war, showed none of the required optimism; and his opera *War and Peace*, based on Tolstoy's novel, had to be repeatedly revised and was not staged until after his death. In 1948 both men were again out of favor, accused of representing "the cult of atonality, dissonance and discord" and of demonstrating an "infatuation with confused, neurotic combinations which transform music into cacophony".

Music for film
By the end of World War II film music had come a long way from the days of a pianist or small instrumental ensemble tucked away in the cinema pit. The first major sound film was *The Jazz Singer* in 1927. The first film to have synchronized sound was Alfred Hitchcock's *Blackmail* (1929), closely followed in Germany by Josef von Sternberg's

It is the duty of the composer, like the poet, the sculptor, or the painter, to serve his fellow men, to beautify human life and point the way to a radiant future. Such is the immutable code of art as I see it.
SERGEY PROKOFIEV, 1946.

Ballet and Dance in Europe and the United States

The Blue Angel, which had a score by Friedrich Hollaender. Gradually, both young and established composers began to involve themselves with film.

Writing music for film involves very precise timings. The demands on both composer and conductor are considerable. When working on documentary films in the mid-1930s, the young Benjamin Britten was renowned for his ability to cut to the precise length of soundtrack required by the final film, without leaving an obvious join – though he had reservations about the result being "music". For the film *Night Mail*, a collaboration with W.H. Auden, Britten was required to write "train noises". Britten's full score for the memorable sequence as the locomotive gets up a head of steam calls for steam (compressed air), sandpaper on slate, rail (small trolley), booms, aluminum drill, motor Moy (a hand-cranked,

▶ **William Walton's music being recorded for Laurence Olivier's *Hamlet* in 1948. Walton had also written the score for Olivier's production of *Henry V*, one of the British cinema's major contributions to national wartime morale. The technical difficulties and theoretical questions underlying the writing of a film score appealed to a number of other British composers, including Benjamin Britten.**

chain-operated camera), hammer, siren and coal falling down a shaft.

For feature films, styles of working could vary considerably. The composer might be brought in at very much the last moment to write a score to fit the edited film, or might be involved from the very beginning in a true collaboration. The Frenchman Georges Auric had a rather eccentric arrangement with Jean Cocteau for *Blood of a Poet* (1930). The music was composed and recorded without regard for the action. Cocteau would then edit by means of arbitrary cuts and *montage* effects, so that the music was as much raw material for his editing creativity as the film itself. Typical of the Hollywood way of working was Dimitri Tiomkin's contribution to Frank Capra's *Lost Horizon* (1937). Tiomkin provided a score to fit the rough cut, a version running some five hours. Thereafter music was trimmed along with film. Tiomkin wanted to express the film's tension between East and West in musical terms, so he used two main themes, a stylized and conventional love theme for the Westerners and a much looser, rhythmically indeterminate melody, with elements of timeless folksong, for the Shangri-La inhabitants.

In Russia, a near-seamless collaboration was achieved between Prokofiev and the director Sergei Eisenstein on the films *Alexander Nevsky* (1938) and *Ivan the Terrible* (1942). Nevsky was the perfect hero to please the Soviet authorities: a noble, brave 13th-century Russian leader. Each night Prokofiev would view the day's rushes with Eisenstein; in the morning the score for the scene would be delivered to the studio. "Prokofiev works like a clock", declared Eisenstein. Even Stalin was delighted by the result.

After Diaghilev's death in 1929, various rival attempts were made to recreate the glittering ambience of the *Ballets Russes*, but it was the brand new companies, which chose to shed the Russian image, that had greater long-term success. In Britain, Marie Rambert and Ninette de Valois set up their own schools and companies, determined to develop a distinctively British style of ballet. The small-scale Ballet Rambert was notable for encouraging the first British choreographers, Frederick Ashton and Anthony Tudor, while de Valois' Vic-Wells ballet was to become Britain's Royal Ballet in 1956. Ashton's restrained, lyrical style was in perfect accord with classical principles, while Margot Fonteyn, the company's leading ballerina, came to define the quintessential purity of the English style. American ballet was a much tougher, more extrovert affair. George Balanchine was invited to the United States in 1933 and founded first the School of American Ballet then the American Ballet, which in 1948 became New York City Ballet. Working with his own specially trained dancers, Balanchine developed the style that was to become the hallmark of American ballet – fast, long-limbed and dangerous, with jazzy inversions of academic steps and positions.

Modern dance emerged during the late 1920s and early 1930s as a systematized alternative to classical ballet. In Central Europe the prime initiator was Rudolf Laban, who set out to analyze all the expressive possibilities of the body, including the relation of movement to space and the connection between psychology and motion. His findings were put to powerful theatrical effect in the starkly expressive dances of his pupil Mary Wigman. In the United States the two great pioneers of modern dance were Martha Graham and Doris Humphreys, both of whom sought to make dance expressive of real emotion and relevant to the complexities of 20th-century life. Both women developed techniques which actively spurned the decorative virtuosity of academic ballet, using abrupt, extreme or contorted physical gestures to express extremes of emotion. Many of the principles of classical ballet were inverted to invest the body with new drama; and movements like crouches and falls made dramatic play of gravity.

◀ *War Theme* by Martha Graham (1941).

THE DEPRESSION YEARS

Time Chart

	1930	1931	1932	1933	1934	1935	1936	1937
Industry	• Majority of production in the USSR now industrial (53%) • Foundation of a large iron–coal combine by the building of plants in Magnitogorsk and Kusnezk (USSR)	• May: Opening of a branch of Ford in Cologne (USA/Ger) • Jun: Collapse of the Nordwolle textile company leads to a banking crisis (Ger)	• Feb: Government assistance program for agriculture (Fr) • Collapse of the match company of I. Kreuger (Swe) • Brazilian coffee destroyed to maintain prices (Bra)	• Aug: Crisis in the lace and wool industry (Fr) • Formation of an international steel trust registered in Luxembourg, the International Natural Steel Export Company	• Apr: Extension of import control over all industrial products (Ger)	• Jan: Decision to destroy up to 10 million cotton spindles in the Lancashire cotton industry (UK) • Nov: Nationalization of the French mining industry	• Jun/Oct: Nationalization of the French armament industry and the military airlines • Nov: Debate on nationalization of the British armament industry	• Mar: New assistance plan for American agriculture, involving the support of prices by the regulation of supply • Jun: Decision to make war preparations in British industry and agriculture
Technology	• F. Whittle obtains a patent for his jet engine (UK) • R. Drew invents scotch tape (USA)	• 1 May: Opening of a radio station near Moscow with the greatest range in the world (USSR)	• 9 Aug: R.S. Willows applies for a patent for his discovery of non-creasing fabric (UK)	• M. Knoll, B. von Borries, E. Ruska and E. Brüche develop the electron microscope (Ger)	• R. Watson-Watt builds a radio navigation system (UK) • Industrial production of synthetic silk and staple fiber (Ger)	• Continuous steel casting introduced in the USA and USSR • 13 Apr: Opening of the London–Brisbane air route	• First standard diesel car produced by Daimler Benz (Ger) • H. Focke constructs the first viable helicopter (Ger)	•Feb: Du Pont applies for a patent for nylon (USA) • G. Eyston reaches 502 km/h in his car *Thunderbolt* (UK)
Finance	• 7 May: Bank for International Settlements (BIS) established in Basle on capital of $500 million • Jun: Issue of the international Young loan of 1.2 billion Marks, to commercialize the German reparations • Bank of England establishes the Bankers Industrial Development Company (UK)	• 1 Jul: Hoover moratorium on war debts and reparations • 13 Jul: Collapse of the German Danatbank causes a banking crisis. Withdrawal of credits granted from abroad and control of foreign exchange ensues. The bank is placed under the control of the government • 21 Sep: Britain abandons the gold standard. End of the leadership of the pound in the world economy	• Mar: Merger of the Danatbank and the Dresdner Bank (Ger) • May: Establishment of the Exchange Equalization Account (UK) • Jul: Foreign exchange control in Japan. Measures against the withdrawal of capital • Establishment of the National Bank for Commerce and Industry as a successor to the National Credit Bank (Fr)	• 4 Mar: Federal Deposit Insurance Corp. established to protect savers. Security Act allows control over the capital market (USA) • 6 Mar: USA abandons the gold standard. US president Roosevelt is authorized to fix a new gold dollar parity • Devaluation of the yen (Jap) • Establishment of the Institute for Industrial Reconstruction (IRI) (It)	• Jan: New gold parity for the dollar. USA raises the gold price from $20.67 to $35 per ounce after abandoning the gold standard. Gold Reserve Act (USA) • Feb: Establishment of the Export–Import Bank with capital of $500 million (USA) • Devaluation of the Czech crown • Severe control of foreign exchange, and devaluation of Belgian, Italian, Swiss and Danzig currencies	• Prohibition of the universal bank system. Belgian General Society eliminates the General Society Bank as deposit bank. Establishment of the Flemish Credit Bank in Brussels (Bel) • Legislation for the German credit system put into force. Note-issuing monopoly by the Reichsbank after the right of issuing notes by the last private central banks is abolished (Ger)	• Devaluation of the Swiss franc and Italian lira • Devaluation of the French franc and a change in the regulations of the Banque de France. Establishment of the Caisse Nationale de Marches d'État (Fr) • Construction of Fort Knox in Kentucky, where half of the US gold stock is laid down (USA)	• Jan: Devaluation of the yen (Jap) • Jul: Devaluation of the French franc and suspension of its gold parity • Establishment of the Institut Nationale de Credit Agricole in Brussels (Bel) • Note-issuing monopoly for the Central Bank of China
Economic Policy	• Jan: Young plan signed by the German government. Amount of reparations fixed at 38 billion Marks payable in 59 annual rates until 1988 • 16 Jul: First emergency decrees issued by the German government to protect the economy • Reduction in prices for raw materials on the world market	• Jun: Beginning of a sharp deflationary policy by the German government • 11 Jul: Negotiations among the governors of the Reichsbank, Bank of England and Banque de France to counter the German crisis of reparation payments. Failure leads to credit restriction by the Reichsbank (Ger) • Jul: McMillan report demands the maintenance of the gold standard (UK)	• Jan: Establishment of the Reconstruction Finance Corporation, an institute for financing the creation of work and encouraging business activity (USA) • Jun: Conference of London on German reparations. Remaining debt fixed at 3 billion Marks • Aug: Chancellor von Papen announces an economic program for increasing business activity by creation of work (Ger)	• Mar: US president Roosevelt announces his New Deal to overcome the economic depression • Mar: Accession to power of the National Socialist party brings a reorganization of economic associations in a corporative pattern and measures to create work (Ger) • Jul: National Recovery Act enforced to achieve an increase in business activities (USA)	• Sep: Adjustment of imports to the German export possibilities, the "new plan" initiated by H. Schacht • Sep: Industrial league prevents the introduction of the forty-hour week (UK) • Establishment of a corporatist economic system by way of confederations and syndicates of employers and employees as supreme economic associations (It)	• Feb: German minister of finance is authorized to finance governmental creation of work without the consent of the Reichstag • Aug: Economic emergency acts in France to abolish the budget deficit and cause an increase in economic activity • Oct: Establishment of the bureau of industrial cooperation for analyzing the best methods for recovery (USA)	• Mar: Mussolini demands the reorganization of the Italian economy into major corporations (It) • 9 Sep: Tripartite Monetary Agreement signed to reorganize the international monetary system after the collapse of the gold bloc (USA/Fr/UK) • Publication of *The General Theory of Employment, Interest and Money* by J.M. Keynes (UK)	• On the order of the League of Nations, G. Haberler produces a study of the theories of business cycles, *Prosperity and Depression* • Oct: Establishment of the Supreme Autarky Council (It) • Nov: Roosevelt's program for increasing business activities published, with an increase in house building and public utilities (USA)
International	• May: French minister of foreign affairs A. Briand publishes his memorandum for the establishment of a United Nations of Europe	• Jul: Conference in London on the German crisis of reparations payments • Sep: Basle standstill agreement for external debts and reparations signed • Sep: Establishment of the Silver Association in London for promoting the bimetallic covering of currencies	• Jan: Establishment of an international bureau for stock exchanges by the International Chamber of Commerce • Feb: Legislation on the final ending of free trade (UK) • Jul: Conference on world trade in Ottawa	• May: Agreement on trade relations between the Soviet Union and Italy and between France and the UK • Conference on the world economy in London demands removal of all trade obstacles, without important results • Oct: Suspension of import tax between France and Italy	• Mar: End of the tariff war between Germany and Poland • Mar: Conference of Valparaiso publishes principles for the regulation of trade relations between the American countries • Dec: American committee for the boycott of German products established	• Feb: Boycott of Germany by the USA. Jewish companies oppose US–German trade relations • Jun: Italy reduces import quotas • Nov: First pan-American economic conference demands an extension of international trade	• Apr: Agreement on trade signed between Germany and the Soviet Union • Jul: Soviet government publishes plans for import restrictions • Dec: Establishment of an Anglo–German company for compensation in trade	• May: Member countries of the Oslo convention condemn all obstacles to trade • Jun: International Labor Conference publishes a declaration on the introduction of the 40-hour week • Jul: Establishment of a German–Belgian–Luxembourg economic committee for the promotion of trade
Misc.	• Beginning of military expansion in Asia by Japan	• Japan attacks and occupies Manchuria • Westminster Statute settled between the countries of the Commonwealth	• First international disarmament talks of the League of Nations ends in failure	• 30 Jan: Hitler becomes chancellor of Germany. Beginning of the Third Reich • Mar: Coup d'état by Dollfuss in Austria	• First meeting of Hitler and Mussolini in Venice. Political collaboration between the two governments begins (Ger/It)	• 15 Sep: Nuremberg laws initiate racial discrimination against the Jews in Germany	• Beginning of the Spanish civil war • Remilitarization of the Rhineland (Ger)	• Sino–Japanese war begins after the Marco Polo bridge incident

48

1938	1939
● Jan: German government urges the exclusion of non-Aryans from all positions in the private sector	● Apr: Preparations for war made in France involving the forming of an economic organization and an increase in production
● Aug: Construction of an oil pipeline from the Atlantic Ocean to Paris (Fr)	● Aug: Transfer of over 30 industrial plants to Manzhouguo (Jap)
● P. Schlack discovers Perlon fiber (Ger)	● P.H. Müller produces DDT (Swi)
● 18 Dec: Opening of the world's first mobile telephone station in Essex (UK)	● 28 Jun: First Atlantic passenger flight by PanAm (USA)
Mar: After the *Anschluss*, the Reichsmark becomes legal tender in Austria. Austrian central banks taken over by the Reichsbank	● Jun: Protest by the board of directors and the resignation of the Reichsbank president Schacht after a law authorizing unlimited credits for the government from the Reichsbank
● May: Devaluation of the French franc	● Sep: Control of foreign exchange, confiscations and reparations determine the international capital markets after the outbreak of World War II
● Apr: Creation of a work program at the cost of $4.5 billion by US president Roosevelt	● Jan: Plan for the recovery of financial and economic power. Reduction of public debts (Fr)
● May: French prime minister Daladier publishes a national economic plan	● Mar: The currency of northern China leaves the pound bloc and joins the yen bloc
● Jun: Transformation of the Japanese economy into a war economy agreed	● Oct: Noiseless war finance begins using treasury bills, bonds and an eightfold increase in cash circulation (Ger)
● Dec: New principles of foreign exchange control in Germany. Disagreement over financing the war industry	● Dec: Agreement on mutual financial aid with France (UK)
● Jun: Belgian prime minister van Zeeland publishes a plan for the enlargement of trade and reorganization of the world economy to counter protectionism	● Mar: Longterm economic agreement signed between Germany and Romania
	● Apr: "Great German" tariff area established
● Jul: Four agreements on economic relations between France and Germany signed	● Sep: Agreement signed on trade relations between Germany and the USSR
● Dec: Pan-American conference in Lima agrees on further development of inter-American trade	● Sep: Establishment of a common financial and economic committee by the Pan-American conference in Panama
● 13 Mar: *Anschluss* of Austria into the Third Reich (Ger)	● 23 Aug: Nazi–Soviet nonaggression pact signed
● 1 Oct: Incorporation of the Sudetenland into Germany	● 1 Sept: German invasion of Poland initiates World War II

"Industry has no orthodoxies; industry is changing all the time, industry is not governed by wise sayings and traditions, it is all the time experimenting; it is opportunist, it is always trying new things; but the extraordinary character of finance is the extent to which it is governed by orthodoxy, it is kept back by maxims and orthodoxies and things handed down and things that were established a long time ago."

J.M. KEYNES, 1930

"It is very easy to produce a simple theoretical exposition which by its very simplicity seems cogent and attractive: but in fact the economic world is very far from simple and any single explanation seems to me to be almost certainly wrong by the very fact that it is single."

OTTO NIEMEYER, 1930

"The main characteristic of the crisis, at any rate during the first two years, appears to have been that an industrial depression set in almost simultaneously with an agricultural crisis, due to quite different causes, at a time when the power of resistance and the stability of the economic situation…were reduced and much smaller than before the war. The industrial depression and the agricultural crisis exercised an aggravating influence upon one another."

LEAGUE OF NATIONS, 1931

"In present conditions any hopes held out to the Germans must be liable to create disappointment… Although things in Germany may seem bad, they will be made infinitely worse if Germany throws in the sponge and does not carry through the Young Plan as long as she possibly can."

SIR FREDERICK LIETH-ROSS, 1931

"Hungarian nationalism has fed ever since 1919 on the open wounds made by the peace treaties which, in their comparative iniquitousness, reached in the Treaty of Trianon the most iniquitous point. Hungary lost… 68.5% of its territory…58.2% of its population…all its gold, silver , copper, salt , and mercury…85% of its forests…56% of its horses,69% of its cattle, 52% of its factories, 57% of its arable land, and 52% of its total wheat production."

JOHN GUNTHER, 1936

"The role played by competition in capitalistic society… must with us be played by the constant pressure arising from the needs of the masses."

NIKOLAI BUKHARIN, c. 1932

Datafile

The causes of the world economic crisis were varied. They lay partly in the overproduction of both industrial and agricultural goods and in the structural problems experienced by almost all agricultural and industrial countries, particularly the old industrial nations of Western Europe but also in the United States. They could also be found, however, in the monetary sphere: in the mistaken monetary and credit policy of the United States, in the negative effects of the stock market crash, in the incorrect handling of the gold standard, in structural deflation and the problems of international debt. In many countries production sank sharply while unemployment increased. The decline in prices of certain products accelerated; the prices of others began to fall. Stock market prices slumped dramatically and exchange rates were further sharply devalued. The decline in world trade showed clearly to what extent the crisis signified a disintegration of the international economy. International trade did not recover until after World War II.

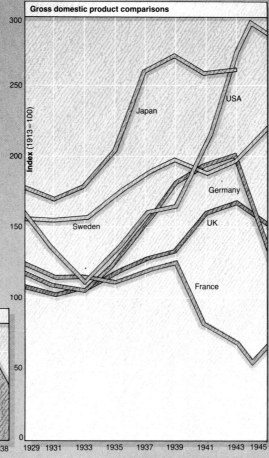

Gross domestic product comparisons

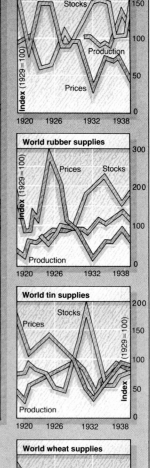

World cotton supplies

World rubber supplies

World tin supplies

World wheat supplies

New York stock market prices

▲ The beginning of the fall in share prices on the New York Stock Exchange in September 1929 was partly an expression of the uncertain economic situation, especially in the United States. It was also itself a cause of the slump into the Depression, resulting in bankruptcy and ruin. Above all, it shattered trust in the capitalist system.

▶ Between 1929 and 1933 world trade shrank by two-thirds. Many countries suffered from the decline in foreign demand, especially the smaller industrial countries and developing countries which exported primary products. The decline was a result of the collapse in national production and restrictive foreign economic policy.

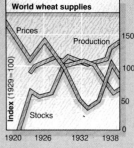

World trade value

▲ During the crisis, all the developed countries had to accept a more or less severe drop in GDP. The upswing in the 1930s, however, varied considerably. A real boom took place only in Germany and Japan. The United States experienced an upswing but 1937–38 saw a renewed crisis. Recovery in Britain was slow, and the French economy stagnated.

▲ Raw materials and foodstuffs were affected by the crisis even more severely than manufactured goods. Production was maintained or even expanded in order to secure some sort of return, despite the fall in prices. Overproduction often accelerated the fall in prices. Government measures to reduce agricultural areas were slow to take effect.

◀ The entire interwar period was one of extremely high unemployment. The Great Depression forced unemployment rates up to a level unique in this century. At the beginning of the 1930s in some countries one in three workers was unemployed, figures that express the extreme wretchedness that the Depression brought with it.

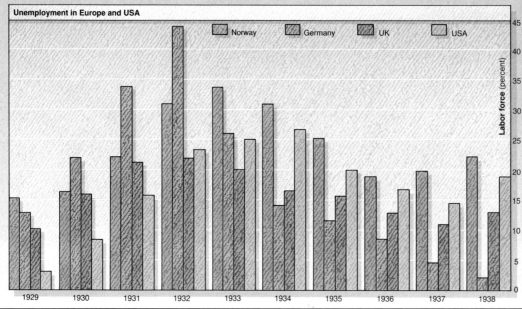

Unemployment in Europe and USA

Norway   Germany   UK   USA

CRISIS AND DEPRESSION

The Great Depression was the biggest crisis ever experienced by the world economy. It hit almost every country: the highly developed countries of Western Europe and the United States; the less developed ones like Canada, Australia, Japan and Argentina; and the underdeveloped countries of Latin America, Asia and Africa just as soon as they became involved in the world market. Many countries experienced the catastrophic breakdown of their national economies, and only a few came through without major damage. The Depression manifested itself in events which had no obvious relevance for many people, such as the complete deterioration of stock prices, the dissolution of the international currency system or the fall of world prices: and also in the immediately felt misery caused by the decline of industrial and agricultural production, the enormous rise in unemployment all over the world and the subsequent reduction in wages. Statistics cannot convey the extent of the effects of the Depression. In 1932, 30 million people were unemployed, while millions more suffered from short hours and extremely low wages in the industrial world alone. The consequences were hunger, higher mortality, apathy and hopelessness, as well as an increase in crime. Political radicalism grew in response to these conditions. As markets for their raw materials and foodstuffs shrank, farmers in developing countries were forced back to subsistence farming despite the fact that people were starving all over the world. In industrial countries farms were abandoned, fertile farm land turned into steppe, and harvests were destroyed in the fields. With the whole world watching, wheat was used to fuel locomotives and coffee was dumped into the sea. And while everywhere in the world people were lining up in their thousands for jobs, newly installed industrial plants decayed for lack of orders.

The world was hit by the Great Depression unprepared. At the end of the 1920s people in the developing nations has no idea of what was coming. Even leading industrialists and businessmen in the West were full of optimism. In the *New York Times* of 29 October 1928, Alfred Sloan, president of General Motors, declared his "conviction that our general economic and industrial situation is thoroughly sound", and at the bankers' conference in Cologne late in 1928 Jacob Goldschmidt, director-general of the Darmstädter und Nationalbank (which finally collapsed in 1931), proclaimed the new revival of capitalism.

Particularly after such claims, the crisis caused a huge loss of confidence in the capitalist system and the liberal world economy. It changed the relationship between state and economy as fundamentally as that between national economies and the world economy.

▼ "The politicians will sit over their breakfast until they are eaten for breakfast themselves." The innumerable conferences which took place all over the world at the end of the 1920s and the beginning of the 1930s produced no concrete results. Instead, they exposed the helplessness with which politicians reacted to the crisis.

The industrial countries

The crisis started in the industrial "center" of the world economy and had its most severe impact there. The GNP of the 16 leading industrial nations fell by 17 percent from 1929 to 1932. In the United States the decline was even bigger, in Western Europe not quite as big. However, in Austria, Poland and Czechoslovakia GNP fell by a fifth. The extent to which the United States was affected can also be seen in industrial production, which fell by 45 percent during this period; in Western Europe the figure was 30 percent.

The effects on international trade were no less serious. The volume of imports of these 16 countries declined by a quarter, the volume of exports even more. As international trade declined, incomes fell in exporting countries, because their markets shrank, and in importing countries, losing their cheapest source. Above all, unemployment increased enormously. As in several European countries, a quarter of the American labor force were unemployed in 1932–33. In Denmark, in Norway, and most significantly in Germany, one in three workers was unemployed. This was the beginning of the process of mass impoverishment characteristic of this period.

Unemployment and poverty

The fate of the unemployed in Belgrade, Brussels, Madrid or Prague was not far different from that of those in Baltimore or Montreal. Early in the morning they went to the employment agency hoping against hope to find some kind of work, at least for this day. Then they waited for hours in long, gray lines, even in snow and rain, usually without success. Lining up for work was followed by lining up for unemployment benefits, if there were any, and then for soup. Certainly, the housewife tried to keep up regular family life, but gradually the atmosphere of poverty spread even to bourgeois homes. Such poverty meant that food had the highest priority over all other necessities, including hygiene. Food was saved for the children. But even worse than material indigence was the feeling of failure and hopelessness. The sheer effort to stay alive dominated everything else. Often it was no longer possible to come up with the rent. Shelters for the homeless were overcrowded. The makeshift homes typical of Depression America also disfigured the cities of Europe and Japan. Shanty towns sprang up in Brussels and Prague. And in Tokyo, along the railroad tracks of Shinjuku, the makeshift shelters of unemployed workers and uprooted farmers joined those left from the time of the 1923 earthquake.

The United States

The United States constituted the dominant part of the industrial "center". It was here that the avalanche began. With increasing speed it took more and more economies into the abyss. In fact, the American economy had shown signs of weakness even before 1929. Investment opportunities were no longer unlimited, as demand fell off during the second half of the 1920s, especially for housing and durable consumer goods. In agriculture, at this time still an important factor in the national economy, real incomes had stopped growing; falling farm prices in the world market posed big problems for American farmers, too. The buoyant bull market at the New York Stock Exchange in 1928 had produced record speculation, and it eventually culminated in the great stock market crash of October 1929, which not only reinforced the recession but finally destroyed confidence in the expansion of the 1920s. Even though New York capital markets were brought back under control relatively fast, the slide into the Depression had started.

The effects on the European economies

The world economy was hit by the events in the United States in various ways. The first blow was the curtailment of foreign loans in 1928–29. This was reinforced by the simultaneous reduction of French and British foreign loans. The boom at the New York Stock Exchange and rising interest rates caused the amount of foreign credits extended by the United States to fall by more than 50 percent during 1928. Many of the countries already severely indebted were primary producers and encountered increasing difficulties as prices for their exports, mainly foodstuffs and raw materials, fell sharply. But such producers of primary commodities were not the only ones to need American capital. Highly developed industrial countries – Germany above all – were also dependent on American credits.

The second blow came with the breakdown of the American economy: foreign loans were further reduced, while import demand contracted significantly. Given the size of the American economy, this was bound to affect the rest of the world, further damaging both exporters of agricultural products and raw materials and industrial nations.

The third blow came in June 1930 when President Hoover signed the Smoot-Hawley Tariff Act, one of the most comprehensive increases in import duty in the history of international trade. The protectionism of this act aggravated the crisis, since debtor countries now found it even more difficult to export goods to the United States in order to earn the dollars necessary to repay their American loans. After the Act American foreign loans dried up completely and American banks intensified their demands for the repayment of outstanding loans.

The crisis was then passed on to European economies through declining American demand

▲ A striking contrast to the glitter of Broadway, New York. Patiently queuing up under the dazzling glare and flicker of the world-famous great white way, hundreds of destitutes lined up every night in Times Square, waiting for the relief kitchen, organized by one of the big newspapers, to open. The situation was similar in all major cities in the 1930s. Everywhere people waited in long queues in order to receive at least one hot meal a day.

for foreign goods, but intra-European trade – more important to the economies of European countries than American trade – was also in decline. The American slump hit Europe at a time when structural problems, insufficient domestic demand, relatively high unemployment, distorted currency parities and problems of international capital integration had already produced an unstable economic situation. As in the United States, a small push sufficed to set off the spiral of recession that kept winding its way farther and farther down. Company expectations of sales and profits were negatively affected by declining demand; thus threatened with overcapacities, companies reduced investments, production and employment. Purchasing power was thus further reduced, limiting opportunities for sales. In many countries investment sank drastically; in some, like Germany, it virtually came to a halt. By the summer of 1932, the economic situation in Europe was grim. Capital and labor were both severely underutilized. Some feared a total breakdown of the economic system.

Financial and monetary collapse

Although the breakdown of the international financial and monetary system did not start in Europe, the European economic situation played a major part. The background was provided by a triangle of debtor-creditor relationships between Germany, the European Allies and the United States, which consisted of reparations, war debts and commercial capital movements: the "debt cycle". Germany needed American capital to fund her war debts, but American capital went to other European countries as well. When the inflow of American capital ceased, European capital exporters – Belgium, France, the Netherlands, Sweden, Switzerland, the United Kingdom – had to curb their capital outflow or even recall foreign capital assets.

▲ The slums of northwestern England, where the textile industry was in depression, were as bleak as those of London's East End. Unemployment and a minimum of state support meant not only economic impoverishment. Many resorted to alcohol which, in turn, put further pressure on family relations.

The Wall Street Crash

The collapse of the New York Stock Exchange in October 1929 has become a symbol of the beginning of the Great Depression. This is to exaggerate its importance, but its consequences should not be underestimated. Before the crash, the sale of shares was often financed with credit. When foreign investors, as well as American banks and institutions outside New York, withdrew their money from the New York market, the crash was triggered. Firms which financed their investments through share issues had to cut back expenditure; production declined and stocks were reduced. And it was not only the professional speculators who took part in share trading: a considerable part of the American middle class had speculated with shares in order to participate in the buoyant market. When the loans with which the shares had been bought could no longer be paid back through the sale of shares, ruin was a not infrequent consequence. The general reduction in consumption caused demand within the United States to fall sharply, along with imports.

▶ An impoverished broker in dire straits.

Germany was one particularly weak point in this system of international capital integration. Here, the complicated transformation of commercial capital imports to the export of reparations payments had to take place. In Germany, moreover, short-term foreign credits were turned into long-term industrial assets to a particularly large extent. A sudden withdrawal of capital meant serious trouble for German banks. Problems could also arise from the extensive indebtedness of the less well-off European countries and the Third World, in which Western European and North American banks had committed themselves far beyond the financial means of the debtor countries; in a crisis, the servicing of debts was by no means secure. A further weak point was the structure of the American banking system, which consisted of a multitude of minor banks with limited capabilities and small reserves. In a lasting crisis they had to recall their credits in order to survive. Between 1930 and 1933

▲ In the major cities of Asia, as well as those of Europe and the United States, there appeared slum dwellings of the unemployed who could no longer afford to pay rent. Sometimes they lived in wooden shacks, sometimes they sought refuge in old drainpipes, as in this Tokyo shanty town; sometimes on the outskirts of the cities they dug holes in the earth. In such wretched living quarters the standards of hygiene were catastrophic; epidemics spread and mortality rose sharply.

◀ Those countries which produced and exported raw materials and foodstuffs were affected by the crisis almost as severely as the industrialized nations. In Australia during 1930, unemployment rose to 25 percent and in 1931–32 was nearly 30 percent. At times one in three Australians was jobless. From 1931, nominal wages fell drastically and from 1932 real wages declined, even if not so sharply. To accept a loss in real wages was, nevertheless, easier to bear than to receive no wages at all. Public charity was organized but unused to coping with unemployment and homelessness on this scale.

almost nine thousand American banks failed. Finally, the lack of sufficient cooperation between the national central banks created yet another weakness in the system.

The flow of capital back to America triggered a series of crises in German banks between 1929 and 1930. Confidence was not improved by the growing popular support for Hitler's National Socialist party. In 1931 the final collapse occurred. In January, Bolivia defaulted on its foreign debt, with other Latin American countries following suit. Creditors rushed to demand instant repayment of their loans. The major Austrian bank, the Österreichische Creditanstalt, which accounted for over two-thirds of total deposits in the Austrian banking system, failed in May, a collapse that was felt in Czechoslovakia, Hungary, Poland and Romania. In June Chancellor Heinrich Brüning declared Germany's inability to continue the payment of reparations, causing a run on German banks. Except for long-term investments, banks recalled their money from business. It was impossible to refinance debts. To prevent the complete breakdown of the German banking system, the German government had to support the banks by purchasing stock.

The financial crisis in Germany and Central and Eastern Europe soon affected the London money market, which was the conduit for the international flow of capital to the countries in this region. Short-term credits were frozen, since the debtors could not pay. The small gold reserves of the Bank of England, the withdrawal of capital from Great Britain and problems of financial policy undermined confidence in the stability of the pound. In mid-September 1931 the flight from the pound and the consequent outflow of gold had reached such an extent that Parliament had to suspend the obligation of the Bank of England to exchange sterling for gold. Within a few months the pound had fallen by 30 percent against the dollar.

Britain's abandonment of the gold standard was another shock for the world economy, since sterling, together with the dollar, was the major international currency and London was one of the most important money and capital markets. Other countries quickly followed this example, and by the end of 1932 the currencies of 32 countries were no longer on the gold standard. They were engaged in a race of devaluation in the hope that this would give them a competitive edge in world markets. When Franklin Roosevelt's administration took over in the United States in April 1933 and also abandoned gold, the gold standard was at an end as the international currency system. Only a few countries – among them Italy, Poland, France, Belgium, the Netherlands, and Switzerland – held on to gold, thereby increasing the pressure on their economies and their currencies.

A week after Great Britain had abandoned the gold standard, the economist John Maynard Keynes wrote: "There are few Englishmen who do not rejoice at the breaking of our gold fetters ... I believe that the great events of the last week may open a new chapter in the world's monetary history. I have a hope that they may break down barriers which have seemed impassable." In reality, however, there was to be no functioning liberal international currency system for a quarter of a century.

When we consider the magnitude of the losses from which the world suffers during a period of economic stagnation similar to that through which the world is now passing, it is impossible not to be impressed by the almost absolute failure of society up to the present to devise any means by which such disasters may be averted.

**LEAGUE OF NATIONS REPORT,
29 SEPTEMBER 1930**

German Austerity Measures

In Germany, Chancellor Heinrich Brüning conducted a deflationary policy of austerity in 1930–31 in an effort to balance the budget. Income tax went up by five percent as early as 1930. Taxes on such items as sugar, beer, tobacco and coffee were raised, and a number of new taxes were introduced. Higher contributions to unemployment insurance were imposed. Civil Service pay was cut, along with old age pensions and other social security benefits. Government investment was radically reduced. As a result the volume of the budget decreased by almost a third between 1929–30 and 1932–33; nevertheless, this attempt to save the economy was unsuccessful.

However, the objectives of this policy were not limited to balancing the budget. In Germany, financial policy in the crisis was an expression of the fundamental revision of social policy and thus reflected sociopolitical conditions in the Weimar Republic. The welfare state element in public financial policy, an important feature of social democracy established after 1918, was to be removed. At the same time, Chancellor Brüning's foreign policy intention must be taken into consideration. Primarily, he wanted reparations to be canceled, which ultimately implied the revision of the Treaty of Versailles. Trying to balance the budget was to signal Germany's willingness and, at the same time, its inability to pay.

▶ **Middle-class unemployed demonstrate in Berlin.**

Reactions to the crisis

The conservative forces in power in almost all industrial countries maintained an unshaken belief in orthodox remedies, and they reacted to the crisis with the tools of orthodox liberal economic policy. Between 1929 and 1931, most strategies employed to overcome the crisis were based based mainly on deflationary policies of austerity. Restrictive monetary and fiscal policies were intended to prevent the outflow of gold and foreign exchange, curb expenditure and raise revenue to balance public budgets; but instead higher interest rates, higher taxes and reduced public expenditure reinforced the cyclical downturn and aggravated the crisis.

The objective was not only to balance the budget but to restore the prewar liberal-capitalist system by the reduction of state intervention, particularly in the area of social policy. The welfare state element in public financial policy was to be removed.

Yet in another area of policy the reaction was markedly interventionist. The collapse of the gold standard was accompanied by foreign trade policies designed by individual countries to protect their national economies from foreign competition in order to soften the effects of the crisis. These measures ranged from arbitrary currency manipulations to the control of foreign exchange and even its complete management by the government. In the area of trade, governments adopted higher tariffs, import quotas, prohibitions and licencing systems. This resulted in the

◀ When Britain went off the gold standard in 1931, many people obtained good prices for articles made of gold. After Britain suspended gold payments, the pound sterling fell by more than 30 percent against the US dollar, which was still fixed in gold.

further decline of trade and, ultimately, the further disintegration of the world economy.

The less developed countries

Outside of industrial Europe and the United States, most countries – accounting for two-thirds of the global population – were still heavily dependent on the production of raw materials and foodstuffs at the end of the 1920s, even though industrial production was gradually increasing. Exports played a special role for these countries, as their development depended to a large degree on the inflow of foreign capital. In more than fifty countries in southeastern Europe, Latin America, Africa, Asia and Oceania, foodstuffs, agricultural and mineral raw materials accounted for more than half the value of their respective exports. Most countries depended on

▼ The financial crisis in central and southeastern Europe soon affected the London money market. Confidence in the pound faded rapidly. Bank of England messengers had to be quick off the mark with news of changes in the bank rate. Within a few months, sterling had fallen heavily in relation to currencies still on the gold standard.

► The 1930s in Latin America began with a catastrophic loss in the value of native raw materials and foodstuffs on the world market. The fall in demand in the developed countries led to oversupply in the producing countries. As stocks grew massive, the price of coffee sank from 22 to 8 American cents, and in Brazil coffee was shoveled overboard into the sea.

two or three commodities: rubber and tea in Ceylon, coffee in Brazil, sugar in Cuba, rubber in Malaysia. This dependence on foreign markets and foreign capital made such countries vulnerable to any changes in international economic conditions.

Thus, the Depression in the industrial countries soon spread outward to make its impact on agricultural southern and southeastern Europe, on developing countries in the Third World and on newly industrialized countries like Japan, Canada, Australia and New Zealand. Most of all, the Depression hit Latin America and Africa, and, though to a lesser degree, Asia. Latin America's GNP (calculated as the weighted average of the national products of Argentina, Brazil, Chile, Colombia, Cuba and Mexico) declined by 13 percent in 1929–32, whereas Asia's GNP (as the weighted average of the national products of China, India, Indonesia, Korea and Taiwan) actually rose slightly during the same period, before eventually declining a little in 1934.

However, national differences were bigger in Asia than in Latin America. Armies of the unemployed did not exist in the cities of the periphery as they did more in the industrial countries, but a process of pauperization took place in rural areas. Japan, Australia and Canada, on the other hand, suffered severe unemployment, even when their national product, as in the case of Australia, did not fall sharply until 1931. As agriculture and industry were hit, farmers who had to abandon their land joined the millions of unemployed industrial workers.

The crisis spread from the center to the periphery as a response to both immediate effects and long-term trends. Primary producers were hit directly by declining demand in industrial countries – a demand that was already stagnating due to improved domestic supplies as a consequence of wartime expansion of farm land and improved agricultural productivity. Natural raw materials were being replaced by synthetics produced in the industrial countries – for instance, fertilizers, silk and light metals; and they were being used more economically. Low population growth and the loss of population in World War I also slowed down demand. Most importantly, an ever-increasing portion of world industrial production originated in countries with agricultural and mineral resources of their own, especially the United States.

But cultivated farm land had been expanded worldwide as a result of World War I, while the exploitation of mineral raw materials had been intensified. For some products, at least, the discrepancy between stagnant demand and growing supply meant potential overproduction. This was true of wheat, sugar, coffee and rubber as well as for tin, lead, wool and cotton. Prices for these commodities declined until 1929, when they fell steeply. Indeed, world market prices in general were falling. On the other hand, demand rose steadily for some products, with prices remaining relatively stable: meat and dairy products, fruit and vegetables, vegetable oils and fats, grains other than wheat, cocoa, copper and oil.

John Maynard Keynes

John Maynard Keynes (1883–1946) studied mathematics and economics at the University of Cambridge in England. He became a lecturer in economics, and in 1911 took up the editorship of the important English economic publication, *The Economic Journal*, and worked in this capacity to the end of his life. He was also a member of various govermental committees, chairman of an insurance company, journalist and publisher.

Keynes became influential because he combined political-economic practice with theoretical considerations. His main work, *The General Theory of Employment, Interest and Money*, appeared in 1936. With it he accomplished a revolution in liberal economics. The experiences of the Great Depression led him to the view that the capitalist system was not, as classical economics had asserted, stable and tending to equilibrium but, on the contrary, unstable. The state must therefore be active to smooth out business cycles.

▼ No economist of his time was so central to the formation of political and economic decision-making processes. Whether as Great Britain's representative at international conferences, as adviser to the British government, as counselor to American presidents or as a journalist, Keynes personified that direction of economic policy that was no longer helpless in the face of crisis but that urged the state to an active battle against the crisis.

This decline in the volume and prices of exports meant a sharp reduction in export earnings. In 40 countries, mostly in the Third World, they fell by more than fifty percent. Augmenting stocks or destroying them – as happened with coffee, rubber and tin – did not at all affect the fall in prices. Supply reacted particularly inflexibly to declining demand, and even during the Depression production really fell for only a few products. For most, it continued or even increased as producers tried to balance income losses from falling prices. By keeping up or increasing output, prices were pushed down still further. Stockpiles reached an extremely high level. As farmers in many developing countries began to find it impossible to offset income losses by increasing their output, since the domestic market was too small, they retreated into subsistence farming.

A vicious circle

Sinking deeper and deeper into the crisis, the world economy was caught up in a vicious circle: as industrial nations demanded fewer and fewer foodstuffs and raw materials, the export earnings and incomes of primary producers fell. In return, the latter reduced their demand for finished industrial products. Even if this was of only minor importance to the industrial countries, the consequences for primary producers were grave.

Furthermore, the collapse of the international capital market had substantial consequences for less developed countries. Capital inflow ceased in

I was a telephone lineman down in Saskatchewan and I saw farmers as poor as any native in a backward nation anywhere on earth. The Government gave them seed grain, registered grain to plant, and this was to be their next year's crop and if things went right ... but those poor bastards couldn't wait until spring to plant, not when they saw their children starving before their eyes, and they boiled the seed wheat, they made porridge and gruel and bannock out of it, and this is the way some of those farmers got their families through the winter.

B. BROADFOOT,
TEN LOST YEARS 1929–1939.
MEMORIES OF CANADIANS
WHO SURVIVED THE
DEPRESSION

▶ It was perhaps in the 1930s that people began to think for the first time about the consequences of exploiting natural resources, as the agriculturally overexploited prairie lands of North America suffered from drought and erosion. At the beginning of the 1930s there was no rain throughout wide stretches of these lands, and the wind blew the topsoil away in dust storms that became a common sight across the prairies. But the conviction that it was possible to control nature still remained unshaken. Steps were taken to avoid such catastrophes in the future by means of dams on the Mississippi, the regulation of rivers and the planting of hedges and trees.

1929–30. As practically all primary producers were debtors (with the exception of the United States), a surplus in trade now offered the only possibility of meeting their obligations. They were the first to be exposed to the double pressure of falling export earnings and continued high interest payments fixed in terms of gold. The flow of capital was reversed: more capital was now flowing back to the industrial nations than was coming in from them.

Just as in the industrial nations, the immediate political reaction to the crisis in the developing countries was to impose restrictive monetary and fiscal policies and reduce currency reserves, but this liberal policy could not be maintained for very long. Argentina and Australia abandoned the gold standard and both devalued in 1929; other Latin American nations, New Zealand and Spain did likewise. Currency controls, higher tariffs, trade restrictions and more devaluations followed.

These measures could not truly solve the problem of debts. A large number of countries, especially in southeastern Europe and the Middle East, defaulted on their debts. There were no effective sanctions for the default or postponement of debts. Also, creditor countries could resort to moral indignation only to a certain degree, as they themselves were late in repaying their war debts and reparations due to financial difficulties. Nevertheless, the debt problem represented an additional burden for all countries involved.

Causes and explanations

There is no generally accepted explanation for the beginning of the crisis, although its causes have been studied since the 1930s. Some of the possible triggers may lie in overproduction and in unenlightened monetary, credit and foreign trade policies. It may also be that the structural problems brought about by the transition to mass consumption in the 1920s, reflecting changes in technology, population growth and income distribution, were partly responsible. What is certain, however, is that it was not until preparations got under way for a second world war that the Great Depression was defeated.

◀ This poor young black woman standing next to a torn poster of a white woman with a tray of food perhaps reflects the shattering of the American ideal of a free but also humane society. The Great Depression revealed anew that it was the poor and the poorest who were particularly affected by economic crisis. The poverty lasted longest in the southern states with their plantation economy where "King Cotton" ruled. The white small farmers were almost as poor as the black agricultural workers, whose subjugation was reminiscent of slavery.

▼ The agricultural depression of the 1920s in the United States was followed by further disaster as drought claimed the prairies. Huge clouds of dust blew over the land, transforming farmland and pastures into desert. Cattle starved, farmers could no longer repay their debts and had to give up their land. Families moved from the now-barren prairie states like the pioneers before them, to the west and north, where there was land and water. In Canada, too, thousands of farms were abandoned.

Datafile

The events of the 1930s affected world production and international trade in different ways. World production experienced a sharp drop during the crisis, but in the course of the 1930s it increased again vigorously, so that at the end of the decade it lay clearly above the 1929 level. This was above all a consequence of the expansion of industrial production. In the less developed countries, and also in some highly industrialized countries, industrialization accelerated. For world trade, the 1930s signified the end of the liberal era. It was already clear in the 1920s that the rebuilding of a liberal world economy after the chaos of the years 1914–18 was only partially successful, but it was not until the 1930s that it disintegrated.

World trade 1937

- 51%
- 3%
- 6%
- 9%
- 15%
- 16%

- Europe
- North America
- Asia
- Latin America
- Africa
- Oceania

Shares in world manufacturing

1928   1938

USA, Germany, UK, France, USSR, China, Japan, Italy

Percent: 0, 10, 20, 30, 40

▲ The 1930s saw the share of Europe and North America in world trade decline slightly. Newly industrialized countries improved their share.

◄ Among the industrialized nations, only the United States and France suffered losses. Japan and the USSR showed clear gains.

▼ It is striking that the value of most of the settlement flows decreased between 1928 and 1938. Britain suffered the worst reversal, and by 1938 was in deficit with all the regions it traded with.

Balance of trade

USA   Rest of world   Europe
UK   Tropics

1928
US dollars (millions): 600, 400, 200, 0, -200, -400, -600, -800

1938
US dollars (millions): 400, 200, 0, -200, -400, -600

Tropics   USA   Other   Europe   UK

The recovery of 1933 from the Depression was anything but dynamic. A few countries that held on to the gold standard, such as France, sank even deeper into the crisis. Countries where the Depression had not been so incisive experienced only a modest upswing. The United States saw considerable rates of growth, but the economy became bogged down again in 1937–38. Properly speaking, among the highly industrialized countries, a real boom took place only in Germany. In terms of the usual macroeconomic indicators – growth, unemployment, trade, prices and so on – the 1930s were a decade of insecurity for most industrial countries, even when the Great Depression was overcome. This can be seen most clearly in the rate of unemployment. In the six years between 1933 and 1938 it averaged 15 percent in the United Kingdom, 16 percent in Sweden, 22 percent in Denmark, and 20 percent in the United States.

In less developed nations the picture was also mixed. South Africa experienced a boom when, after the devaluations, the price of gold rose and gold production expanded from 1931 on. Japan, too, showed dynamic economic development. In Australia, on the other hand, national product grew only modestly. In Canada it grew faster, yet unemployment remained relatively high in both countries. For many people, those were hard years full of bitter memories: ten lost years. As one Canadian recalled, "I never throw away vegetable scraps without thinking, 'I wonder if there is something I can use these for?' That's the Depression thing. You were hungry for so many years, not starving but hungry, and it's like some men I know, some men who have to have three hundred dollars or so in their wallet, just something to fall back on. Because for so many years when they were kids, you understand, or young men, they had nothing. Not a bean." (B. Broadfoot, *Ten Lost Years 1929–1939: Memories of Canadians Who Survived the Depression*.)

The expanding industries

Generally it was the automobile, electrotechnical and chemical industries which sustained the recovery in the highly industrialized countries, while other sectors, such as mechanical engineering, also now developed positively. In terms of motorization, Europe had fallen far behind the United States after World War I; in 1929, with a total of half a million cars, the European automobile industry reached just 11 percent of American production. In the 1930s, however, Europe started to catch up. While American production was hit very hard by the Depression and recovered only slowly, European production, with the exception of France, soon reached full capacity. Together, the four big car-producing

RECOVERY AND ECONOMIC PROGRESS

countries in Europe – the United Kingdom, Italy, Germany and France – averaged a quarter of American output during the 1930s, and in the recession year of 1938 nearly half. As a branch of the economy, the expanding automobile industry required more and more resources as its demands influenced the whole industrial structure. In 1938, for example, the American automobile industry generated the biggest demand for strip steel, bars, sheets, malleable iron, alloy iron, gasoline, rubber, plate glass, nickel, lead and mohair.

Western Europe also recovered at least part of the American lead in other durable consumer goods. Vacuum cleaners, washing machines, refrigerators, record players, radios and telephones – all kinds of household appliances made their way into more and more homes, carrying the expansion in the electrotechnical industry. Apart from the necessary purchasing power, this sort of

mass production depended upon two preconditions. First, new techniques of mass assembly had to be introduced, with all the corresponding possibilities for increasing production and productivity. Second, sufficient capacities for energy production had to be built up. The spread of household appliances, the rising consumption of electricity for lighting and cooking, and the growing demands of industry led to an enormous increase in electrical generating capacity.

The chemical industry, too, owed its expansion partly to consumer goods. Various kinds of plastics and synthetic fabrics were developed for new consumer industries. In addition, a whole range of other products entered the market permanently, such as artificial fertilizer, pharmaceuticals and dyes. Throughout the 1930s and 1940s, innovation and invention took place in all modern sectors of industry.

▼ **The United States remained unchallenged as the major supplier of consumer durables. The radio, in particular, spread very fast.**

▶ Japanese cabinet ministers inspect Japanese-made woollen goods in 1933 – a mark of the importance of the Japanese textile industry, which survived the crisis relatively well. Japan sold woollen goods, as it did cotton, within the boundaries of the British Empire, in South America and in China at state-subsidized dumping prices. The young textile industries in the less developed and underdeveloped countries suffered particularly from this Japanese competition.

▶ After the disintegration of the gold standard, various new currency groupings came into being. These groupings broadly reflected existing patterns of trade and political alliance.

▼ Krupps smelting works, Rheinhausen, Germany. Among the highly industrialized countries, a real boom only took place in Germany. It was based on rearmament, in which the heavy industries were of prime importance. In contrast, the share of consumer goods industries in production as a whole perceptibly declined.

World production and world trade

The 1930s produced different effects on the geographic distribution of world industrial production across individual countries and regions. There were "winners" and "losers". Europe belonged to the former, partly because Germany and some other Western powers built up their arsenals in the second half of the 1930s, and also partly because young industries started to develop in Eastern and Southern Europe. If the Soviet Union is also taken into consideration, the European share rose from just over 40 to over 46 percent, as during those years the Soviet Union's industrialization accelerated. Japan, India, New Zealand, South Africa and Chile were also among the "winners". Nonetheless, the overall share of the Third World countries rose only a little, from about seven to eight percent. The United States was the only real "loser".

While world production resumed its rise after 1932 and suffered only a slight reverse in 1937–38, the 1930s marked the end of an era for world trade. Apart from the two world wars, no decade in the 19th or 20th centuries had seen world trade so persistently stagnant. In the decade between 1927 and 1937, trade in primary products increased slightly, while that in manufactures decreased. An increase in trade in mineral raw materials was entirely responsible for the growth in the share of primary products.

As early as the 1920s economists believed they could give good reasons for the declining importance of world trade. Technological progress was to make possible the substitution of synthetics for natural raw materials and a more economical use of the latter. The spread of industrialization was to enable more and more countries to produce necessary industrial goods themselves. With income rising, a smaller portion would be used to import goods and a bigger share would go into service industries. Rising economic instability in industrial nations and the growing political emancipation of developing countries would lead to more restrictive trade policies in an effort to minimize the risk of the global economy's getting away from national control. Not every economist believed in the diminishing foreign trade

Currency Blocs c.1930

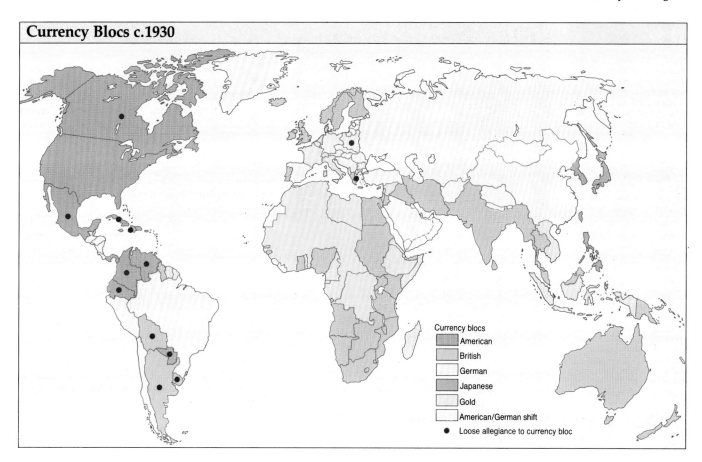

Currency blocs
- American
- British
- German
- Japanese
- Gold
- American/German shift
- ● Loose allegiance to currency bloc

hypothesis, which was to be refuted by the period after World War II. But it was generally accepted that world trade would have to suffer from national protectionism in a world without an international currency system and without an arrangement for international trade in capital and goods.

New currency groupings

With the retreat from the gold standard, a number of regional currency systems came into existence, largely reflecting trading and political links. The sterling bloc united Great Britain with Portugal, Scandinavia, Estonia and Latvia, as well as the Commonwealth countries. A dollar bloc was formed around the United States, including Canada and some Latin American countries, while a yen bloc was set up in Southeast Asia. The gold bloc was made up of countries that held on to the gold standard even after 1932: France, Belgium, Italy, Switzerland, Poland and The Netherlands; in 1936 it dissolved again, when France went off gold. The area in central and southeastern Europe that was dominated economically by Germany could be called a Reichsmark bloc. The currency areas could be seen as an expression of global economic disorder: there was no longer any generally accepted world currency system.

The reduced flow of capital

The collapse of the international capital market was no temporary phenomenon either. It took almost a quarter of a century before it completely functioned again. Investment was determined more by political considerations that by those of

profit. What capital still flowed tended to go to those countries with whom close links already existed – from London to the Commonwealth and other members of the sterling bloc, from France to other members of the gold bloc. It also flowed between Sweden and other Scandinavian countries, between the United States and Canada, and between the Latin American countries. Less and less was invested in the underdeveloped debtor countries, but more in other industralized creditor countries; less in Europe and more in the United States; less by private and more by public institutions.

Efforts at stabilization

In the 1930s international cooperation was at a low point. In the summer of 1933 a World Economic Conference was held in London, but this turned out to be a complete failure. No agreement was reached to fix new exchange rates, to cut tariffs, or to adopt stabilizing measures, despite the emphatic recommendation of the newly elected President Franklin D. Roosevelt that the Conference "must establish order in place of the present chaos by a stabilization of currencies, by freeing the flow of world trade, and by international action to raise price levels". It was the last attempt before the outbreak of World War II to solve international problems by international cooperation. By the beginning of July, Roosevelt was advocating a unilateral move, the "compensated" or "commodity" dollar, on the grounds that the "sound internal economic system of a nation is a greater factor in its well being than the price of its currency in changing terms of the currencies of other nations".

▼ As motorization accelerated, American oil companies began to drill for oil in other regions of the world and to acquire the rights to the exploitation of such oil fields. Here, Canadian Indians sell land rights to oil companies for exploration.

▲ Guns or butter? More arms or more trade? It was already clear to critical contemporaries in 1933 that the new regime in Germany was not concerned with job creation and better living conditions, but with rearmament.

▶ The New York World's Fair of 1939 served as a symbol of the nation's industrial and economic power.

▲ "Work and bread", the slogan of the German National Socialist party, lured people with promises of satisfying the most basic needs. In the face of the massive impoverishment during the crisis, this was both clever and dangerous. Such promises were only partially kept. By the middle of the 1930s Germany had, indeed, achieved full employment, but the standard of living remained very low. The regime could, in fact, offer little more than work and bread.

The adoption of bilateralism

Instead of international cooperation, national protectionism increased in the form of currency management, arbitrary currency manipulation, tariff walls, import quotas and prohibitions. Increasingly, bilateral agreements – between pairs of trading partners – replaced traditional trade agreements, saving diminishing currency reserves by reducing the need for settlement in gold or scarce foreign exchange. Such agreements frequently involved either direct exchanges of goods of equal value, or settlements made through special clearing accounts in terms of the two countries' own currencies. Thus, the multilateral system of trade was dismantled in favor of bilateralism, and despite criticism of this development from some quarters, the restrictionism of international trade continued, amidst general skepticism and uncertainty concerning the future development of international trade.

Since bilateral agreements were no alternative to multilateral cooperation, however, various countries tried to reach closer cooperation in trade policies on a regional level. Agreements were made in Southeastern Europe, by Scandinavia, The Netherlands, Belgium and Luxembourg (the so-called "Oslo-group"), and by Italy, Austria and Hungary (the Rome Agreement of 1934). The United States entered into liberalization agreements with several Latin American countries that also concluded similar agreements among themselves. Most importantly, the Commonwealth agreement made in 1932 created the Imperial Preference System, under which Commonwealth countries benefited from lower tariffs and easing of import restrictions, while countries outside were subject to increased restrictions. The amount of trade within the various regions grew sharply as a result.

Cartels and commodities

In the interwar period, falling prices, potential overcapacity and restrictive trade relations led to the proliferation of international cartels in manufactured and semifinished goods such as steel, chemical and electrotechnical products, as well as oil and aluminum. The cartels were supposed to regulate production quantities, stabilize prices, organize sales, and, if possible, secure monopoly profits, as one member of the cartel acted as monopolist. Ultimately, the international cartels were only mirror images of the national ones. During the 1930s capital concentration and the elimination of competition reached unprecedented heights in many countries.

International commodity schemes were really the only effective form of bilateral cooperation in the 1930s. The governments of countries producing and buying such things as sugar, copper, rubber, coffee and tea tried to stabilize – or even increase – production, prices, sales and ultimately earnings. Unfortunately, these commodity schemes, whether bi- or multilateral, could not replace a liberal international economy. They merely represented emergency measures adopted in order to offset at least the worst consequences of global economic disintegration. They created no trade but merely served to mitigate the

negative consequences of a severe depression on each country's own national economy and to shift its costs to other countries.

Government economic policies

Increasing government control over foreign trade and the partial withdrawal from world trade did not mean that governments decisively changed their policy and adopted anticyclical measures, although orthodox-liberal policy had obviously exacerbated the crisis. But in the United States, the Roosevelt administration turned to new directions with its New Deal policies in 1933. And in Sweden the Social Democrats took up anticyclical monetary and fiscal policies as early as 1932, creating additional purchasing power with public works, work creation programs, the improvement of social benefits as well as other measures. The significance of this policy for the course of the economy is difficult to measure. While recovery was fully under way in Sweden from 1935 on, allowing the policy of budget deficits to be discontinued, the American economy was already set for the next crisis beginning in 1937.

The fascist governments of Italy and Germany reacted to the crisis in a special way, national socialist economic policy being particularly successful with regard to the reduction of unemployment and the growth of the national product. German economic policy after 1933 consistently pursued rearmament, which contributed to the country's recovery.

Japan probably achieved the fastest and strongest recovery from the Depression, a recovery determined by the government's anticyclical polices and reinforced by its emphasis on rearmament. The three measures that were taken in order to counter the problems of foreign trade and weak domestic demand and investment – the

devaluation of the yen, reduction in interest rates, and increased government expenditures – were highly successful: the volume of exports doubled between 1932 and 1935, while the national product rose by a quarter.

In contrast, economic policy in other countries helped to exacerbate the downturn far into the 1930s. The crisis hit France relatively late and less severely. Huge gold reserves had tempted policymakers to stick to the gold standard and thus to fixed exchange rates, and rather than devalue or introduce exchange controls, French governments between 1931 and 1936 tried ineffectually to reduce costs and prices by deflationary policies. It was not until the Popular Front took over the government in 1936 that the gold standard was abandoned, the franc was devalued, and expansionary monetary and fiscal policies were adopted. From 1937 on, the French economy started to recover. Other countries that held on to gold – Belgium, The Netherlands, Switzerland and Poland – pursued similar economic policies.

The less-developed countries

Latin America and Africa were both severely struck by the crisis in 1929–32. Thereafter they experienced a distinct recovery, though income rose more slowly than in the 1920s and 1940s.

In Asia the crisis had only limited effects. The general recovery of national economies throughout the world made the reduction of stocks possible: this occurred most of all tin, wheat, cotton, silk and sugar.

Nevertheless, it was a difficult decade for less-developed countries. Capital inflow from industrial countries was still interrupted. Investment projects could not be continued. Servicing debts, where indeed it was possible, was a strain on the balance of payments. Generally, the debt problem remained unsolved. For the majority of Third World countries, the disintegration of the world market meant worse export opportunities. Although export earnings rose strongly, they did not reach the level of the 1920s again. Producers and exporters of basic foodstuffs suffered less than exporters of more sophisticated consumer products such as coffee. International commodity agreements to limit production usually discriminated against small domestic farmers rather than the big plantations owned by American or European investors. The devaluation of the yen and the growth of Japanese exports posed new problems for a number of Asian and African countries. Recovery was interrupted in 1937–38 by the recession in the United States, which mainly hit primary producers. The increase in

Roosevelt's New Deal

▲ Roosevelt's New Deal in action in this works program in New York. The crisis fundamentally changed the relationship between society, state and economy in the United States. The New Deal became the symbol of a capitalism with a more humane face, of concern for the socially disadvantaged. It set in motion unprecedented state activity in order to overcome economic problems.

During the "Hundred Days" of Roosevelt's first administration, programs were initiated to deal with a number of domestic problems. The National Recovery Act of June 1933 introduced industrial codes on production and prices as well as new regulations to protect labor. The Tennessee Valley Authority was set up in May 1933, investing government with control over the hydroelectric dam and the nitrate plants at Muscle Shoals on the Tennessee River, as well as power production, flood control and shipping on the river. New agencies to carry out relief measures were established. The unemployed were offered jobs in public works, and in agriculture direct payments to farmers were made

to reduce output and raise prices. The legal position of trade unions was improved, helping them to increase workers' wages and purchasing power. The banking crisis was tackled by the introduction of bank deposit insurance. Roosevelt hoped these measures would end the crisis.

The sudden economic downturn in the United States in 1937 caused Roosevelt's liberal advisers to urge him to resume deficit spending. He was hard to convince. J. M. Keynes himself joined in the effort to persuade Roosevelt to change his mind; at present, he said, more spending on public works, and particularly on housing, was needed. But Roosevelt was unmoved by his arguments, preferring to balance his budget.

prices was interrupted, although there was no sharp fall as there had been in 1929 because, among other things, European rearmament programs had created a growing demand for raw materials from overseas. But exports and imports declined, and Latin American GNP stagnated, while Asian GNP dropped by three percent.

For many less developed countries, the 1930s brought a reorientation towards national resources. Partial detachment from the international market seemed the best option for most Latin American countries, and internal development in the form of import substitution replaced external development. Policy changed direction to support this switch. By abandoning the gold standard and stopping debt payments, these countries at least partially avoided deflationary pressures. At the same time, they moved to expansionary monetary and fiscal policies in order to finance domestic industrialization. In Europe, too, the less-developed countries experienced an expansion of industrial production based, among other things, on import substitution.

Colonial policies in Asia

The weaker recovery of Asian developing countries resulted not only from the fact that the crisis had been less severe there, but also from the continuation of restrictive deflationary policies in the colonies of the United Kingdom and The Netherlands. The British Colonial Office demanded that each colony should balance its budget. Thus, harshly austere policies were pursued and taxes ruthlessly collected. In British India customs duties, which had already become the most important source of government revenue, had fallen considerably owing to the decline of foreign trade. This made government even less able to make any tax concessions to farmers. Even the salt tax, chosen by Gandhi as the focus of his campaign against British rule, was not reduced but, owing to the crisis, increased substantially even at the price of increasing anti-government agitation. The specter of government bankruptcy in British India, which would have entailed the bankruptcy of the British government, looked dangerously real. Therefore, any devaluation of the rupee, as demanded by Indian nationalists, had to be averted, lest a panic of creditors caused by devaluation precipitate immediate bankruptcy. Thus, deflationary currency policies were added to austere fiscal policies in order to preserve the overvalued exchange rate of the rupee at any price at all.

China suffered from domestic disturbances in this period and, after 1937, from the war against Japan. The Japanese colonies Korea and Formosa (now Taiwan), on the other hand, profited from the Japanese recovery. In Asia, there were no efforts of industrialization comparable to those of Latin America, though there were spectacular individual cases like the Indian sugar industry. To promote import substitution, protective tariffs and other trade barriers would have been necessary; but these would not have been accepted by the industrial countries without retaliation. Colonial powers conceded protective tariffs only for particular items, if at all, mostly in order to get rid of foreign competition.

African countries

The situation was similar in Africa where British, Belgian, French and Portuguese colonial administrations or the national governments tried to compensate for income losses due to declining foreign trade by raising taxes and reducing expenditure on infrastructure and welfare services. Big developmental projects were stopped, particularly in some West African countries. Increasing government interventionism certainly pointed towards future developments. *Laissez-faire* had never been very strong in Africa, and the drift of official policy in the 1930s was clearly towards an expansion of the public sector and the adoption by the state of responsibility and powers for management of the economic system.

In general, the Depression reinforced protectionist tendencies on the part of the colonial powers and increased their willingness to control colonial national economies more intensely. By 1941 the majority of British colonies were embedded in a system of price controls.

Import-substituting industrialization

The import-substituting industrialization practiced in the less developed countries was concentrated mainly on foodstuffs and textiles, with the remainder divided mainly among the metal-producing, metal-processing and chemical industries. However, no advanced technologies were used in production and no high-value-added manufactures were produced. Certainly there were countries like Brazil that experienced a breakthrough in industrialization in the 1930s, and others like Egypt or Southern Rhodesia that made real industrial progress. But even in Latin America, where a number of countries put their industries on a broader basis. Output growth was accompanied by relatively little fresh investment and technical change. The import-substitution industries were not necessarily low-cost, and the plant and equipment for them had largely to be imported. Moreover, new industries tended to remain enclaves of modernity in a general sea of backwardness, showing few indications that they could become the instruments of a more general structural transformation. Instead, they often tended to reinforce economic dualism.

On the average between 1919 and 1939 more than one-tenth of the men and women desiring work were unemployed. In the worst period of the depression well over 25 per cent were left in unproductive idleness ... War time has taught us valuable lessons ... (that) full employment must be achieved in ways consistent with a free society.

AUSTRALIAN WHITE PAPER, 30 MAY 1945

Saudi Oil

In Saudi Arabia, which was founded as a Kingdom in 1932, the international economic crisis caused the flow of pilgrims from eastern grain-producing countries to break off almost overnight, thus depriving the ruling dynasty of its main source of income. Due to the deterioration of grain prices, Indian, Persian and Indonesian Muslims, who usually made up the majority of pilgrims, had not been able to build up any reserves to pay for the long journey to the holy Islamic shrines at Mecca and Medina. In search of new sources of income, the Saudi Arabian king then opened the country to financially potent American oil companies.

At the same time, the large American oil companies had been particularly hard hit by reforms being carried out in various countries, especially in Mexico, where 17 British and American oil companies were taken over during March 1938 as part of General Cardenas's revolution, which included land redistribution and nationalization of the railways as well as expropriation of the oil companies. To balance these losses, the American companies were looking for alternative areas of exploration, and were only too eager to accept the opportunities offered by Saudi Arabia.

Oil, for which there was a growing demand in Western countries, was one of the few resources available in Saudi Arabia. In view of its own financial position, and the need to secure those in power and maintain a feudal way of life, King Saud granted licenses to the American oil companies and opened the country to them. It was to prove the beginning of the road to riches for Saudi Arabia, which proved to have

enormous oil reserves. However, it was not until the early 1950s that Saudi Arabia, along with other oil-producing countries of the Middle East, began to insist on new agreements with the foreign companies which would give it a property share of the vast profits of the oil industry. In 1951 agreement was reached with the Arabian American Oil Company (ARAMCO) to share its profits with the Saudi government even then, only a small share of the revenue stayed in the country.

▲ King Saud of Saudi Arabia is entertained to luncheon aboard ship by his American hosts. The Depression, allied to a developing sense of nationalism, led to a cautious attempt to promote native national resources and to reduce dependence on Western finance.

THE MILITARY–INDUSTRIAL COMPLEX

In most industrialized countries since 1900 there has developed a close cooperation and mutual dependency of the interests of the military, industrialists and politicians. From this has arisen the so-called military–industrial complex, a juggernaut that has moved under its own impetus to fund and build large programs of weapons manufacture. The impetus of this complex has had profound effects on social, economic and political decision-making.

The complex results from the interdependent interests of five groups in society. First are the politicians, to whom military equipment gives muscle in the international arena. Second, the industrialists themselves may win fortunes from large contracts for researching, developing and building new weapons of war, and who achieve considerable influence in the bargain. Third, the scientists may find funds forthcoming for their research projects funds as part of a military program while unavailable elsewhere. Fourth, the generals, admirals and air marshals have an insatiable demand for new products, and the availability of new technology provides the opportunity to devise new battleplans. Finally a strong defense industry provides a substantial proportion of the workforce with secure employment even in times of depression.

In the period before World War II, Germany was considered the country in which the military–industrial complex was most firmly established, and in the 1930s the Nazi party relied on armaments manufacture to provide secure jobs. By the end of the decade, the Nazis, the military and industry were closely interlinked and a clear separation was no longer possible. After 1945, the conditions of the Cold War meant that the United States and the Soviet Union made an important part of their industry dependent on military expenditure. These are simply the most important examples, however; the military–industrial complex exists wherever weapons are produced.

Although the proportion of total public expenditure accounted for by military spending fell in most industrial countries after World War II, the economic importance of the armaments industry grew. As the state took on responsibility for stable economic development, the jobs in the armaments industry, which relied directly on government contracts, became more important. And, as military technology became more sophisticated, it began to product spinoffs in the form of products for commerical use.

However, the logic of the military–industrial complex was not inexorable. As the armaments of the superpowers were being negotiated away, particularly in the second half of the 1980s, experiments were made in converting military works into factories making civilian products without loss of jobs. Many people argued that civil production had more benefit for humanity, as the products of the arms industry exist only to be destroyed, whether on the battlefield, or as a result of successful arms-control negotiations.

▶▶ Soviet leaders and generals during Red Square parade in Moscow, 1950: in the East politicians, generals and industrialists worked closely together in a military–industrial complex.

▶ John Heartfield's satirical photocollage attacked the emphasis on military production: "Hurray the butter is finished! Göring in one of his speeches: Ore has always made an empire strong. Butter and lard have made people fat at best."

▶▶ World War I was the first war in which arms production became the dominant sector of industry. Here the massive German steel works of Krupp produce gun barrels.

▼ Hitler visiting a shipyard in Hamburg in 1935. The military–industrial complex grew in the 1930s in Germany as in no other country.

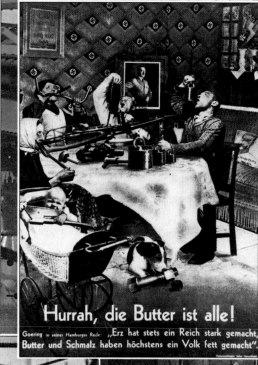

Hurrah, die Butter ist alle!

Goering in seiner Hamburger Rede: „Erz hat stets ein Reich stark gemacht, Butter und Schmalz haben höchstens ein Volk fett gemacht".

▶▶ Not only are politics involved in the military-industrial complex, in the course of the 20th century science has also played an increasingly important role in the invention of military weapons. The American "Star Wars" program in the 1980s introduced a great deal of government money into scientific research.

▶ The arms industry is an export industry. How dangerous such export business is has been shown increasingly, since more and more underdeveloped nations have become able to buy modern weapons. This aircraft and concomitant missiles are on display in an airshow of 1976.

ЛЕНИН

Datafile

In the 19th century sulfuric acid was commonly regarded as "the barometer of industry", because it was used in such a wide variety of processes. In the 20th century this was no longer so, mainly because of its disproportionately high use in fertilizer manufacture. In its place power consumption, and particularly power consumption per person, came to be seen as an index of national industrial activity.

▼ Fossil fuels have been increasingly used through electricity as an intermediary. The industrialization of the Soviet Union after the 1917 Revolution relied heavily on a program of electrification, but the United States was by far the world's largest consumer.

▼ The registration of patents is a useful pointer to industrial activity. These figures for plastics patents 1931–45 reflect intense interest in Germany, stimulated by the substitutes (*Ersatz*) program. By now the inventive individual was being eclipsed by the big chemicals companies created in the 1920s.

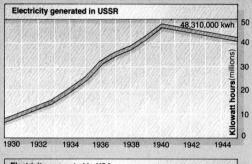

Electricity generated in USSR

48,310,000 kwh

Plastics patents 1931–45

16%

84%

Total 5,132

☐ To firms
☐ To individuals

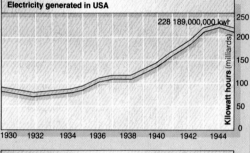

Electricity generated in USA

228 189,000,000 kwh

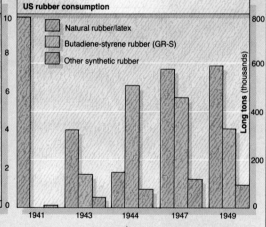

Plastics patents awarded

IG Farben
Du Pont
Eastman Kodak
Dow Chemical
ICI
American Cyanamid
CIBA
Monsanto Chemical
Hundreds

US rubber consumption

☐ Natural rubber/latex
☐ Butadiene-styrene rubber (GR-S)
☐ Other synthetic rubber

Long tons (thousands)

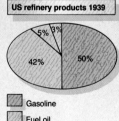

Crude oil output 1938

6%
0.5%
3.5%
13%
62%
15%

☐ North America
☐ Latin America
☐ Eastern Europe
☐ Middle East
☐ East Asia
☐ Other

US refinery products 1939

5% 3%
50%
42%

☐ Gasoline
☐ Fuel oil
☐ Illuminating oil
☐ Lubricating oil

▲ Until the Japanese largely cut off its supply of natural rubber in World War II, the USA had little interest in synthetic alternatives except for special purposes. During the war they mounted a crash program to manufacture general-purpose synthetic rubber.

◄ Before World War II the USA produced more crude petroleum and refined products than the rest of the world combined.

The 1930s and 1940s saw a significant change in the role of science in many societies. At the beginning of the period the applications of science had already profoundly influenced the pattern of life in the Western world, though with considerable regional variations. The telephone, for example, was far more rapidly adopted in Sweden than in the rest of Europe. From the 1920s most countries had national systems of radio broadcasting. Motoring was transforming the transport field. The cinema had become a popular form of mass entertainment.

The list is impressive, and could be extended, but the public gave little credit to the scientists who had played an essential role in bringing about such developments. The motor industry was identified with the industrial leaders, such as Henry Ford in the USA and William Morris in the UK, rather than with the technologists who had developed the new alloys needed for engines and chassis; with the heads of the great oil companies rather than the engineers who sank the oil wells and invented the new chemical processes essential to maintaining the flow of petrol. In radio popular broadcasters were better known than the new race of electronic engineers who invented the complex thermionic tubes and other components necessary for radio transmitters and receivers. In the film world it was the directors and stars – the Hitchcocks and Garbos – who were esteemed rather than the technologists who had developed equipment and processes.

That this should be so is not altogether surprising, for most of these scientific and technological advances had developed gradually, so the public only slowly became aware of them. Scientists were also generally ignored by the publicity services commanded by the captains of industry. Indeed, most had no desire for publicity, preferring to be judged by their scientific peers rather than by the public at large.

The war changed all this. Advances which had been kept secret, or at least not publicized, were slowly revealed. The strategic significance of radar, the degaussing of ships to protect them against magnetic mines, the proximity fuse, aerosol-dispersed insecticides to control the insect vectors of disease, even the Biro pen which pilots could use at high altitudes without leaking, were all revealed to a suitably impressed public. But the biggest single factor was undoubtedly the atomic bomb. At the time, the bombing of Hiroshima and Nagasaki in August 1945, followed almost immediately by the unconditional surrender of Japan, seemed little short of miraculous. Only later, as the full horrors began to be seen in historical perspective, and the implications for the future of the human race had to be faced, were misgivings to be voiced.

POWER FOR INDUSTRY

The practical social consequences of research and development aimed primarily at wartime needs were considerable. Radar, for example, was immediately adaptable to the burgeoning civil aviation industry. The cavity magnetron which generated the intense centimeter-wavelength radiation for radar eventually entered the kitchen in the microwave cooker.

But the most marked and important change was in the public attitude toward scientists. Long regarded as a remote breed who carried out esoteric experiments in the remoteness of their laboratories, they emerged as real people who could change the history of the world. Young people, and those who advised them, saw science as not only the salvation of mankind but a highroad to fame and fortune. Without science, life's battle might be lost before it had properly begun. This change of attitude was strikingly reflected both in the enhanced importance attached to science in education – especially tertiary education – and in the media. For a time science rode the crest of the wave.

▼ A crucial feature of Soviet policy after the Bolshevik Revolution of 1917 was to invest heavily in science and technology. This typical poster (1932), by Alexei Kokorekin, urges the need to "Unite the power of science with the creative energy of the working class".

Electricity generation and distribution

For many purposes requiring electricity, such as telegraphy, only a low-power source was required, and various forms of battery sufficed. A more powerful sustained supply – such as that needed for lighting – was feasible only when reliable mechanical generators became available from the 1880s. Thereafter progress was steady, but haphazard. Public supplies became increasingly available in urban areas but there was no standardization of voltage or frequency – in some areas frequency was irrelevant because only direct current was available. This was discouraging for the consumer: electrical appliances could not be transferred from area to area because of their differing ratings. Moreover, with only local markets to supply the appliance industry too was fragmented.

The British experience typifies the general course of events throughout the western world. There the key event was the establishment of a government committee in 1925 to consider national electricity supply. Its recommendation

was that a gridiron of supply lines should be set up to connect all the supply areas. An eight-year program to construct the Grid was begun in 1928: by 1935, when the scheme was almost complete, nearly 5,000km (3,000mi) of primary transmission lines were in operation.

To unify supply, frequency and voltage had to be standardized. In 1926 three-quarters of the electricity supply in Britain was three-phase with a frequency of 50Hz; as this was also common in Europe it was agreed to adopt it as standard.

Nevertheless, there were considerable areas where it was different: northeast England was generally 40Hz and part of London was 25Hz. In some areas, such as part of north London, only direct current was available.

By 1935, when the Grid was largely complete, it was still not possible to transmit power freely from point to point, because of voltage differences. There were over 600 supply undertakings, providing electricity at voltages ranging from 100 to 480 volts: not until 1945 – after

▼ One of the most significant and dramatic technological developments of the 20th century was the spectacular growth of the electrical industry, an industry which had no earlier counterpart. This picture of New York in the 1930s epitomizes the prodigal use of electricity. Not until the OPEC oil crisis of 1973 was fuel conservation to be a matter for serious international concern.

generating and distribution systems and app-liances had been modified – was it finally pos-sible to standardize nationally at 240 volts. By that time generating capacity had risen to 12,000-MW, compared with 5,000MW when the Nation-al Grid was first approved. Since 1928 the number of houses wired for electricity had increased threefold (from about 2 million to 6 million).

Whenever electricity flows through a conduc-tor, such as a metal wire, power is lost in the form of heat. Sometimes this is a desired effect – as in an incandescent filament lamp – but in the trans-mission of electricity it is wasted energy. This can be minimized in two ways. Firstly, by using cables that are good electrical conductors; second-ly, by transmitting at high voltages.

Of the commonly available metals the best con-ductor is silver but this is too expensive for general use. The next best is copper and initially this was widely used. After World War I, how-ever, the price of copper rose considerably and increasing use was made of aluminum, which although not such a good conductor was a good deal cheaper and much lighter. Two defects had to be overcome, however. The first was its poor mechanical strength, a problem when cable has to span long distances between pylons: this was overcome by wrapping it round a supporting steel core. The second was corrosion. This was solved by developing special resistant alloys.

The question of transmission voltage is com-plicated, but the basic fact is that losses diminish in proportion to the square of the voltage. Conse-quently, substantial savings can be effected by using very high voltages, but there are inherent penalties. The most important are those pre-sented by generation and insulation. In Britain 132,000 volts was chosen for the main power lines but for the US Hoover Dam in the mid-1930s 289,000 volts was specified for its 500km (300mi) main transmission line. For local distribution these voltages must be stepped down by trans-formers in substations.

Sources of light

Until the 19th century artificial light was for all practical purposes synonymous with a naked flame. Not until the advent of electricity was there any fundamental change. This gave birth, well before the turn of the century, to the arc lamp and the familiar incandescent filament lamps. Of the two, the incandescent filament lamp – since made literally in billions – was by far the most familiar and convenient, but its efficiency was low.

The domestic consumer was not unduly bothered by its wasteful use of electricity, because the consumption was quite small. The case was very different for big users, however – factories and commercial premises of all kinds and, especially, local authorities obliged to provide lighting for kilometers of streets and large public places. There was, therefore, an incentive in the 1930s to develop more efficient electric lamps and interest turned to ones based on quite a different principle – the discharge of an electric current through a gas. In 1901 the Cooper-Hewitt lamp had appeared (in the UK), in which the discharge was through mercury vapor: this gives a bluish

light. In 1910 Georges Claude demonstrated in Paris a different form of discharge lamp, one filled with neon gas: this gave a characteristic reddish yellow light. It was developed in two forms: long tubes for advertising displays and a more com-pact form for street lighting. Progress was slow, however, and the now ubiquitous neon lighting was not widely adopted until the 1930s. Like the mercury vapor lamp, the light from a neon lamp is monochromatic but in a region of the spectrum to which the eye is particularly sensitive.

The neon discharge lamp has about three times the efficiency of incandescent filament lamps, but it is unsuitable for domestic use: apart from pro-ducing a monochromatic light unacceptable in this context, it is expensive and bulky.

In these circumstances interest switched back to the mercury discharge lamp. One reason for its relatively low efficiency is that part of the radiation it emits is in the ultraviolet region of the spectrum which is not only invisible to the human eye but harmful to it, so that it must be filtered off and wasted. But if this invisible light falls on certain substances, known as phos-phors, they glow and emit visible light. By suit-ably blending phosphors the emitted light can be made to approximate to normal daylight, or to warmer colors if desired. The fluorescent lamp, which first appeared in the mid-1930s, consists essentially of a tube, coated on the inside with an appropriate mixture of phosphors, in which an electric discharge passes through mercury vapor. After World War II it was widely adopted for commercial and industrial purposes.

▲ Lenin's equation for modernizing the Soviet Union was: Electrification plus Soviet power equals Communism. The great rivers of Russia favored the exploitation of hydroelectric power. In 1922 he proclaimed that "Dnieprostrol (above) will be the great monument of the electrification of the USSR".

▼ In London a similar message – "Power: the Nerve Centre ..." was spelled out on the posters of the Underground.

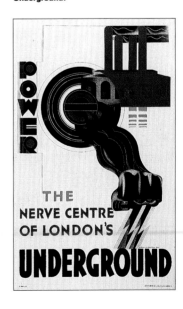

▲ In the 1920s the refining of crude oil to satisfy the growing demands of the automobile for gasoline – and of diesel engines for the heavier fractions – had become a major industry worldwide. This picture shows the Texas Company's refinery at Port Arthur, Texas, which operated the oil industry's first continuous thermal cracking process.

▼ Although it was particularly identified for many years with the United States, oil production was already an international business by the turn of the 20th century. The Nobel brothers operated oilfields in the Caspian in the 1880s. This picture shows drilling in Kuwait.

Oil refining

The petroleum industry is today so closely identified with transport that it is easy to forget that its origins had nothing to do with this. When E.L. Drake sank his first oil well in Pennsylvania in 1859, thus starting a great new industry, the first automobiles were still some 30 years in the future. His main target was lamp oil, and to obtain this viscous crude oil had to be fractionated (broken down into constituents) by distillation. This process yielded some useful by-products, including lubricants and a wax suitable for candles.

The lightest product of all, obtained in large quantities, was an embarrassment. It was highly flammable, with a low flashpoint, and was difficult to dispose of, save for limited use as a solvent. Yet its production was unavoidable, for it came off the still before the fractions actually required. However, it was these very qualities that made it invaluable when the pioneers of the automobile industry, notably Gottlieb Daimler in Germany, sought to use the internal combustion engine as a power unit for road vehicles. As a liquid it was easily handled and transported and it was so volatile that it could easily be vaporized to form an explosive mixture in the cylinder. Moreover, it was cheap and abundant.

It was not long before the tail was wagging the dog. With gas lighting given a new lease of life with the advent of the Welsbach mantle (a construction of asbestos impregnated with "rare earth" oxides which emits brilliant light when heated, invented in 1885), and increasing use of electric lighting, the demand for lamp-oil and candles slackened. At the same time the demand for petrol rocketed and, paradoxically, a situation arose which was exactly the opposite of that existing in the early days of the industry. Then, unwanted petrol had to be made to produce sufficient lamp-oil and other desired products: by the 1920s large quantities of unwanted higher fractions accumulated in order to meet the demand for petrol. Moreover, by then engine design was more sophisticated so even narrower fractions of the petrol fraction were required.

Basically, petroleum is a complex mixture of hydrocarbons, differing from each other in the number and arrangement of carbon atoms joined to each other to form individual molecules. In principle, therefore, one means of balancing supply and demand would be to "crack" some of the longer-chain molecules and so convert them into shorter ones of the required length. One way of doing this is simply to heat the higher fractions strongly – to around 500°C – in order to rupture some of the carbon-carbon bonds. Such a thermal cracking process was introduced about 1912, but was not widely practiced until the 1920s. Apart from producing more high-grade motor fuel, it also yielded as by-products hydrocarbon gases suitable as raw materials for the American chemical industry. However, these gases were not always desired in preference to a better yield of petrol and there was therefore much interest in alternative catalytic cracking processes which yielded a lower proportion of gas. The first major success here was that of the French engineer

E.J. Houdry; after some ten years of development work by a consortium of oil companies – at a cost of around 10 million US dollars – his process first became operational in 1936. In a variation introduced a little later – the so-called fluid process – the catalyst is differently handled, making it easier to control the composition of the product.

These cracking processes made it easier for the oil refineries to balance supply against demand, but by the mid-1950s the demand for high-octane fuels for new high-compression automobile engines was such that even some straight-run petrol fractions had to be subjected to catalytic reforming. But the refineries had also to provide fuel for an internal combustion engine with rather different requirements. This was the diesel engine, devised by the German engineer Rudolf Diesel around the turn of the century. In this, the fuel in the cylinder is ignited not by an electric spark but by the heat generated by the compression of the fuel mixture by the piston. It requires a rather heavier fuel, which is injected into the cylinder.

The development of polymers

The modern plastics industry effectively dates from 1907 when almost simultaneously L.H. Baekeland in the USA and James Swinburne in the UK patented the first phenol-formaldehyde plastic, subsequently known as Bakelite. The discovery was timely, for the material was a good insulator and could easily be molded into the multiplicity of small items needed for the electrical industry and for the electrical components of automobiles. For these purposes the brown color of the plastic did not matter but the later colorless formaldehyde resins based on urea and melamine found wider application as they could be attractively colored.

The 1930s saw the advent of another transparent plastic, polymethylmethacrylate, which became familiar under trade names such as Perspex and Plexiglass. Initially it was almost entirely used for the windshields and cockpit covers of military aircraft, for which it was ideally suitable, but after the war it found many other uses as a lightweight substitute for glass.

After the Nazis' seizure of power in 1933, Germany paid much attention to developing domestic substitutes for essential imports, of which one of the most important was rubber. This was required both as an insulator for electrical cables and for the tires of motor vehicles. For the first purpose PVC (polyvinylchloride) proved superior to rubber, being more durable, and it was also manufactured in the USA for this and other purposes, such as architectural sheeting and pipes. For tires, Germany developed Buna synthetic rubbers, but between the wars the USA was interested only in synthetic rubbers for a few special purposes. This situation changed dramatically when Japan conquered European and American rubber plantations in Asia (1941–42): in a crash program the USA managed to produce synthetic rubber at the astounding rate of nearly a million tonnes a year.

The Haber-Bosch nitrogen fixation process developed in Germany before World War I represented a major advance in chemical engineering. It was effective only at pressures some 200 times greater than atmospheric, far higher than had ever before been achieved in a large-scale manufacturing process. In the 1930s Imperial Chemical Industries in Britain embarked on an investigation of high-pressure chemistry generally. In special laboratory equipment they were able to attain pressures up to 2,000 times greater than atmospheric. In 1935 they succeeded in polymerizing ethylene, a simple gas consisting only of carbon and hydrogen. The new product, polyethylene (polythene), proved to be an excellent electrical insulator, repelling water. It was tough and could be easily molded. This combination of properties suggested a specialist use in submarine cables. Trials made in 1938 were so successful that ICI commissioned a commercial plant with an annual capacity of 200 tons. This came on stream on 1 September 1939, the day on which Germany invaded Poland and precipitated World War II in Europe.

This date was very significant, for the first major use of polythene was as an insulator in the development of centimeter-wave radar, for which its unique combination of properties proved virtually tailor-made. It arrived on the scene too late to be incorporated in the defensive radar chain constructed in Britain before the war but was crucially important in the shipborne and airborne radar equipment developed later.

At this stage it still appeared that polythene's main use would be in the electrical industry, as an insulator: expectations were that production would be at most a few thousand tonnes per

► Polymers – exemplified by bakelite and rayon – began to come into use long before there was any clear understanding of their nature. Some chemists believed them to be giant molecules, each containing thousands of atoms; others that they were aggregates of quite small molecules. The first view, powerfully advocated by Hermann Staudinger, professor of chemistry at Freiburg in Germany (1926–51), proved correct. Belatedly, he received a Nobel prize in 1953.

Man-made Fibers

The textile industry is literally as old as civilization but until the end of the 19th century there was virtually no change in the raw materials it utilized. These were primarily the natural vegetable fibers cotton and flax and those of animal origin – wool and silk. The first break with tradition came around the turn of the century, when C.F. Cross and E.J. Bevan in 1892 invented viscose rayon, made by a chemical process from cellulose. Manufacture was first taken up in Britain by Courtaulds in Coventry.

By the mid-1930s world production of rayon (largely viscose rayon) was around 750,000 tonnes a year, comparable with wool at around 1.5 million tonnes, but far short of cotton at over 6 million tonnes. Nevertheless, rayon was sufficiently big business for the chemical industry to explore other possible manmade fibers, especially wholly synthetic ones.

The first to achieve a major success was Du Pont in the USA, where in 1935 W.H. Carothers discovered the fiber-forming potential of polyamides (a kind of polymer). To transform these into a marketable product was a difficult task but Nylon 66 came on the market in 1939. It was an immediate success, especially in the stocking market: nylons and stockings soon became virtual synonyms. Later, nylon was used in many other ways – in fashion fabrics, ropes and fishing lines.

In Britain a chemically different sort of fiber – a polyester – was patented in 1941 but was not substantially developed until after World War II. It was marketed by ICI in Britain and the rest of the world, except the USA, as Terylene; in the USA as Dacron. This found many applications in the clothing industry, as fabric and knitwear but not as stockings; like rayon its relaxation time was wrong so that stockings bagged.

◀ Model wearing artificial clothes and (inset) nylon research.

◀ Growing understanding of the chemistry of polymers in the 1930s made it possible to develop new ones systematically instead of empirically. One of the earliest fruits of this new approach was polymethylmethacrylate, a transparent, light-weight material marketed under various names such as Perspex and Plexiglass. Becoming available just before World War II, almost all available supplies were used to make cockpit covers for military aircraft, such as this German JU87 Stuka. Later is found many uses as a substitute for glass, for example, in roofing. Its attractive physical properties led also to other uses in opaque varieties colored with pigments.

year. This prediction was utterly confounded by events. Although the electrical outlet remained important, polythene proved highly successful for the manufacture of a wide range of moldings, such as toys and household goods. It also made excellent film. Production worldwide soared, especially with the advent of low-temperature low-pressure processes in the 1950s: no more than 1,000 tons in 1945, it had risen to a million tons in 1960 and five million tons ten years later. What had started as a specialist chemical emerged as a basic world commodity with an importance akin to rubber or cotton.

The reason why plastics are all based on long carbon chains is simply that this element is virtually alone in being able to unite atom-to-atom in this way. The only other element which has this property – and to only a very limited extent – is silicon. During and since the war a range of silicon plastics – the silicones – have been produced for application where their anti-adhesive properties, water repellency, and heat resistance justify their high cost. They range from fluids to jellies and tough flexible solids.

Basically, plastics are of two kinds: thermosetting and thermoplastic. The former – such as urea-formaldehyde – set permanently solid when they are heated; the latter – such as polythene – can be repeatedly softened and hardened by heating and cooling. In either event they have to be shaped by molding, casting, extrusion through dies, or in other mechanical ways.

A major development in the plastic industry has been in the ability to make very large articles, such as baths or lengths of gas or water main. There is, however, an upper limit to what can be achieved by this means and if only a small number of items are to be made the considerable cost of a mold may not be justified. In such circumstances large moldings – such as the hulls of small boats – can be made by coating a former, often of wood, with a paste of plastic and reinforcing glass fiber. The plastics used are epoxy resins, generally familiar as "Araldite" and similar household adhesives. Here the setting is effected not by the application of heat but by chemical reaction between two components.

The cheapness and ease of fabrication of plastics led to some unexpected uses. In 1958 there was a worldwide craze for Hula-Hoops, most of them made of polythene. While it lasted, many millions were made: one New York store sold more than 2,000 in a single day. Later a similar boom arose with a craze for skateboards.

The Struggle of Science in Italy

Between the 16th and the early 19th centuries Italians made many notable contributions to science, but by the late 19th century Italian science had become stagnant. The political unification of Italy in 1870 had failed to restore a position of prominence and, if anything, the gap widened in the 1890s, when the pace of development in pure and applied research set by other European countries – especially Germany – quickened. It was only on the eve of World War I, in the context of mounting international tension, that the goverment began to heed the calls of Italian scientists for the reform of the country's scientific institutions. However, scarcely any action was taken before the 1920s, and even the creation of the Consiglio Nazionale delle Ricerche (National Council of Research) in 1927, under the chairmanship of Guglielmo Marconi, yielded a disappointing harvest. The resources were too limited and too thinly spread to generate substantial research programs.

In the early 20th century, mathematics was (as in the 19th century) the only sector in which Italy retained a truly international reputation. The situation was less favorable in other sectors. Inadequate facilities, and a tendency to focus on rather narrow experimental problems, detached Italian physics from the profound theoretical developments changes that led to the emergence of relativity, quantum mechanics and nuclear physics. Galileo Ferraris created an important school of electrical engineering in Turin (the forerunner of the "Galileo Ferraris" National Institute of Electrical Engineering opened in 1935), and Augusto Righi conducted brilliant experiments on electricity in Bologna, but neither of them succeeded in building a research school. The decline of this individualistic tradition was eclipsed by the emergence of a new breed of capable "academic" managers in the 1920s. The most remarkable product of this change was the creation of a research center attached to the University of Rome, where Orso M. Corbino brought together an outstanding team, including Enrico Fermi, Emilio Segrè, Franco Rasetti and Edoardo Amaldi. Their work on atomic physics flourished until 1935, but by then not even their reputation could secure the funds that were necessary to continue their research. This, with the growing influence of fascism, triggered a diaspora from which Italian physics did not recover until the 1950s.

The reorganization of science after World War II was slow and fraught with financial and organizational difficulties. While the Consiglio Nazionale delle Ricerche retained its central role in sponsoring research, other national and private agencies were created, with responsibilities that often overlapped. Applied research achieved the most visible results. Giulio Natta, for example, with the support of industrial as well as governmental funds, developed the study of polymers for which he was awarded a Nobel prize in 1963. Physics began to gather new momentum in the late 1950s, chiefly through the launching of European cooperative projects in the nuclear field, such as CERN, which was strongly supported by Italy.

Splitting the atom

In retrospect, it is a little surprising that the atom-splitting experiment of J.D. Cockcroft and E.T.S. Walton at Cambridge in 1932 attracted the attention it did. There was no general notion of the potential possibilities of atomic power, even though the decision to attempt the construction of an atomic bomb lay less than ten years ahead.

For an explanation of why the experiment captured the public imagination we must look to traditional views about the nature of atoms. Despite the accumulated evidence that atoms had structure, the old belief that they were indivisible died hard. News that two Cambridge scientists had in fact deliberately split an atom thus had the effect of undermining dogma.

Put in its simplest terms, the experiment was a microversion of the familiar coconut shy at the fair, when a powerfully hurled wooden ball breaks open a larger nut. In the Cockcroft/Walton experiment the ball was a positively charged hydrogen atom (proton) – electrically accelerated to a high speed – and the coconut was an atom of lithium. On traditional theory the mass of the projectile and the target should have exactly equaled that of the two new particles: in fact, there was a slight discrepancy exactly accounted for, in terms of Einstein's theory, by the amount of energy released. Thus although there was a long way to go, and the road ahead was not clear, the possibility – and no more – of deliberately converting mass to energy had been established. For the moment, however, this was ignored: the pioneers were intent not on providing a new

▼ The discovery of artificial radioactivity by the French physicists J.F. Joliot and his wife opened up new avenues in atomic physics. Joliot (right) is seen here in his laboratory in the early decades of atomic physics, the dangers of exposure to radioactivity were not entirely appreciated. Marie Curie died of leukemia in 1934, presumably caused by an excessive intake of radioaction; so too did her daughter Irène (who married J.F. Joliot in 1926). Even after World War II servicemen were exposed to radiation during open-air testing of atomic bombs.

▲ ▶ The atom-splitting experiment of J.D. Cockcroft and E.T.S. Walton – carried out in 1932 in the Cavendish Laboratory, Cambridge – was a highly significant event in the history of physics. Until then, one of the basic doctrines of science was that atoms were indivisible: now a typical cloud chamber picture (above) provided evidence for all to see that a lithium atom could be disintegrated by a fast-moving proton. This picture shows their original apparatus, with Walton inside the "hut". Cockcroft and Walton were awarded the Nobel Prize for Physics in 1951.

In my own experimental work, we used to hold up a fluorescent screen in our lab, and we judged the intensity of the radiation to which we were exposed by the intensity of the glow. If it was too bright we added another millimeter of lead shielding. It is remarkable that we are alive and well today!

J.D. COCKCROFT

source of energy but with satisfying their curiosity about the ultimate structure of matter.

The essence of the new method for investigating atomic structure was to provide increasingly faster and more energetic particles – on the principle that a rifle bullet will penetrate further into a target than a pea from a peashooter. The velocity a particle acquires from an electric field is determined both by the potential difference and the length of the path it travels. To increase the latter, E.O. Lawrence and D.H. Sloan in the USA conceived the ingenious idea of using a combined electric and magnetic field to make the particle travel in a spiral, shaped like the hairspring of a watch. In this way, a long path can be contained

within a relatively small space. Such a device came to be known as a cyclotron and by 1939 Lawrence had built one at Berkeley, California, with a power more than 50 times greater than that of Cockcroft and Walton. With a 200-tonne magnet, this was already an expensive machine but Lawrence even then had a far more ambitious machine on the drawing board. This was designed for a 5m (16ft) magnet weighing nearly 4,000 tonnes and containing 300 tonnes of copper wiring: its power was no less than 200 MeV. In the event this was not at first used for research, as intended, but was diverted to the Manhattan Project to separate uranium isotopes for the first atomic bombs.

THE PLANNED ECONOMY

The Soviet Union was hardly affected by the economic crisis which affected most of the rest of the world in the late 1920s and 1930s. After the Revolution of 1917, it had largely withdrawn from the world market. By the end of 1928, Stalin had taken power and embarked on an ambitious program intended to transform the Soviet Union into a modern nation.

Two five-year plans were to form the basis for this enormous restructuring of the national economy. The first, which concentrated on iron and steel production, began on 1 October 1928 and was declared complete on 31 December 1932. It was consolidated and broadened by the second plan, from 1933 to 1937. Both involved the abandonment of the market economy; instead targets for local industry were set by the Supreme Economic Council. Resources were also directed by the state, and despite some confusion and distorted statistics, the achievements were spectacular.

Between 1928 and 1937 industrial production rose by 12 to 18 percent annually. In particular, mechanical engineering expanded strongly, while a number of new industries were introduced. Tractors, trucks, aircraft and so on were mass-produced for the first time, and the number of industrial employees increased from just over four million to nearly 11.5 million during this period. New roads and railroads, as well as new factories, sprang up all across the Soviet Union, as well as power stations to service the new demand. In contrast, per capita personal consumption fell and the production of industrial consumer goods grew much more slowly than that of investment goods.

The relentless collectivization of agriculture – abolishing private property and reorganizing agricultural production into large collective farms, which were themselves set high production targets by the state – was central to Stalin's plans. Between late 1929 and the end of 1931, 20 million individual farms were turned into collectives. Those who would not willingly join were dealt with ruthlessly. The number of people working in agriculture dropped from 71 to 51 million between 1928 and 1937 (many of them dead, others forcibly removed from the land) and grave famines ensued, especially in 1932–33.

Despite the successes of the five-year plans, the system in the 1930s was by no means planned perfectly. Yet the Soviet Union developed into an important industrial power; mass unemployment was abolished and millions of unskilled or poorly trained peasants received basic training in industry. The human costs of this policy, however, were also enormous.

▶ The industrial worker in the five-year plan was promoted as a modern hero. The photographs of Arkadi Schaichet – such as this image of a young man in a new cotton factory in Balakha in 1930 – expressed this quality dramatically.

▶▼ Consumer goods including clothing were given far lower priority than heavy industry, and despite such images of enthusiastic labor in textile mills, consumer output fell below 1928 levels through the 1930s and most of the 1940s.

▶ The first five-year plan placed great emphasis on tractor production. This poster encouraged Soviet tractor engineers to work harder, indirectly to improve the agricultural situation. Without incentives or profit, the economy relied on such propaganda to raise output.

▲▶ China under Communism also experienced a centrally planned economy. During the 1960s, students, bureaucrats and teachers were directed to the fields in order to improve agricultural production, and to avert the dangers of urban unemployment.

РАЗВЕРНЕМ
НАСТУПЛЕНИ

◄ Power and electricity were at the heart of Stalin's industrialization plans. Here the third turbine is being installed in the new hydroelectric power station in Dneprogues. Water and coal were the main sources of energy.

▼ Tractors being delivered to a *kolkhoz* or collective farm in 1930s. The bucolic image hid the reality of starvation, forcible emigration and widespread opposition to collectivization, which led many peasants to slaughter their own animals.

ОЦИАЛИСТИЧЕСКОЕ
В ГОРОДЕ И ДЕРЕВНЕ!

THE
FADING
DREAM

Time Chart

	1930	1931	1932	1933	1934	1935	1936	1937
Rural life	• Feb–Mar: Reports of 40 kulaks per day murdered by agents of Stalin. Thousands of peasants flee to Poland • Southern and midwestern USA hit by unprecedented drought	• 10 Jan: Molotov, head of the Council of Commissars, predicts half of Soviet agriculture will be collectivized by 1932 • UK, USA, France, Belgium and Canada join to stop Soviet grain dumping	• Feb: France begins an assistance program for agriculture • New farmland opens up in the Netherlands with the drainage of the Zuider Zee • Famine in the Caucasus and the Ukraine (USSR)	• 12 May: Agricultural Adjustment Act becomes law (USA) • World price of wheat hits an historic low point	• May: Dust storms blow 300 million tonnes of topsoil from Kansas, Oklahoma, Texas and Colorado into the Atlantic (USA) • "Okies" and "Arkies" (farmers from the Dustbowl) begin the trek to California	• Apr: Increasingly severe dust storms in Kansas, Colorado, Wyoming, Texas and New Mexico (USA) • Resettlement Administration is created by executive order to move people to better land (USA)	• Nazi Germany undertakes a four-year program to replace raw materials such as fats and livestock fodder with synthetics (ersatz) • Drought reduces the American harvest	• Drought finally ends in the USA but stem rust attacks the wheat crop
Industry and labor	• 12 Mar: All-India Trade Union Congress authorizes Gandhi to commence civil disobedience demonstrations • Majority of USSR production is industrial (53%) • Unemployment passes two million in the UK, and four million in the USA	• 15 Sep: 12,000 Royal Navy sailors at Invergordon strike against pay cuts (UK) • 30 Nov: Merger between His Master's Voice and Columbia creates Electrical and Musical Industries (EMI) (UK) • Unemployment reaches 4.75 million in Germany, 7 million in the USA, and 2.66 million in the UK	• Jan: Reconstruction Finance Corporation established to finance the creation of work and to encourage business activity (USA) • 14 Apr: New Zealand sees its worst riots in history after cuts in civil service pay • 20,000 US businesses go bankrupt and 1,616 banks fail	• 18 May: Tennessee Valley Authority is created in Roosevelt's New Deal to develop the area's resources (USA) • 5 Aug: Roosevelt establishes a National Labor Board under the National Recovery Act to ensure the right of collective bargaining • 30 Aug: Air France is created	• Sep: Industrial League prevents the introduction of the 40-hour week (UK) • 1 Sep: 400,000 US textile workers begin a three-week strike • Italy establishes a corporatist economy. Confederations of employers and employees act as supreme economic associations	• 5 Jul: Labor Relations Act takes effect and guarantees the freedom of trade unions (USA) • Nov: France nationalizes the mining industry • Germany introduces the eight-hour day	• 26 Feb: Hitler opens the first Volkswagen factory • 5 Oct: Jarrow Protest March begins with 200 unemployed men and a petition bearing 11,572 signatures (UK) • United Rubber Workers of America pioneer the sit-down strike in action against the Goodyear Tyre and Rubber Company	• 2 Mar: United Steel allows its workers to join unions • 29 Mar: US Supreme Court upholds the minimum wage principle for women • 30 Apr–26 May: 30,000 London bus workers strike • German Jews are excluded from positions in industry
Government and people	• 31 Mar: Congress enacts the Public Road Building Act, providing funds for state highway building jobs (USA) • 1 Apr: Government abolishes the Poor Law Guardians (UK) • 30 Apr: Women's insurance law enacted in France • 19 May: White South African women given the vote; coloreds remain without vote	• 16 Jan: Electoral reform eliminates plural voting in the UK • 31 Jul: May Committee recommends £96 million in spending cuts (UK) • 16 Oct: Spanish government legalizes divorce • Universal suffrage introduced in Ceylon	• 17 Apr: Emperor Haile Selassie abolishes slavery in Abyssinia • 24 Sep: Poona Pact is signed, after Gandhi's fast in prison, giving voting rights to untouchables • Brazil, Thailand and Uruguay extend voting rights to women on equal terms with men	• 14 Mar: Nazis ban kosher meat and leftwing newspapers • 8 May: First gas chamber execution carried out in the USA • 6 Jun: Congress approves the National Industry Recovery Act. Congress gains tremendous control over industry, administered by the National Recovery Administration (USA)	• 19 Jan: Roosevelt orders $21 million for US war veterans • 29 Sep: Conscription is introduced in Poland for both men and women • 30 Oct: Mussolini orders all 6–8 year olds to join a special premilitary training corps (It) • 20 Nov: Depressed Areas Bill introduced in the UK	• 6 May: Beginning of the Works Progress Administration, to provide employment for millions in a series of public works programs • 27 May: US Supreme Court declares the majority of US president Roosevelt's "New Deal" legislation illegal • 27 Nov: NZ Labour government enacts a major program of social reforms	• 21 Feb: New Spanish government grants amnesty to 30,000 political prisoners • 7 Apr: Blacks are barred from office in South Africa by the Native Representation Act. Instead, they are represented by three elected white representatives • USSR revokes a 1920 decree which legalized abortion	• 9 Jan: Italian government bans interracial marriages in its African colonies • Jan–Feb: First general elections held in India • Fatwa issued by Islam's Grand Mufti permits Muslims to use contraceptive measures to which both men and women agree
Religion	• 31 Dec: Birth control proclaimed a grave and unnatural sin by Pope Pius XI • Haile Selassie, new Ethiopian emperor, is hailed as the living God by Rastafarians, thus fulfilling the prophecy of Marcus Garvey	• 25 Mar: Muslim and Hindu riots at Cawnpore kill hundreds (Ind) • 31 May: Pius XI condemns fascism after priests are attacked (It) • Joseph Franklin Rutherford renames his group Jehovah's Witnesses (USA)	• 30 Sep: Pius XI condemns Mexican anticlericalism	• 7 Feb: Mustapha Kemal bans Arabic prayers and "Allah", the Arabic word for God (Turk) • 27 Oct: Protests against Jewish immigration in coastal towns of Palestine	• Jan: Pastors denounce the Nazi regime but homes of such clergy are attacked by the police (Ger) • 5 Aug: 100 Jews and Arabs are killed during rioting in Algeria • Nazis rewrite the Psalms to minimize reference to the Jews	• 19 Mar: British troops fire on a crowd of Muslims rioting against Hindus, killing 27 people (Ind) • 15 Sep: German Nuremberg laws legitimize antisemitism • 17 Sep: Jews are denied German citizenship	• 19 Apr–25 May: Riots in Tel Aviv between Palestinians and Jews leads to eleven deaths and 50 injuries. The Arab rebellion continues until 1939 (Pal) • Oct: Hindus and Muslims riot in Bombay (Ind)	• May: Government decree forbidding the veiling of women leads to riots by Albanian Muslims • 7 Jul: British government Peel Report suggests a partition of Palestine into Arab and Jewish states
Events and trends	• 12 Mar–6 Apr: Gandhi's march to the sea in protest against British laws controlling salt production (Ind) • May: Stewardesses first employed by United Airlines (USA) • Abortion becomes a crime in Fascist Italy • First supermarket opens, on Long Island, New York (USA)	• 22 Jan: Doctors in London claim the discovery of a vaccine against polio (UK) • Feb: Japan is first to televise a baseball game • 1 Jun: Mussolini bans all Catholic youth organizations (It) • 11 May: Austrian Kreditanstalt goes bankrupt	• 30 Jan: Prohibition of alcohol is lifted in Finland • Jul: With 230 seats gained in an election, the Nazis become the biggest party in the Reichstag (Ger) • Oct: Iraq enters the League of Nations, thereby gaining full independence from Britain	• 22 Mar: Roosevelt signs bill legalizing wine and beer, thus ending the Prohibition (USA) • 25 Jul: Hitler announces plan for a compulsory sterilization program to racially purify Germany	• 15 Jan: Serious earthquake in the Bihar Province of India and in Nepal kills 10,000 people and leaves 500,000 homeless • 3 Sep: Evangeline Booth becomes the first woman general in the Salvation Army (UK) • Durex condoms for men first produced	• May: Yellow River floods drowning 50,000 and covering hundreds of square miles • Alcoholics Anonymous founded in New York • Amended Irish criminal code makes the sale, importation or advertisement of any birth control device a felony	• Tampax Inc is founded to commercially produce tampons (USA) • Great purge begins in the USSR as Stalin eliminates his political enemies • Publication of J.M. Keynes' The General Theory of Employment, Interest and Money (UK)	• Publication of George Orwell's The Road to Wigan Pier (UK) • Jamaicans riot against British rule • Nationalist riots in Trinidad and Tobago
Politics	• 21 Jan–22 Apr: Five Power Naval Conference agrees to limit size and quantity of naval ships and submarines	• 14 Apr: King Alfonso leaves Spain, and the country is declared a republic • 11 Dec: Statute of Westminster creates a Commonwealth of equal and autonomous Dominions	• 18 Feb: Japan establishes a puppet state (Manchukuo) in Manchuria	• 30 Jan: Hitler becomes Chancellor of Germany and proclaims the Third Reich (Mar) • Falange, the Spanish fascist party, is founded by Antonio Primo de Rivera	• 30 Jun: Hitler wipes out rival leadership of the Nazis during the Night of the Long Knives • 2 Aug: Hitler assumes the title of "Führer" on the death of Hindenburg (Ger)	• 19 May: Sudeten Party, many of whose members are Nazis, becomes the second strongest party in Czechoslovakia • 3 Oct: Mussolini's troops march into Abyssinia	• Mar: Germany remilitarizes the Rhineland • 18 Jul: Beginning of the Spanish Civil War with the Nationalist insurrection	• 7 Jul: Japan attacks and later occupies northeast and east China • Irish Free State renamed Eire, with a new constitution and dominion status within the Commonwealth

1938	1939
● By pooling milk from various herds, US dairies eliminate the occasionally fatal "milk sick" disease ● Crop planting restrictions eased in a new Agricultural Adjustment Act (USA)	● 3 May: UK farmers offered £2 per acre to plow up and reseed unused pastures ● Swiss chemist Paul Müller introduces DDT as an effective, inexpensive pesticide
● 18 Mar: Mexico nationalizes its petroleum industry and expropriates US and UK oil companies ● Apr: US president Roosevelt establishes a $4.5 billion work program ● 27 Jun: Employers in Vienna give all Jews two weeks notice (Aut)	● 19 May: Trades Union Congress decides not to oppose conscription (UK) ● Aug: More than 30 industrial plants are transferred to Manzhouguo (Jap) ● 22 Dec: Female arms workers in UK demand the same pay as males
● 3 Jun: UK government announces its intention to distribute gas masks to all schoolchildren ● 30 May: All Czechs and Slovaks aged 6–60 must undergo defense training ● 1 Sep: Mussolini orders the expulsion of all Jews who entered Italy after 1918 ● Social Security Act provides state medical service in New Zealand	● 1 Jan: All women under 25 years ordered to do one year's civilian service for the Reich (Ger) ● 5 Apr: Government announces plans for the evacuation of 2.5 million to the country in the event of war (UK) ● 30 Aug: Beginning of the evacuation of children from cities in France and Britain
● 14 Jul: Italy officially adopts antisemitism ● 9 Nov: Kristallnacht: 7,000 Jewish shops looted and hundreds of synagogues burned during a night of Nazi violence (Ger)	● 20 Jan: King Farouk declared the Caliph (spiritual leader of Islam) (Egy) ● 27 Feb: British White Paper issued outlining plan for independent Arab-Jewish state in Palestine ● 28 Oct: Jews are required to wear the Star of David
● 22 Oct: First xerographic image is produced, by Chester Carlson (USA) ● 21 Dec: UK announces plans to spend £200,000 on air raid shelters ● Nestlé Company of Switzerland introduces Nescafé coffee	● 20 Feb: Nylon stockings go on sale for the first time (USA) ● 23 Jun: Irish government outlaws the Irish Republican Army (IRA) ● British government begins delivery of free air raid shelters to thousands of homes
● 30 Sep: Munich Agreement between Britain, Germany, France and Italy allows for the German annexation of Sudetenland (Czech)	● 1 Sep: German troops invade Poland, causing Britain and France to declare war on Germany on 3 Sep

"The remedy is for people to stop watching the ticker, listening to the radio, drinking bootleg gin, and dancing to jazz; forget the 'new economics' and prosperity founded upon spending and gambling, and return to the old economics based upon saving and working."

R.C. LEFFINGWELL, 1930

"Except for the comparatively fortunate owners of modern tenement flats, the wage-earning classes of this country still live in badly planned, inconvenient little houses which harbor dirt, involve incessant labor, and are totally unequipped with the most elementary devices for saving time and toil."

VERA BRITTAIN, 1932

"My work incapacitates me for the full enjoyment of my leisure time…consequently, much of my leisure time…is frittered away in lounging aimlessly about."

BRITISH MINER, 1934

"With what pleasure we read newspaper reports of crime! A true criminal becomes a popular figure because he unburdens in no small degree the consciences of his fellow men, for now they know once more where evil is to be found."

C.G. JUNG, 1934

"The German Constitution of 1918 granted equality before the law to all citizens. Women entered politics, the professions, the civil services. Between thirty and forty-two sat in each of the various Reichstags as deputies between 1919 and 1933 – a higher proportion than in any other country… But the Nazi movement has reversed all that… …Wherever possible women in administrative positions have been replaced by men."

WINIFRED HOLTBY, 1934

"(There is) a growing indifference to religion…Not only is church attendance declining, but Sunday School classes are melting away. It is becoming increasingly difficult to evoke interest in the things of the Spirit. God has been forgotten."

A. SALTER, 1939

"Those poor women with so many children and babies were queuing up for bread…and we climbed up lamp-posts and told them that we would win the war…we actually…believed it. But those good ladies looked at us in such a way…"

TERESA PAMIES on the Spanish Civil War

Datafile

The 1930s saw challenges to capitalism as an economic system and to political liberalism. Right-wingers as well as Marxists saw in the world crisis of the Great Depression the imminent demise of capitalism; and the authoritarian politics for which the crisis provided fertile ground fundamentally questioned political liberalism. The upshot was that the planning of economic development and social change, with the state intervening in most spheres of life, became widely accepted. For ordinary people the effects of these years were contradictory and sometimes divisive, as some experienced long-term unemployment while others benefited from falling prices and the increase of domestic comfort.

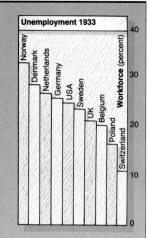

Unemployment 1933

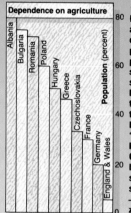

Dependence on agriculture

◀ **Eastern and southern Europe remained primarily agricultural.** Almost everywhere the traditional peasant economy had been proven an adaptable system. Big estates survived in Poland and Hungary. Change was taking place, however, and the "sociographer" Gyula Illyes wrote in 1936: "The 'wind of progress' blew keenly over the *pusztas* (the Great Plain of Hungary), breaking in through the farm servants' windows and scattering [them] like chaff" – referring to the modernization of agriculture.

▲ **The 1930s were "the time of troubles".** Among the major powers Germany was hardest hit, largely because of its heavy dependence on international credit. By 1933, the year in which Hitler came to power, almost one-third of the working population was unemployed. It was *not* amongst the groups most affected by unemployment, however, that Hitler's support lay, but rather among the large self-employed labor force in agriculture and in handicrafts.

▶ **Following the passing of the National Labor Relations Act in the United States in 1935**, which gave government backing to rights to join trades unions, there was massive growth in union membership. The history of labor in Europe in this period, in contrast, is generally one of defensiveness, at least until the war years.

US Labor Union membership

New Nazi members 1930–33

7% — 5%
22% — 34%
32%

Total 670,000

- Manual workers
- Self-employed
- White collar workers
- Public servants
- Domestic employees

◀ **What was most striking about the membership of the Nazi "workers" party was the underrepresentation of the working class** (then 45 percent of the German population). Around half of the new manual worker members were unemployed. Peasants provided the Nazis with their overwhelming support after 1929.

▶ **The industrialization of the Soviet Union under "Five Year Plans"**, launched in 1928, led to an enormous and rapid expansion of the nonagricultural work force. This permitted a great deal of social mobility. The 1939 Party Congress plausibly claimed that "The Soviet intelligentsia is yesterday's workers and peasants".

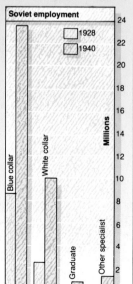

Soviet employment

In the 1930s different approaches to social change crystallized and came into conflict. The assumptions of democratic liberalism in industrial societies were threatened. Fascism and Nazism, born from the social tensions generated by industrialization and liberal democracy in Italy and Germany, came to offer an alternative, authoritarian model of social change. In Eastern Europe and the Soviet Union, meanwhile, there were radically opposing experiments in changing economically backward societies – one building on existing peasant communities; the other on centralization of authority to bring about rapid industrialization.

The responses of the capitalist democracies established the notion of the possibility of planning economic development and social change – even in the United States. The central issue left by this period was that posed to himself in his diary in May 1940 by British prime minister Winston Churchill's private secretary: "Will state control, once instituted, ever be abandoned?" By 1945 the world confronted two models of development and change, that of Soviet communism and that of capitalism. But by then both involved state intervention in a way which challenged liberal values.

Social consequences of the world crisis

"On the morning of October 24, 1929", wrote the American author Fredrick Lewis Allen, "the towering structure of American prosperity cracked wide open". The fall of New York's Wall Street stockmarket dragged the economy of the whole world into the Great Depression. It led to a sharp reduction in industrial production, slashed the already deficient demand for primary commodities, and threw millions of industrial workers into unemployment. It also destroyed the livelihoods of millions more peasant producers, even in parts of the world remote from Wall Street – bringing far-reaching changes in their societies and hastening the overthrow of colonialism.

The American economy spiraled downward from the day of the crash through to mid-1932. As industrial production dropped there were as many as 5 million vagrants, with (in the words of the historian M.A. Jones) "jobless men roaming the countryside looking for work or congregated on the outskirts of big cities in colonies of cardboard shacks known as Hoovervilles" – a play on the name of the then president (Herbert Hoover), who spurned state intervention. Meanwhile in industrial Europe Germany was hardest hit. In Britain unemployment remained at over 1.5 million throughout the 1930s, stretching the system of unemployment relief to the limit and leading to the introduction of a bitterly resented means test for benefits. France, with its more autonomous

UPHEAVAL AND UNCERTAINTY

economy, was affected later but then saw unemployment remain high from 1932 right up to World War II.

European and American agriculture was already depressed in the 1920s. Farmers everywhere struggled because of falling prices. In France, where farmers still made up a third of the work force, small peasants were those hardest hit as prices for farm produce fell much more sharply than those of industrial products. Between 1931 and 1935 peasant incomes fell by a third. A Peasant Front was formed in 1934, seeking a political system more in sympathy with agriculture. There were demonstrations and a milk strike which saw peasant landowners (as opposed to farm laborers) banding together in collective action for the first time. The Depression brought great hardship to German peasants too, and their similar grievances over falling prices were allied with resentments against both big business and

The social impact of the Wall Street Crash

Fascism and its supporters

Antisemitism

France and Britain under threat

Socialism in one country

Collectivization in Stalin's Soviet Union

The peasant societies of Eastern Europe

▼ **Unemployed workers in the United States waiting for relief payments. For the millions of unemployed in North America and Europe the 1930s were the "hungry thirties".**

socialists, making many of them strong supporters of Nazism. In the United States decline in foreign demand and the withdrawal of government price support saw prices falling from 1920. Part of the New Deal legislation in the 1930s was the Agricultural Adjustment Act (1933) which attempted to increase prices by curtailing production. Benefits went mainly to larger farmers.

Amongst the deeper and longer-run causes of the slump was the fact that by 1929 productive capacity had far exceeded the level of consumer demand. This in turn reflected the inequality of income distribution in America as in Europe. An important aspect of the responses of governments to the slump was intervention to stimulate demand in the economy. In America Franklin D. Roosevelt's New Deal entailed the massive expansion of Federal expenditure. Part was for the employment of several million people in work relief projects. Blacks, who had been especially

hard hit, benefited from these and began to vote massively for the Democrats for the first time. State recognition of the needs of the underprivileged was expressed also in welfare legislation in which the United States had hitherto lagged behind Europe. In 1935 the Social Security Act and the National Labor Relations Act were passed, the latter encouraging unionization to raise wages and purchasing power, and expanding the role for government in labor relations.

In America the minority of trade union leaders who formed the Committee on Industrial Organization (CIO) in 1935 had some success, against the craft traditions of the American Federation of Labor (AF of L), in organizing all workers in particular industries into single unions. By the end of 1937 it claimed to have more members than the AF of L and pioneered a new technique of industrial action, the "sit-in". The growth of industrial unions accelerated the decay of the old "drive system" of labor management. Corporations encouraged the integration of unions into a new collective bargaining structure. They also began to experiment with the development of "internal labor markets", that is the incorporation of a section of the work force in a secure and privileged career structure. The increasing importance of blacks and of women in the work force – notably during and after World War II – made for a growing heterogeneity, giving employers an opportunity to manipulate sex and race differences to enhance their bargaining power.

Experiences of fascism

The rise of fascist movements predates but was later intensified by the economic crisis. Contemporary Marxists saw in fascism the "death agony" of capitalism. Many representatives of landed and business interests took a similar view, regarding the economic crisis as opening up opportunities

to bolshevism; but they also considered it to be insoluble within the confines of parliamentary democratic rule. They therefore looked to authoritarian means to quash organized labor. At the same time, however, the elites required mass support in order to establish authoritarian rule, or at least to legitimize it. A potent base for such support existed in the eclectic mixture of nationalism and racialism that characterized Benito Mussolini's first steps to build a fascist movement in Italy.

Who supported fascism in Italy, and what kind of a regime was established? The fascist movement in its early phases was predominantly young and radical. "Old men of power", and notably the corrupt oligarchic politicians of the rural south, were targets of the anger of the petty-bourgeois fascist base described by the historian J. Steinberg: "young ex-officers, now students without degrees, lawyers without clients, doctors without patients, accountants without accounts". In the Tuscan city of Livorno in April 1921, for example, over 48 percent of fascist activists were lower middle-class (largely white-collar employees), compared with a working-class presence of just 8.5 percent (and that in an industrial city). Peasant smallholders, especially sharecroppers in what became the fascist stronghold in Central Italy, supported the fascists; landless laborers did not. Italy had no major conservative party in which a scared, angry middle class might take refuge. Liberalism itself remained fatally fearful of mass-participatory politics, while the propertied classes were also mistrustful of the main Catholic party, the Partito Populare, because it was a socially radical peasants' party. Thus, even as early as 1921, the middle and upper ranks of the middle classes were prominent among the fascists (19 percent of members in Livorno). The working class had been seen as a threat to state and church alike, and to the material interests of the defenders of each. Fascism, and the restoration of law and order which it promised, provided the ruling elites, even at the eleventh hour, with an opportunity to recover much of the ground they had lost.

Mussolini seized power in Italy in 1922 and in 1926 established a one-party fascist dictatorship, when all opposition parties were formally abolished. Only working-class organizations, however, felt the full force of "totalitarianism". Borrowing from Fordism, the regime encouraged new techniques of production, but in contrast with the USA, Italy's industrial innovators after 1926 no longer had an independent labor movement to contend with. In theory the regime favored "Corporatism", in which key decisions are supposedly made through negotiation between organized interest groups. In fact in fascist Italy corporatism was an illusion: workers could not choose their own leaders and management was given a free hand. While the Italian economy clawed its way out of depression after 1929 this situation allowed wages to be depressed and consumption to be sacrificed to the needs of heavy industry. But it took the strains imposed by war finally to cause the fragmentation of the coalition of interests represented by fascism.

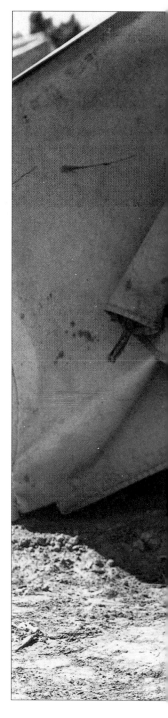

◄ A Nazi election poster, promising "Work, Freedom and Bread". Similar imagery and slogans were used in the Soviet Union, but here the literal message was less important than the impression of purposefulness and strength. The breakdown of law and order was an issue on which the Nazis successfully appealed to a frightened middle class which had lost confidence in the institutions of the German republic. Paradoxically the one serious prospect for the restoration of order lay in the suppression of Nazi violence.

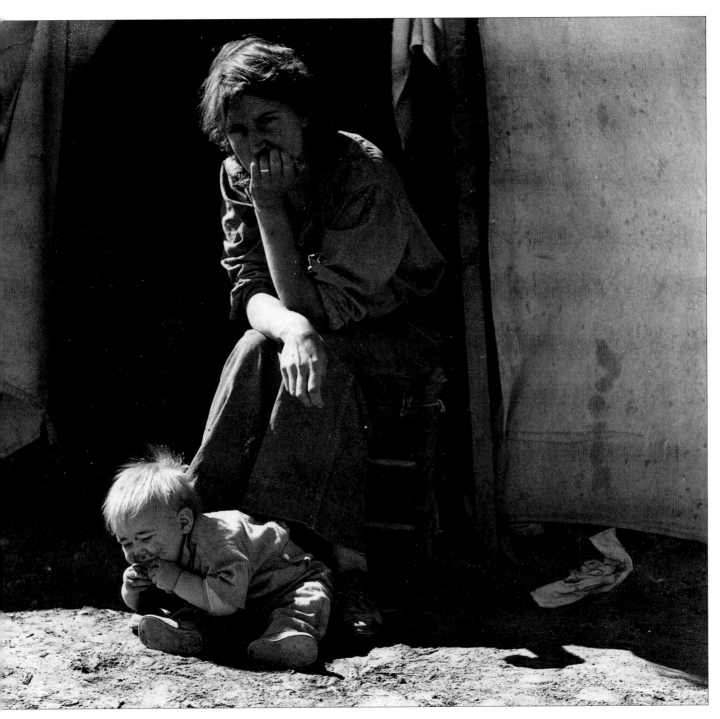

The authoritarian regimes imposed in Portugal from 1932, in Austria in 1934-38 and by the Francoite forces in Spain in 1938-39, were instances of long-established Catholic, military and landlord conservatives adopting a fascist coloring.

Fascism offered order, efficiency and strong government. It rejected pluralism in favor of "corporate" or "organic" national unity and solidarity. It promised a new social order based not on birth or economic status, but on service to the nation and to the fascist movement – a kind of meritocracy. Like socialism it rejected the insecurity of the unregulated market economy and it favored state and corporate regulation. But in contrast to socialism it did not contemplate wholesale expropriation of private property, and it repudiated class as an organizing principle. Instead, it aimed

supposedly to transcend class divisions and to enforce national solidarity and consensus. It capitalized on the widespread disenchantment with "old-style" party politics, and repudiated economic and political liberalism. Fascism thus constituted a fundamental challenge to smug Western assumptions that as other countries "developed" they would become more and more like pluralistic Western democracies pursuing liberal policies.

German society in the thirties

Nazism was both a more virulent and more consistently totalitarian variant of fascism. The democratic history of the "Weimar Republic" in Germany was effectively ended with the onset of the world economic crisis in 1929, when, in the

▲ A young mother and her child, migrants from Oklahoma to California, 1937. Drought, dust storms and erosion together with the unintended effects of state intervention drove small farmers from the Dust Bowl of the Great Plains in Oklahoma and Arkansas to become migrant laborers in California. Their plight, which became legend in John Steinbeck's novel *The Grapes of Wrath*, was shared by many others in different parts of the world. Jobless men roamed America. Poor farmers everywhere suffered notably during the Great Depression.

absence of a stable coalition in the German parliament, the Reichstag, traditional political and military elites sought to fill the power vacuum that was left. It was the failure of those elites to manage the political crisis of the early 1930s that caused them to look to the Nazi leader Adolf Hitler to bolster the narrow base of their rule.

In the early 1920s the Nazi party had been only one among a number of small racialist groupings on the fringes of German politics. In 1923 it had attempted to overthrow the Bavarian government but after 1925 it demoted violence to a tactic and shifted its emphasis to the ballot box. The Nazis appealed to nationalism and racism and presented demands which included reduction in taxation and increases in food prices appealing above all to the middling classes and peasantry. They came to form its mass base. Big business threw its weight behind the Nazis relatively late in the day. The Depression had served to reinforce industrialists' determination to dismantle

the Weimar welfare state and to put an end to independent trade unions. It was not actual trade union power they baulked at but merely its potential as an impediment to the dismemberment of social welfare provision. Neither those business interests who rallied to Hitler at the last, nor the many conservatives who voted Nazi in the elections of 1932 and 1933, fully understood the nature of the power they had helped set in motion. But the destruction of the political and economic wings of the labor movement was welcomed.

As had happened in Italy a decade earlier, the revolutionary rhetoric of much of the left had given both the working class and its enemies an exaggerated impression of its strength – in fact now reduced because of the split between communists and social democrats, and by the sheer weight of unemployment (one-third of the work force in 1932). Labor's real weakness was exposed by the passivity of its responses to Nazi power.

The Nazis were aware of proletarian hostility to the new regime from its inception. They responded first with brutal coercion and then by attempting to integrate the working class within the fabric of the "Third Reich". Unemployment was rapidly reduced and real wages increased by 19 percent between 1932 and 1938. The all-out offensive on workers' living standards which some industrialists had hoped for was a luxury the regime felt it could not afford. Indeed, wages were augmented by new social provision on the part of the state (though capital gained far more than labor from economic recovery). Most workers reacted to the Third Reich with indifference or passive consent, or with a mute but stubborn resistance to its ideological claims.

The dictatorships at war

Until the very last months of World War II, the Nazi regime maintained order and morale remarkably well. Although levels of absenteeism rose and the authorities worried about falling productivity, there is little evidence of a working-class attempt to undermine the war effort. (Britain, too, experienced these phenomena – and more militant forms of industrial action). What impresses in the end is the Nazi regime's ability to mobilize labor for the war. Only the attempt to drive women back into the labor market (which flew in the face of the Nazis' own family policy) failed. The shortage of labor was made up instead by the massive recruitment of foreign labor from occupied territories, foreshadowing postwar dependence on immigrant labor. In wartime most served under conditions of virtual slavery.

It is a chilling testimony to the coercive power of the Third Reich that resistance activities remained marginal and largely individual to the very end. In Italy and Austria ordinary people did play some part in their own liberation; in Germany a flowering of anti-fascist committees postdated the war.

▲ A button from the tunic of a young woman, who was obliged to perform a "Year of Duty" for the Nazi state, before starting regular work. The year was usually spent in either agriculture or domestic service. It was not enforced thoroughly and was strongly opposed by industrialists who feared it would lead to cuts in labor supply.

Jews and Antisemitism

The fate of the Jews in 20th-century European societies can be traced back to prohibitions and privileges imposed on Jews in medieval Europe. They were determined not by Jews themselves but by Christian elites, which accorded Jews unique religious toleration – on condition that they engaged in usury (moneylending at interest) with which Christians would not demean themselves. Medieval church rulers built on scriptural authority to portray Jews as the killers of Christ and to encourage pogroms (unprovoked violent attacks). The Lateran decrees of 1215 obliged Jews to distinguish themselves from Christians by their clothing so that their separateness might be regulated. Racial elements began to contribute to the antisemitic arsenal. The association of Jewishness with long, hooked noses dates from this time.

While persecution of the Jews therefore long predated the modern world, the social position of Jews and the dynamics of prejudice against them altered dramatically during the 19th century. In 1800 most of the large Jewish population in Central Europe was economically peripheral and rural, but as the 19th century proceeded liberal sentiment increasingly approved their emancipation (removal of civil disabilities) and social assimilation. But emancipation was slow and uneven.

Three specific factors contributed to the emergence of a genuinely popular antisemitic movement from around 1880. First, Jews proved remarkably adept at using the educational avenues for advancement now open to them. Second, where they had previously been dispersed, Jewish communities now concentrated in the growing industrial cities. Third, the mass immigration of Jews into Central Europe to escape persecution in the Jewish "pale" (settlement area) of western Russia caused widespread resentment. Where Jews had once been despised for their poverty and ignorance, now they were envied for their wealth and education. In the new conditions of mass participation in politics, the pressures of small-town and peasant prejudices forced the adoption of antisemitic rhetoric by threatened conservative and even liberal political elites,

which reached its culmination in the antisemitism of the German Nazi party.

The role that antisemitism played in the growth of the Nazi party has, however, frequently been exaggerated. Much of the German electorate voted Nazi in spite of rather than because of racial rhetoric. The execution of the Nazi holocaust in World War II, when about 6 million Jews were systematically murdered, owed far more to planners and technocrats than to the brutish violence of the perpetrators of pogroms.

After World War II antisemitism was suppressed, but it revived in the late 1980s when across Europe attacks on synagogues and the desecration of Jewish cemeteries became commonplace. The antisemitism of the early 1990s shared one characteristic with that of the late 19th century: both were concomitants of nationalism, which needs to draw attention to aliens at home in order to forge the bonds of new cultural and ethnic communities.

▲ Nazis organize the boycott of Jewish shops in prewar Germany (top). *Cahier Jaune* (above) was a wartime French antisemitic journal produced by collaborators in occupied France.

France, Britain and the fascist threat

Though French society was shot through by political turbulence and bitterness, in the 1930s, and in spite of the war-time Vichy regime's fascist sympathies – as in its antisemitism – French political culture as a whole remained resistant to fascism. In Britain contemporaries widely anticipated that political "extremism" would flourish as a consequence of the Slump, but in the event parliamentary government in general and the Conservative Party in particular adapted easily to the challenge. The economic hardships of the 1930s did give rise to a more humane and also more technocratic approach to social issues. But if the intellectual high ground moved to the left in the course of the decade, it took the war to translate it into political effect.

It is possible to exaggerate the leveling effects of the war, even within the working class. Although women entered the workforce to an unprecedented degree, there was no recognition of the principle of equal pay for equal work, let alone of equality of opportunity. Yet there was an undoubted general leveling of incomes and a significant improvement in wage levels. The permanence of these changes and of the welfare reforms instituted under the auspices of the wartime coalition government in Britain help to explain the popularity of the Labour Party in 1945 and its victory in the general election of July 1945.

Stalin's revolution from above

From 1929 to 1953 social change in the Soviet Union was directed by Joseph Stalin, whose 50th birthday in 1929 was used to launch the "cult of personality", ie of the party leader. Thereafter, even those Communist party faithful who believed in more humane forms of socialism were unable to halt the Stalinist juggernaut. This was

partly from fear of the dreaded security police. More fundamentally, however, the party faithful shared the belief that, in the ousted Bolshevik leader Leon Trotsky's words, "The Party in the last analysis is always right, as the Party is the sole historical instrument given to the proletariat for the solution of its fundamental problems".

Stalinism grew out of the doctrine of "socialism in one country", which Stalin elaborated following the economic collapse and political retreats of the early 1920s. He warned that "the land of proletarian dictatorship cannot remain independent if it does not produce the instruments and means of production in its own country". Hence "industrialization is to be understood above all as development of heavy industry, especially machine-building". With this came a reductionist interpretation of socialism as state-regimented industrialization, collectivization of agriculture and military modernization, to which all other goals should be subordinated.

Soviet agricultural development, however, failed to keep pace and this, together with a state

▲ This English advertisement reflects the centrality of "the home" and the commitment to a form of suburban life which was found pleasing by more and more people in Britain. This was the "age of disguise". Surburban architecture simulated past grandeur, while the restricted space of suburban homes meant that furniture now had the trick of folding away into nothing or revealing unexpected secondary uses.

▶ Watching the coronation procession, London, 1937. The enthusiasm of the British people for their monarchy was undiminished by the abdication of Edward VIII (1936). The coronation of King George VI was an occasion of national unity. The idea of the nation as a family was one which the new king aimed to depict.

◀ Loading bicycles at the Gare St Lazare, Paris, for the holidays in 1936, the year in which holidays with pay were introduced in France. The same rights were extended to 11 million people in Britain in 1938. Now the common people, too, could go for seaside holidays which had long been fashionable for others. The 1930s also saw a great vogue for hiking and the development of an interest in the conservation of the countryside – nowhere more so than in Hitler's Germany.

policy of holding down bread and grain procurement prices for the benefit of townspeople, caused a growing shortfall in peasant grain deliveries to the towns. "What is the way out for agriculture?" Stalin asked the December 1927 party congress. "Perhaps to slow down our industrial development...? Never!... The way out is to convert small scattered peasant farms into large amalgamated farms based on...collective cultivation of the land on the basis of new higher techniques". It was · time to "systematically eliminate" capitalists from agriculture and craft industries.

According to an official *History of the USSR* (1977), "As of 1928, there were more than 1 million kulak farms [farms held and run by relatively rich farmers]... In two years around 600,000 kulak farms were expropriated and more than 240,000 kulak families were deported... At the end of 1932 there remained approximately 60,000 kulak farms". Since kulaks were prohibited from joining collective farms, and since kulak households were relatively large, so-called "dekulakization" presumably left at least 5 million people (including Russia's best farmers) either destitute or languishing in labor camps. Indeed, any peasant opposing rural collectivization was liable to be denounced as a "kulak". Thus "dekulakization" also served to intimidate the

Collective Farms and Rural Development

◄ Members of a collective farm prepare a tractor. "All the objections raised by science against the possibility...of organizing large grain factories of 40,000 to 50,000 hectares each have collapsed", Stalin proclaimed in 1929, "We can now accomplish...what was considered fantasy several years ago." He later declared that collective farmers could "utilize neglected land, obtain machines and tractors and thereby double or even treble labor productivity".

▲ "Peasant woman, go to the collective farm", urges this Soviet poster. For peasant women, however, the problem was not so much going to the collective farms as ever getting out again. In the 1930s the Soviet Union introduced internal passports and residence permits which severely restricted peasant mobility. By the 1940s most collective farmers were women, with little hope of escape from their allotted stations in life.

peasantry at large into joining either collective farms (*kolkhozi*), in theory autonomous agricultural cooperatives, or state farms (*sovkhozi*), which were funded and controlled by the state. The autonomy of collective farms was more formal than real. In practice they were controlled by local party cells and were assigned mandatory plan targets and delivery quotas.

By 1935 most peasants had reluctantly joined *kolkhozi*, which they rightly regarded as a form of serfdom, on account of the attendant regimentation, supervision and restricted household autonomy. Even the system of workdays or workpoints used to tot up each person's labor con-

In the 19th and early 20th centuries communists cherished the idea of creating social equality and increased efficiency in rural societies by forming large, communally run "collective" farms not in private ownership. The Soviet Union was the first state to implement this idea, between 1929 and 1935. After World War II other communist states pursued similar policies. However, among the millions of words of early communist theory about agriculture and peasantries there was little guidance on how collective farms were to be structured and managed. In practice the collectivization of Soviet agriculture was carried out by hundreds of thousands of urban workers, party officials and Red Army soldiers with little knowledge or experience of farming. They threw together landholdings into large farms, which were subject to party and state control. Collectivization included the "liquidation" of several million of the most successful farmers, the so-called *kulaks*. So it is not surprising that Soviet agricultural output, productivity and incomes fell sharply instead of rising as communist "economists" had naively anticipated.

Nevertheless it is difficult to sustain dogmatic verdicts "for" or "against" rural collectivization. As with private agriculture the forms, contexts, objectives and results have been extremely varied. It is more meaningful to refer to specific forms and circumstances in which rural collectivization has been successful or unsuccessful in promoting rural development. There has been a widely held but mistaken belief that rural collectivization embodies a particular rural development strategy or option. It really embraces a wide range of strategies and options which have widely differing results. Rural collectivization has assumed a wide variety of institutional forms: (1) "collective farms", formally self-managed and self-financing agricultural producers' cooperatives; (2) "state farms", financed by the state, employing workers who are state employees with statutory benefits; (3) China's vast "people's communes" (1958-80), federations of collective and state farms with increasingly centralized services, local government functions and burgeoning rural industries; (4) Bulgaria's giant unwieldy "agrarian-industrial complexes", 170 of which were established in the 1970s; and (5) various "transitional forms", such as "mutual aid teams" and purchasing or marketing cooperatives. In some cases collectivization has built upon existing village or communal institutions and practices, as in North Vietnam; but in others it has set out to destroy and supersede them, as in the Soviet Union under Stalin.

Il terremoto ucraino nella Russia in rivolta mentre quasi tutti gli uomini validi sono incarcerati, le donne e i bambini, affamati e percossi, costretti a sgombrare i loro villaggi, sono confinati nei boschi, in campi di concentramento sorvegliati dalla soldatesca... (Disegno di UGO MATANIA)

◀ A prison camp for the wives and children of Western Ukrainian "rebels". In squandering so many millions of lives in forced labor camps and prisons and through brutal collectivization of agriculture, the Soviet regime profoundly alienated and demoralized the peasantry, especially in the Ukraine. After the famine in rural areas in 1932–34 many Ukrainians came to believe that the Soviet regime was pursuing deliberate policies of genocide or "war by starvation" against the Ukrainian peasant nation. The ordeals of the 1930s were so terrible that when the Germans invaded the Soviet Union in June 1941 many Ukrainian and Byelorussian villagers greeted them as "liberators".

tributions and entitlements was adapted from Russian serfdom and subsequently transmitted to other communist states! In the process of collectivization, however, the Soviet Union experienced major famines in several regions and lost half its livestock. According to the careful estimates of F. Lorimer and S. Wheatcroft, "excess mortality" totalled 5.5 million in the 1930s.

Stalin's "Workers' State"
In the 1930s the Soviet regime enjoyed great prestige from its lasting elimination of mass unemployment – in dramatic contrast to the mass unemployment in the capitalist world. The industrial work force in fact grew much more than expected because Plan targets were repeatedly and arbitrarily raised. Labor productivity did not rise as rapidly as expected. (Enterprises found it easier to meet increased targets by taking on additional workers than by raising the productivity of a largely inexperienced and untrained work force.) The consequent labor shortage encouraged enterprises to hoard scarce labor, and planned industrialization spawned a mushrooming bureaucracy. These became enduring features of the Soviet planned economy.

This expansion of the "modern sector" work force permitted massive upward mobility. Between 1926 and 1939 some 23 million peasants moved into town work and 10–15 percent of Soviet workers were recruited into administrative, managerial and technical posts. Under Stalin, there was always room at the top for those prepared to live dangerously, never knowing when it would be their turn to be arrested and imprisoned. According to S. Fitzpatrick, " the essence of the special relationship between the Party and the working class...was that the regime got cadres [administrators and managers] from the working class" and "the regime's commitment to the working class had much less to do with workers *in situ* than with working-class upward mobility".

Operations shall begin at daybreak. Upon entering the home of the person to be deported, the senior member of the operative group shall assemble the entire family of the deportee into one room...In view of the fact that a large number of deportees must be arrested and distributed in special camps and that their families must proceed to special settlements in distant regions, it is essential that the operations of removal of both the members of the deportee's family and its head shall be carried out simultaneously, without notifying them of the separation confronting them.

SOVIET SECRET POLICE ORDER FOR DEPORTATION

◄ Peasants outside a church in Yugoslavia. In 1942 representatives of Eastern Europe's peasant movements met to produce a joint statement of their philosophy and goals. "Believing, in the words of the Bible, that we are all members of one body", it began, "we maintain that the raising of the peasant's standard of life is the necessary precondition for the progress of the whole nation... The main basis on which a sound and progressive agricultural community can be built up is that of individual peasant-owned farms. We do not, however, believe that the peasant can live in isolation, and we recognize the desirability of voluntary cooperation in land cultivation." However, "peasants themselves should control marketing, credit and the supply of agricultural equipment by their own institutions, democratically organized."

We work fourteen hours a day in the fields, and we have no money.... A kilogramme of oil for my lamp now costs me sixty eggs. It is too much, for to sell eggs I must walk to Czernowitz, or take the horse out of the fields for a whole day. It is not worth it, just to get some oil, so we sleep when it is dark.

PEASANT FARMER'S WIFE
ROMANIA, 1932

Peasantist movements in Eastern Europe

In Eastern Europe in this period major peasant movements emerged in almost every state. They were engaged in a common quest to end "feudal" landlordism and to build in its place democratic societies based on peasant proprietors united in cooperative movements. The natural constituency for peasantism was still considerably larger than that for Marxist socialism or fascism or liberalism. Only in Slovakia, Slovenia (in Yugoslavia), Hungary and Poland did agrarian parties remain strongly under ecclesiastical (Catholic) influence, and only under the reactionary Sanacja and Horthy regimes in, respectively, Poland and Hungary did landed oligarchies survive almost intact. But even here peasant parties eventually united in support of radical programs prior to their electoral victories in 1945. The peasantist Agrarian party was the dominant party in successive governments in interwar Czechoslovakia, the Romanian National Peasant party dominated Romania in 1928–31, and interwar Croatia (in Yugoslavia) was dominated by the radical Croatian Peasant party.

In Europe since the late 19th century large-scale industrialization and the spread of Marxist socialism had increasingly distanced urban-industrial workers' movements from peasants and fostered often bitter ideological divisions between them. However much Marxist parties attacked the exploitation and alienation inherent in capitalist industrialization, they fully intended to move or "progress" in the same direction as capitalist industrializers, only their industrial society would be under the control of socialists or communists. It would be capitalist industrialism without the capitalists.

By contrast, the peasantist movements aspired to move in an altogether different direction. They envisaged a "cooperative society", distinct from both capitalism and Marxist collectivism. In their view, full democracy would only be achieved if peasants were to break the political monopoly of the urban and rentier classes, so that society could be governed "from below, not from above". Voluntary, democratic village cooperation was expected to address every need of village life, though collective agriculture on the Soviet model was rejected because of its suppression of peasant autonomy.

The very survival of peasant movements and democracy were closely intertwined in Eastern Europe. Both were under recurrent threat from the fascist or royalist authoritarian right and from the Marxist left. But unfortunately, except in liberal Czechoslovakia, the peasantist movements failed to retain and expand their footholds in government. They were mainly the victims of the singularly vicious conjuncture of world Depression and fascism. In Eastern Europe, as elsewhere, the Depression and plummeting tax and export revenues scuppered schemes of democratic social reconstruction by causing public expenditure cuts, widespread bankruptcies and foreclosures, and increased ethnic tension. As in Western Europe such conditions were a fertile breeding ground for both urban and rural fascism. Furthermore, the continuing popularity of the peasantist movements and their proven ability to make effective use of the democratic rights written into most East European constitutions, frightened the ruling groups as the socialists never had done and made them prime targets of the political malpractice and persecution perpetrated by monarchs, dictators, fascists and corrupt urban "machine politicians".

These political and economic setbacks forced the peasantist movements into a period of intense introspection and self-renewal from which they reemerged strengthened in 1945, though not before they had undergone the ordeal of fascist domination and war, during which millions of peasants demonstrated extraordinary capacities for active and passsive resistance.

► Threshing in progess in Poland. Vladko Maček, leader of the Croatian Peasant party in the 1930s, declared that East European peasants who had only recently freed themselves from "feudal serfdom" would not readily accept forms of collectivism which "turn the peasant into a serf of the state". However, "it is possible to turn the village into an economic unit." Peasants produce "partly for the needs of the family and partly for the market". The former "should remain the business of the peasant family", but the latter was already evolving "toward cooperative production as a common concern of the village as a whole."

ETHNIC MINORITIES

An ethnic group is one held together by common traditions based on race, religion, language, culture, or a combination of these. These traditions act as a force for unity within the group, providing it with an identity which it seeks to maintain against outsiders. Often the group is a minority one, under pressure from a mainstream culture which seeks to devalue or destroy its heritage; in such cases the need for a common identity becomes all the stronger.

Such ethnic minorities originate in many ways. Some, the Australian Aborigines or North American Indians for example, were the original inhabitants of their continents but were almost overwhelmed by an irresistible influx of European settlers. The Jews were scattered from their homeland in the Middle East and existed as minorities throughout Europe and elsewhere for many centuries. Their communities were particularly successful in maintaining their religious and cultural traditions in face of long periods of persecution. The ancestors of today's American blacks were forcibly transported from Africa as slaves. In the 19th and 20th centuries many millions of voluntary migrants have sought new lives in the richer parts of the world. Their own ethnic traditions have traveled with them.

There is a common feeling among minority ethnic groups that their traditions are undervalued by the majority culture. All kinds of subtle discriminations can exist in order to exclude a minority culture from a full life in the host community. In extreme cases, as in the Nazi treatment of the Jews in Europe in the 1930s and 1940s, a long-established and economically successful group may even face extermination.

In the United States for many years there was an active policy of breaking down ethnic roots in an attempt to create an all-American culture from the melting pot. Many second-generation immigrants were torn betweeen the cultures of their parents and the mainstream American life which seemed to offer the only path to economic success. Often it was the third generation who reacted and successfully rediscovered their ethnic roots.

Although discrimination and persecution are common experiences for ethnic minorities, some succeed in both maintaining their traditions and achieving economic or political success. Chinese communities overseas have achieved a dominance as traders in many Asian countries. In South Africa, the Afrikaners, forming only ten per cent of the population, achieved absolute political control of the country from the 1940s.

▲ ▶ The gypsies are one of Europe's oldest and most persistent ethnic minorities. With no national home and living nomadically, gypsies have faced discrimination and persecution over centuries. This picture shows traveling gypsies in central Europe in the 1930s.

▶ Jews throughout Europe had been forced in medieval times to live in segregated "ghettos". Even when they became free to move, many chose to remain in the ghetto areas, such as this Jewish community in Poland in the 1930s. Such ghettos were common in central Europe.

◀ In the 1970s and 1980s the Aborigine peoples of Australia have become increasingly aware of their cultural heritage and the way that their land rights and traditions have been devalued by the white majority. These children have joined a demonstration for their rights.

▼◀ The white Afrikaner minority in South Africa fought to defend their traditions and livelihood against other whites and the black majority. They achieved political supremacy in the 1940s, instituting the policy of apartheid. This farmer's wife illustrates Afrikaner defiance.

▼ Many cultures have fought to maintain their identity and Muslims have felt particularly affronted by Western cultural dominance. The picture shows a single sex girls' school in Britain run on traditional lines for Muslim girls.

Datafile

The arrival in the 1930s of new consumer goods like instant coffee and potato crisps prefigured the postwar development of consumer society. For many people in the West, outside agriculture and the old industrial areas, in which unemployment bit deep, this was a period of increased comfort, more leisure and a pleasing domesticity. This was the context of declining fertility, smaller families and a new awareness of the relationships between men and women as individuals. Yet states were concerned about the sheer numbers of their peoples, and a renewed emphasis on the roles of women as mothers conflicted with the trend toward greater freedom for women as individuals.

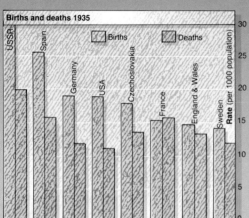

Births and deaths 1935

◀▲ The changes which had taken place in the world economy are marked by the growth of New York and Tokyo well beyond the great European cities. The relative slowing down of the expansion of the latter's populations reflected the fact that western Europe began to complete the "demographic transition" to low birth rates and low mortality. Children were no longer considered an economic advantage. The French population started to decline, in spite of the encouragement of populationist policies.

▼ The British National Insurance Acts of 1920 and 1921 established unemployment insurance (known as "the dole"), but it was severely stretched by high and persistent unemployment. Yet, though the dole was often near the margin of adequacy, it was usually just sufficient to keep people from desperation.

▶ After 1920 retail prices fell almost continuously until 1934, and only gradually thereafter. Thus real wages generally increased. In Britain those employed in new industries (mainly in the Midlands and Southeast) became better off and a social divide opened between this area and those of old heavy industry.

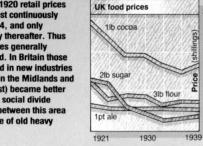

UK food prices

◀ These data show the high level of aspiration for higher education among young Americans (and, considering it was wartime, a surprising lack of interest in military service). The belief that higher education was the right of all Americans was encouraged by the "G.I. Bill of Rights", which provided for tuition fees and maintenance grants for ex-servicemen. By 1956, when it ended, it had permitted several million to go through college. The war years in America especially, and in Europe to a lesser extent, ushered in expansion of higher education, which would later make the idea of "the meritocracy" – a new elite, recruited by merit rather than by birth – seem realistic.

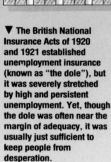

UK family dole budget 1934

Total £1 9s 0.5d

- Food
- Rent
- Fuel
- Insurance
- Balance

US students' plans 1943

Girls

Boys

- Further education
- Work
- Armed services
- Marriage
- Don't know

In spite of the impact of the Great Depression upon the millions who experienced unemployment in Europe in the 1930s, average living standards improved modestly. Prices fell faster than wages so that average real wages increased and there was more money available to spend on modest luxuries. With the expansion of chain and department stores the range of foods on sale increased. Canned and processed foods became more widespread. Instant coffee, breakfast cereals and potato crisps attracted consumers and diets improved as the consumption of meat, milk, vegetables and fruit increased. But scientific investigations still suggested that (in Britain) a high degree of poor nutrition and ill-health was intrinsic to the lives of the poor, especially children, whether or not their parents were unemployed, while in the United States the heavy toll of the Depression is reflected in the finding in 1940 that almost half of the first batch of 2 million conscripted men was medically unfit, largely because of malnutrition. Yet death rates in the United States continued to decline, reflecting higher standards of medical care.

The domestic use of electricity increased further, and with it that of electrical gadgets. The radio became the center of home entertainment. In Germany by 1932 one house in four possessed a radio; in France before the outbreak of World War II there were about 5 million sets. The political use of broadcasting became very significant. In the USA President Franklin D. Roosevelt's "fireside chats", initiated in 1933, played a part in his construction of a new consensus in American politics; the propaganda uses of the radio in the war are notorious. Cinema-going expanded hugely – in Britain in 1939 new cinemas were opening at the rate of three a week. For the mass of the people holidays became a feature of life for the first time. When holidays with pay were introduced in France in 1936 many families made their first visit to the seaside. The idea that suntanned bodies were attractive began to take hold.

Demographic decline and the family

By the 1930s the industrialized world had seen the last stages of what has been called the "demographic transition": a move from high birth rates and high death rates to a pattern of low birth rates and low mortality. Fertility was being limited; fewer children were created; and people lived longer. This development, which began roughly during the later 1870s changed family life and the position of women in particular.

From about 1900 onward the main effect of fertility limitation had been to compress childbearing into the early years of marriage. Thanks to the lower birth rate and the general fall in adult mortality, women could now expect to live far longer

STATES AND FAMILY LIFE

after the birth of their last child (30–35 years compared with 20 in the 1850s). For the first time in history both parents could look forward to a period together without the cares of bringing up children. Falling adult mortality also meant that the duration of marriage, unbroken by divorce, had risen from about 20 to 35 years by 1900 (45 in 1990), with all the obvious implications of the need for readjustment between marriage partners. Sexuality gradually became dissociated from biological reproduction. At the same time improving standards of living encouraged the desire to limit fertility.

The way in which marriage, the family and women's roles were defined and regulated in the 1930s through population policies, illustrates how unprepared most nations were to accept the interrelationship between industrialization and low birth rates. This in turn made it difficult for policy-makers to accept that the family should act

▼ The arrival of the family car greatly changed people's leisure options. Here a family had traveled from their small town to a "community sing" at Pie Town, New Mexico, USA.

as a self-regulating institution, responding to the industrial situation by controlling its own size according to its means, and to the life expectancies of both parents. These policies affected women in particular. Their struggle to control their own fertility and sexuality was directly opposed by political and ideological policies and pressures to bear more children.

After the huge losses of men killed in World War I the 1920s began to show a conclusive fall in the rate of population growth and the world economic crisis of the early 1930s accentuated the established trend toward smaller families. Overall population structures were changing throughout the industrialized world, but changes were more apparent in those countries that had suffered especially large losses of life in World War I. In France, Germany and Romania people noticed a disproportionate number of old people and a "surplus" of women (1 million in Germany), for

whom there were no husbands, giving rise to concern about so-called "population deficiencies", and the longterm implications of such loss of manpower or potential fathers. As Europe appeared to be becoming mainly middle-aged, it was feared that the population decline would gather momentum throughout western and northern Europe. Rational demographic thinking changed into populationist obsession notably in Germany, where the maintenance of racial purity added a sinister element to the generally reactionary measures employed to encourage larger families. Populationist thinkers in many countries featured propaganda supporting the cult of the family and advocated fiscal encouragement for large families. In France, where abortion had been relatively widespread, laws were enacted to forestall further "race suicide": both abortion and the sale and supply of contraceptives were forbidden. Generous family allowances and medals for large families were introduced to encourage motherhood. In 1931 the papal encyclical *Casta Conubii* declared all except "natural" family limitation to be sinful. In Catholic countries population policies thus simply swam with the tide – or were pursued for militaristic or political reasons, as in Italy, despite its relative overpopulation.

In America as in Britain the response to family limitation and planned parenthood was in general no more favorable. While contraception continued to become more widely available in a few American states, and the number of advice centers set up also increased (from 29 in 1929 to 746 by 1941), about half of the states maintained the Federal Comstock Law of 1873 which forbade the import and distribution of contraceptives, many until as late as 1968. In Britain family planning became more respectable through Marie Stopes' advocacy of contraception as a means to improve the race. In 1930 the British government accepted that birth-control information should be provided "on specific medical grounds" for controlling the fertility of women "unfit" to have children. It was not until 1949 that this was extended to all married women. Thus in Britain the emphasis remained on family policy, on insurance benefits and on unemployment assistance to support and strengthen the family during the long years of high unemployment and financial hardship, rather than to help control the number of mouths that had to be fed. In Scandinavia policies were more enlightened. Sweden began to provide public finance for contraceptive clinics in 1936, together with new family benefits. Abortion was legalized in 1938.

While the prohibition of contraception indicated that effective techniques existed, the majority of women were still only marginally affected by the rise of new and safer birth-control methods. All classes practiced birth control in some form, but it was middle-class couples who were most able to exercise choice about when and how many children they might have. Those with limited resources – the poor, industrial workers – tended to have more children anyway. Prohibition of contraception, heavy penalties for abortions and pressure on women to have more children thus potentially affected most those who

could least afford large families. It was among the poor that "backstreet" abortion was often the last desperate resort to restricting their brood of small children.

While the demands made by society thus came up against the limited resources of private families, the contradictions in the prevailing social and economic system became more obvious. The "Welfare State" was only in scaffolding in the 1930s; public assistance only helped the poorest. Thus during the interwar years the opposition to married women working or to planned parenthood came close to being punitive to many families. Meanwhile, however, many couples resisted public policy and quietly restricted the size of their families. Their attitudes began to create new values and expectations of family life which in due time would make an impact on public policy.

Women and the family under Stalin
From the Bolshevik Revolution of 1917 onward the Soviet Union had professed equality for women. Employment and education statistics suggest that the Soviet commitment to equality of opportunity continued during the 1930s. The total number of women workers rose from 24 percent of all workers in 1928 to 39 percent in 1940 and 56 percent in 1945. The female share of the greatly increasing numbers of students in higher education similarly rose from 28 percent in 1927 to 43 percent in 1937 and 58 percent in 1940. These changes, however, were forced on the Soviet Union and mainly resulted from the acuteness of urban labor shortages (engendered by forced industrialization) and, after 1937, by the drafting of millions of men into the armed forces.

Most female labor reserves lived in cities and were members of workers' families. Their recruitment was therefore cheaper than that of men from the countryside, since they could be brought into production without major outlays on new housing or social amenities other than child-care facilities. Women were mainly channeled into the least-skilled and lowest-paid jobs with the poorest promotion prospects. Any profession

▲ Soviet poster encouraging sport: "To work, build and not complain! We have been shown the path to a new life. You may not be an athlete but a gymnast you must be." Stalin's regime glorified physical prowess.

◄ Russian peasant woman suckling a child. By the mid 1930s the Soviet regime was alarmed by sharply falling birth rates and in 1935 outlawed abortion. But abortion had only been widely accepted by townspeople. In rural areas preindustrial forms of family limitation must have prevailed instead, such as amenorrhea (suppression of ovulation by suckling).

▼ Russian women plasterers. In 1935 women were surprisingly prominent among manual workers. They accounted for 24 percent of workers in coal mining, 23 percent in iron-ore mining, 32 percent in chemicals and 24 percent in engineering.

which acquired a preponderance of women became relatively low-paid, even if it had not been so at the outset – the prime example being medicine. Women remained greatly underrepresented in managerial and skilled positions, and continued to encounter considerable male chauvinism, resistance and harassment.

Increased employment of urban women was not compensated by reductions in their household burdens: Soviet men rarely lifted a finger in the home. Urban housing was extremely cramped (urban housing space per person actually declined from 5.8 square meters in 1928 to 4.9 in 1932, 4.5 in 1940 and 3.9 in 1944. The Soviet Union had been very slow to develop and provide labor-saving household appliances, public laundries, efficient retailing and wholesaling, private automobiles and convenience foods, so Soviet women spent inordinate amounts of time on housework, shopping, public transport and queuing – looking after the men.

Until 1935–36 the family as a social institution was under attack as a custodian and perpetuator (in conjunction with organized religion) of pre-revolutionary and counterrevolutionary values. The Stalin regime even encouraged children to denounce their own parents and grandparents as

counter-revolutionaries. After that time, however, the regime abruptly reversed its policies. In 1936 it was proclaimed that "the family is an important social institution under the protection of the socialist state....Disrespect toward parents, neglect of one's obligations towards father and mother...are psychological features of the social and moral decay of the personality, gravely harmful to...socialist society. Conversely, the strengthening of family relations...is one of the essential elements of consolidating the new order". The regime had suddenly rediscovered the usefulness of the family as an anchor of social and political stability in a period of turmoil, as a prop for authority, as a means of disciplining and socializing Soviet youth, and as an inexpensive agency of social control and of care for the aged, the sick, the disabled and the orphaned. This was associated with an increasingly urgent perceived need for strong measures to raise birth rates to offset the disastrous demographic consequences of Stalin's Purges and of the liberal abortion policy of 1920–35. In 1936 there was a major tightening of divorce procedures. The Soviet state also mounted a fascist-style glorification of motherhood, preparing the ground for the distinctly conservative Family Laws of 1944, which were also a

Young people are causing the...Party agencies much anxiety. Both boys and girls are trying by every means possible to dodge the year of Land Service.... There is a section of youth that wants the romantic life. Whole bundles of trashy literature have been found in small caves.

REPORT ON GERMANY, 1938

Youth Movements

By the beginning of the 20th century the particular problems of the phase of "youth" were recognized, and in Britain a contemporary expert wrote: "The miscellaneous associations represented by clubs, lads' brigades, boy scouts and the like, have all been called into existence for the express purpose of exerting some measure of control over the transition period which separates the boy from the man". Of all these youth movements the most important, which spread rapidly across the world, was the boy scouts. Founded in 1907–08 by Robert Baden-Powell, the scout movement arose in

GIOVENTU' FASCISTA

specific circumstances, reflecting the preoccupation of Edwardian England with the maintenance of its Empire. The Boer War (1899–1902) had shaken British self-confidence, and seemed to expose Britain's moral, physical and military weaknesses. These ruling-class fears, existing concerns about social order, and even specific problems about the fitness of army recruits, were addressed by the scout movement. Baden-Powell grafted ideas drawn from Ernest Thompson-Seton, who celebrated American Indian culture and woodcraft, as well as from his own experience of army scouting, onto those of Christian social reformers. It was an appealing mixture, but the rapid growth of the boy scout movement owed nothing to chance. Rather it was the result of skillful publicity, and thoroughly political. As Baden-Powell wrote: "Our business is to pass as many boys through our character factory as we possibly can" – inculcating in them obedience to authority, values of service and uncritical patriotism. It was an ideology rooted in the self-interest of the upper classes.

The youth movements of communist regimes, of the Italian fascists, and of the Nazis in Germany served quite similar objectives. In Nazi Germany the *Jungvolk* (for those aged 10–14), the Hitler Youth and the parallel organization for girls, the *Jungmädel*, bore the main responsibility for carrying out Hitler's exhortation "Be hard, German youth, and make yourselves hard" – through the mixture of sport, war games and propaganda. The ideological extremes of Nazism are reflected in this prayer of the Hitler Youth: "Adolf Hitler, you are our great *Führer*. Thy name makes the enemy tremble. Thy Third Reich comes, thy will alone is law upon the earth. Let us hear daily thy voice and order us by thy leadership, for we will obey to the end and even with our lives. We praise thee. Heil Hitler!" Yet it seems that as many adolescents were bored by it all as were fired with enthusiasm!

◄ Italian youth magazine, 1932.

response to the damaging effects of World War II upon family life and sexual responsibility.

In 1936 a much-publicized "Conference of the Wives of Engineers in Heavy Industry" endeavored to exalt and rehabilitate the role of the Soviet manager's "kept wife" as a hostess, housekeeper and charitable patron of downtrodden working-class women, an almost comical expression of the incipient "embourgeoisement" of the new Soviet ruling class. All in all, however, Soviet women gained significantly more duties and burdens than power or status.

Women and family in Hitler's Germany

In the 1930s policies toward the family and women in the advanced industrial nations shared certain basic trends but differed strikingly in their commitment to their objectives. Under the National Socialist (Nazi) regime in Germany (1933–45) policies associated with the revival of a quasi-sacred image of motherhood, like other aspects of Nazi social policy, were carried to extremes. Paradoxically, the notion of the public, masculine and private, feminine sspheres was institutionalized yunder Hitler as a rigid social system of male

supremacy, based on images polarized of man and woman – of the "valuable" and "valueless". The pressuures to which women were subjected were antagonistic; social welfare measures were restrictive and compared with reactionary policies in other countries women's oppression in Nazi Germany was antifeminist in the extreme.

Yet it would be wrong to dismiss Nazi policies toward women as purely reactionary. They never resulted in a true "bondage of pure housewifery" as envisaged by the famous slogan *"Kinder, Küche, Kirche"* (children, kitchen, church), which was to remind women of their proper place in the home. When Gertrud Scholtz-Klink claimed leadership of all the Nazi women's organizations, she also saw to it that "her" women would retain or even enhance their own "female sphere of action in society". Extraordinary contradictions were apparent in the Nazis' policies, which both exploited women and subjected them to repressive protection. This suggested that both reactionary and progressive views were at work as the regime attempted to deal with the tensions within an economic and social structure in which "modernity" (city life, the small family, women's

▲ Flight before the advance of war, in Spain during the Civil War (1936–39). These Spaniards forced on the move anticipated the fate of perhaps as many as 50 million Europeans who were to be expelled from their homes to become refugees during World War II. When the war was over Germany – in defeat and within reduced frontiers – found itself faced with the task of settling 10 million displaced persons. For all the destruction which it had wrought, World War I had not torn apart whole societies in the way that happened during World War II.

new freedom) coexisted uneasily with essentially preindustrial conservative political and social ideologies.

Antifeminism played an important role in the regime's attempt to enforce the unity of a conflict-ridden society, and ultimately, to generate mass support for its expansionist and population policies. Fueling antisemitic feelings, Adolf Hitler declared the concept of women's emancipation to be a construct of Jewish intellectuals. The repudiation of women's (much exaggerated) independence and the repeated attacks on the feminist movement also reassured conservatives and reactionaries for whom women's emancipation symbolized all they hated and feared.

Explaining his mystifying success with women in 1932, Hitler promised, "in my state the mother will be the most important citizen." And in the last election for nearly sixty years in which the whole population was to enjoy any freedom of choice at all, in March 1933, the women's movement (the BDF, boasting a membership of about one million), buoyed by nationalism and the urge

to serve, gave support to the Nazis, and actually expressed a wish for Hitler to introduce a "biological policy" to preserve the German family and laws to protect it from "asocial" persons. Families excluded from the sphere of acceptability included those that were considered "hereditarily defective, racially mixed or asocial, alcoholic, lacking an orderly family life" and "in which children [were] a burden to the state."

On the other hand, the expansion of women's employment between 1925 and 1929 (20 percent) and the growing proportion of women students at universities had been sufficiently sharp to activate antifeminist resentment. This grew during the Depression after 1929. In 1933 the Nazi regime simply turned the clock back and reduced the number of women students (from 18.9 to 12.5 percent) and removed women (where expedient) from the overcrowded labor market, especially from positions of responsibility or from well-paid jobs. Predictably too, it was the "new", allegedly mannish woman who came under attack – women who defied traditional conventions of

femininity. To correct such unnatural development the Nazis channeled the education of young girls "into a deeper conception of the nature and values of womanhood, and of women's duties and responsibilities to the family and the 'Volk' [nation]" – a program that the Women Teachers Association had already formulated in 1921.

Yet the Nazis never urged the total exclusion of women from the labor market, nor was their objective of a separate curriculum for girls fully realized. Despite its antifeminist policy, by 1939 the regime was forced to encourage the return of some professional women into employment and young girls to take up academic study, if only to fill posts men had left empty as the war took them to the front. Women's employment as cheap labor was also essential to both the rearmament program and the war effort, especially after 1939, when labor shortages threatened the regime's war aims. Still, the Nazis were never quite able to set aside their reservations about the reemployment of women, and so failed to enthuse women into further service for the nation, and their increase in employment during the war was minimal. For various reasons the role of the housewife really did seem preferable to many women. As real wages had risen by some thirty percent by 1939 the family was financially better off than ever before and women experienced a real easing of their load. The Nazis' attempts to mobilize women for the war effort were also fairly half-hearted, threatening as they did to destroy a large part of the regime's basis of popular support.

The threat "to emancipate women from emancipation" (in the words of the Nazi ideologue Alfred Rosenberg) was real, however, as all notions of personal freedom and rights were to be replaced by total subservience to the state. Thus women were expelled from political office and stripped of their civil rights. A strict hierarchy of male dominance in public life was established, and while this served to appease male fears of female transgression, it also brought the regime closer to its real concern, which was with women as bearers of the future master race. Increasingly eugenic policies (gene and race care) were to expose the hypocrisy of the Nazis' cult of motherhood. While Jewish and gypsy women were portrayed as sluts and whores, the ultimate offer for women to partake in the reconstruction of society as "mothers of the Volk" was only directed at certain "valuable Aryan" women. Those who lacked in "social value" or were "racially and hereditarily impure" were vilified or murdered and excluded from bearing and rearing children (and men from begetting them) with compulsory sterilization as the principal deterrent, or by abortion of "defective" pregnancies, practiced secretly until it was introduced by law in 1935. The "birth achievement" demanded of acceptable women was calculated carefully according to the numbers of those who were not to give birth.

For the desirables, massive programs to revive motherhood were implemented. Propaganda projected images of the mythic sturdy peasant family, of radiant mothers and healthy children exalting the family as the "germ cell" of the nation.

All notions of personal freedom and equality were to be replaced by a new collective responsibility toward the State. Collective joy would make private happiness obsolete. As unquestioning servants of the Volkidee (the community and recovery of the German people), women, declared Goebbels in 1933, had "the most beautiful of all roles, namely to bear children for country and Volk."

This emotional appeal was enhanced by material incentives such as marriage loans, child bonus and benefits for large families and punitive taxes for the unmarried. Yet throughout the Third Reich, the propagation of the myth of the "lost family" of preindustrial times as a "bulwark against the tides of alienation", and the provision of financial incentives to strengthen the family, were flagrantly contradicted by Nazi social policy. Housing needs were almost totally neglected. The demand for absolute loyalty to the Führer (Hitler) undercut the authority of the head of the household. Children were encouraged to inform on the political attitudes of their parents. The socialization of children itself was concentrated outside the family in youth organizations. For ordinary people the home was drained of its emotional meaning by Nazi policy. As the demands of the armaments drive increased, more and more men had to live away from home and women had to cope on their own. As unmarried women began to get official encouragement to bear illegitimate children, so (in the words of British historian T. Mason) "the official shining ideal of the integrated stable and prolific family began to look more and more like a monstrous deception".

► Soldier and children. Families were split up during World War II, even in countries which did not experience displacements of people. Many women became workers and carried responsibility for their families – some of them discovering that they were more capable than their menfolk. Yet the war did not bring about great change in the class and power structures of European societies. The sharing of experience by people from different backgrounds was part of a broader "social levelling", but also strengthened social cohesion.

LOVE AND MARRIAGE

How men and women display affection, engage in relationships and build economic security differ considerably despite the universal importance of ceremony to celebrate sexual union. In the West monogamy – no more than one spouse at a time – is universally the law and the nuclear family unit (man, women, children) predominates though to a lesser extent than in mid-century. In large parts of Africa and Asia polygamous marriage – in which a man may take several wives – persists, and larger family groups live communally. Almost everywhere women are subordinated to the men of the household but their status and mobility vary considerably. The seclusion imposed on veiled Muslim brides of the Middle East and Asia is far from the experience of the liberated middle-class American women or West African women farmers and traders.

The age at which people marry and have children varies between societies, as it has in the past. In the west it often used to be later than it is now.

Love and marriage are associated with the most intimate and private parts of life and interference in them is strongly resisted. This has not stopped the state from intervening very directly in personal relations during the 20th century. The *kibbutzim*, the communal farms prominent in the Israeli state since the 1940s, offered a communal alternative to conventional Jewish marriage and family life. In socialist countries the ideals of "revolutionary love" and the proletarian family were promoted. These fell short of sexual licence, considered to be a bourgeois aberration, but inequality between men and women in the home was denounced. Collectivization (the move away from private property) was aimed not only at increasing agricultural and industrial production but also at undermining the authority of the male household head. Altered family forms were not sustained although personal relations were transformed. Following the communist victory in China in 1949, marriages arranged by parents for their children were outlawed. Here the youth brigades took on the task of educating young men and women in the mysteries of modern courtship in which they initiated and made the decisions.

In the West, the late 20th century witnessed a revolution in sexual relations and family forms. Young people claimed greater autonomy and independence for themselves. Choice of partner increasingly lay with the couples involved rather than their parents. Many lived together without formalizing their unions through religious or civil ceremonies.

Such changes do not go unchallenged and family lobbies promoting traditional and conservative values remain strong and vocal. The seductive promise of romantic love, popularized in films, ballads, novels and magazines as well as the enchantment of ceremony, ensures the enduring allure of Valentine cards, engagement rings and white weddings.

▲ An advertisement for skin creams. From the early 20th century advertising told Western young women that their skins had to be softer and younger. Ignoring such injunctions could preclude romance and love.

▶ From the 1930s the screen kiss of Hollywood films reinforced the idea of romantic love and after World War II spread it worldwide.

▲ The explosion of popular sex education from the 1960s is represented above all by the immense worldwide sales (in numerous languages) of the British book *The Joy of Sex*. The creation of new expectations of sexual fulfilment has also given rise to anxieties for many men and women.

▲ The wedding, in South Korea, of 6,516 couples belonging to the Unification Church (Moonies). Here the symbols of purity associated with Western weddings are employed as part of a religious creed that repudiates local custom.

▲ In India child marriages (as here) are less common than they were, and the age of marriage has gone up. In many societies marriage is the outcome of a contract arranged between families. Sometimes the marriage is formalized when the parties are children and becomes effective later.

◄ A divorcing couple at a Soviet court. The Soviet Union has usually pursued liberal family policies. Ensuing social problems were contained within the authoritarian structures of the state, but threatened to become overwhelming as state authority retreated in the late 20th century.

Datafile

The social and economic impact of the Great Depression in Africa, Asia and Latin America was mixed, depending on what raw materials were exported and to where. In general, however, the major effects were negative, driving many out of export production and reducing cultivated acreage and mining activity. Many rural producers experienced a new kind of crisis: one due to failure of markets instead of the rains. The turmoil which was caused contributed to popular risings against colonial powers. But the Depression and World War II also gave opportunities for some countries to industrialize further. Japan accelerated its drive to industrialize with success.

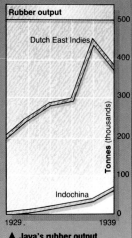

Rubber output

Dutch East Indies

Indochina

Tonnes (thousands)

1929 — 1939

▲ Java's rubber output fluctuated with world output. Indochina, just starting real production, expanded slowly through the 1930s. Loss of export revenues led colonial governments to increase domestic taxation, sometimes provoking rebellion.

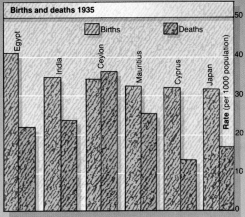

Births and deaths 1935

Births Deaths

Egypt · India · Ceylon · Mauritius · Cyprus · Japan

Rate (per 1000 population)

◀ The Japanese death rate was still characteristic of a poor country and worse than many. Ceylon's death rate exceeded its births. But for most, the tempo of growth in the birth rate was quickening.

▶ The Bengal famine was one of the worst famines ever. The rice price soared while wages stagnated. The capacity to buy, 100 in December 1941, fell as low as 24 in May 1943. Nationalists blamed the British for reserving the crop for its armies, and for preventing grain movement. Between 3 and 6 million perished.

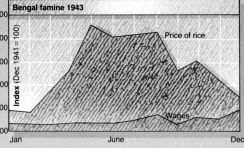

Bengal famine 1943

Index (Dec 1941 = 100)

Price of rice

Wages

Jan — June — Dec

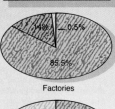

Indian employment 1939

14% — 0.5%

85.5%

Factories

14%

45%

Plantations

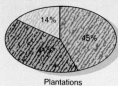

Men
Women
Children

◀ Women and children were vital workers in India. The war boom increased the need for them in factories and mines, although on the plantations numbers declined. Women were paid much less than men for the same work and there was no provision for special needs (such as childcare), in spite of factory legislation.

▶ Bombay gangers traditionally recruited mill labor from their home villages, distant from the city. Many came from an arid district far south of the city, Ratnagiri. Rural poverty did not drive workers out, but social networks drew them in, fitting them to special tasks in the mills and special urban localities.

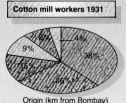

Cotton mill workers 1931

8%   4%

9%

38%

15%

26%

Origin (km from Bombay)

1–160
161–320
321–1,200
over 1,200
Unidentified migrants
Born in Bombay

The Great Depression of the 1930s had contradictory effects on societies in Africa, Asia and Latin America. It was devastating for commercial farmers and for mining operations oriented to exports, but where governments had autonomy in setting tariffs it also stimulated industrial growth – notably in Latin America. These economic changes intensified social contradictions and helped to change the character of nationalist struggles. Meanwhile the whole relationship of the West to the rest of the world was profoundly affected by the remarkable rise of Japan.

The modernization of Japan

From the 1868 Meiji Restoration – a coup against the old Tokugawa dictatorship by a group of disaffected *samurai* (members of an aristocratic caste of warriors) – the new Japanese government strove to create a powerful modern state. It copied from Europe and America whatever social changes seemed best suited. The development of

DUSK OF EMPIRE

The transformation of Japan

Life in Tokyo

The end of the promise of empire

Life in Bombay working-class districts

The status of women in sub-Saharan Africa

the armed forces was crucial, initially to defend the country against foreign intervention when all around the Great Powers of Europe were expropriating countries, but quite rapidly to prosecute the purposes of new Japanese imperialism. It was the drive to war, not for markets, which provided the basic stimulus to the economic transformation of the country.

Extraordinary sacrifices were required from the Japanese people, which was possible only through a combination of an ethic of heroic devotion with tight and fearful social control. Initially after the Meiji Restoration industrialization was entrusted to unemployed samurai rather than the old merchant class, so that the modern management cadre was instilled from the beginning with the ethic of service. Thus, a distinctive economic system was created, governed in part by quasi-feudal loyalties of warlords and retainers rather than market competition. In the first instance the fervor of patriotic sacrifice governed only the

▼ ▶ A Yokohama fish stall (below). By the 1930s Japan combined traditional dress and culture with elements of great modernity – such as this commuter train (right). Some found the combination hard to reconcile.

managers and owners of business; the mass of workers, recruited from poor village families and organized labor gangers (subcontracted by firms to perform particular tasks), were excluded. However, by the 1920s an increasing proportion of the work force in the largest corporations was being inculcated in the warrior ethic.

A dual structure was gradually emerging. On the one hand there was a class of extraordinarily large firms or groups of firms (the *zaibatsu*) with privileged subcontractual relationships to the state; on the other there was a mass of unstable small and medium enterprises that supplied goods to the large companies as subcontractors (or dealt with the local retail trades). In the first, companies moved to offering their work force a lifetime of employment. In the second, the turnover of workers was high, pay and levels of productivity were much lower, and conditions far inferior.

Education was a precondition for the rapid pace of growth. Only two years after the British introduced universal compulsory primary education, Japan followed suit. By 1904 98 percent of the relevant age group were in school. By the 1920s most farmers, for example, were literate. In higher education growth was equally impressive. In 1918 there were five universities and 104 high schools and colleges; by 1945 there were 48 and 342 respectively. Especial encouragement was

Life in Interwar Tokyo

City life in Japan had deep roots. In the early 19th century Tokyo (then called Edo) already had a million inhabitants and was probably the largest city in the world. With the great economic expansion of the 20th century cities grew quickly. By 1930 Tokyo contained almost 6 million people.

On the surface at least, city life for the majority was traditional. In new districts of Tokyo old class divisions were perpetuated on the ground – between samurai, merchants and artisans. Samurai areas, for example, were situated in the best locations, on high ground. Most people were packed in a dense mass of tiny crowded streets and higgledy-piggledy two-storey dwellings. Their traditional thin walls gave no privacy – even less during the day when they were removed. Families lived in one room. Washing was hung on bamboo poles pushed out from the first storey.

Most streets and lanes were unpaved and were muddy in winter and dusty in summer. Opening on to the narrow lanes were masses of shops, tiny restaurants and workshops for tailors, clogmakers and carpenters. In the lanes themselves stood tea, noodle and soup stalls. Street life was in continual movement, with itinerant craftsmen, story-tellers and hawkers of beancurd; with salesmen and junk-collectors; with children running free or at play, with girls carrying their infant siblings on their backs.

By the 1930s the urban birth rate was falling, but the majority in Tokyo were young and drawn from the lower classes. They were garrulous, warm-hearted and open and still embedded in traditional culture with its kabuki theater, suomo wrestling, geisha houses and traditional sentimental music.

By the 1930s there were increasing numbers of white-collar workers – managers, shop assistants, clerks. They wore western suits and aspired to escape from the old crowded cities. The great earthquake of 1923 encouraged dispersion of the population to new suburbs, with consequent commuting to work. The better-off were more westernized and formal in behavior. They favored orchestral music, modern drama, foreign films and ballroom dancing. For some of the intelligentsia the spread of new values was difficult to reconcile with Japanese traditions. Yet secular values had not eroded traditional beliefs in Japan as they had in Europe during early industrialization.

▲ A Tokyo alley. Notice how narrow the lane is with dwellings virtually looking into each other. Most houses were made of bamboo or wattle – airy in summer but bitterly cold in winter. There was no heating. Most families depended on communal bathrooms and latrines. Most people, and virtually all women, wore traditional dress – like the woman in the picture with a baby tied to her back.

given to military engineering, leading to the development of important Japanese prototypes.

In the 1930s Japan shared in the universal slump in agriculture which produced a rapid spread of rural indebtedness, but simultaneously, the value of industrial output soared and the dual structure of industry was even further exaggerated. Small enterprises took the full strain of the slump, while the large continued to make rapid growth. By 1932 the smallest companies paid wages which were only 26 percent of those paid by the largest firms and offered nothing like the large firms' stability of employment, health services, sports, educational and cultural activities. A male worker in a large company expected all his lifetime needs to be met by the firm; in return, he would expect to make whatever sacrifices were required to ensure the prosperity of the company. Sacrifices there were, and not merely in freedom of thought and action. Up to 1936 real wages fell almost continually. In textiles, an extreme case with a high proportion of women workers, the nominal average wage rate declined by 60 percent. Furthermore, as war production expanded and the armed forces vastly increased their recruitment, there were severe labor shortages. They were never allowed to be expressed in wage pressure; at most, during World War II, smaller firms moved to offering lifetime employment. Military discipline, expressed through wage and price controls as well as forced labor, now governed the civilian labor force.

From the late 1920s rightwing political views became increasingly important in shaping Japanese opinion, particularly in the armed forces. These views emphasized equality and anticapitalism: all should be equal under the emperor; the wealth of the zaibatsus was responsible for the impoverishment of the peasantry. They affirmed that military discipline ought to be the norm in society, not working for profit or pay. And finally, that Japan's cause was anti-imperialist – there could be no peace until the Anglo-American domination of the world had been overthrown and space made for the newcomers, Germany, Italy and Japan.

Japan was thus fully prepared when World War finally arrived, but to no avail, for in the end, despite the prodigious results of an extraordinary social discipline, the sheer economic weight of the giant American economy overwhelmed the country. The final spectacular triumph of feudal Japan was thus the prelude to catastrophe and the demise of feudalism.

The Depression and rural social change

As in Europe and America, rapidly and drastically falling agricultural prices had profound effects in Asia, where commercial cash cropping had grown in importance in the 19th century and had been booming in the 1920s. The slump brought a new kind of crisis to peasant cultivators who had been drawn into a greater dependence upon money and who, with the fall in prices for the commodities they produced, were left unable to pay for the essentials they needed. At the same time supplies of credit dried up, and the richer peasants, landlords and money lenders were also

hard hit. A South Indian proverb runs, "After ruin go to the city" – this was the fate of many members of the village elites in the 1930s. In Southeast Asia the Depression delivered the coup de grace to an agrarian social order already weakened by the effects of commercialization and colonial rule. As the fall in prices drove many households into deficit, the fall in exports led to a severe loss of government revenues from customs dues. To compensate for this the French in French Indochina and the British in Burma sought to increase head taxes, provoking peasant resistance in the Saya San rebellion in Lower Burma in 1930–31 and the brief establishment of peasant soviets under the influence of the fledgling communist party in northern Annam. The legitimacy of the colonial state and of the power of the rural notables of the old order were shattered as such guarantees of livelihoods as had existed in village economies were no longer honored.

It was also instability in relative prices rather than a fall in production which lay behind the terrible Bengal famine in 1943. In the circumstances of wartime inflation and the policy of restricting the movement of foodgrains imposed by the colonial government, fears about a shortfall in the rice harvest in Bengal provoked hoarding and a price spiral so that rice prices far outstripped the wages of agricultural laborers and rural artisans. They made up the majority of the three million or more victims of the famine. Famine resulted not so much from absolute decline in the availability of food as from price changes which eroded the spending power of those depending on wages.

▲ Women did much of the hard work in Japan's fields, particularly planting the rice seedlings in standing water. Conditions for peasant families were very harsh, and for women, even worse.

▼ Physical education at a Tokyo school. Strict regimentation in school and at work created a powerful collective discipline and spirit of sacrifice that stood Japan well in war. The country had a high level of education, practical rather than religious; it was intensely patriotic.

The rising tide of nationalism

In the colonial and noncolonial developing countries the Great Depression demolished the economic promise of empire and the two World Wars demolished the twin assumptions of the moral superiority and military invulnerability of the imperial powers. In the colonized countries, national movements were either created or grew into an increasingly significant force. In India the Congress mainstream, however, remained a loose coalition of interests that could not, until quite late in the day, confront social questions lest it undermine the coalition. Mass radicalization finally forced Congress to greater militancy to retain its position of leadership. It also forced the adoption of a social program to relate the national question to mass interests. Tenant farmers, sharecroppers and the landless were now offered agrarian reform, rent reductions, security of tenure and the abolition of zamindaris (a peculiar Indian form of landlordism, originating in tax farming). For the prosperous Muslim landlords, faced with the appalling prospect that the British could no longer be relied upon to protect them either at home or abroad, Congress's attack on landlordism, modest though it was, was frightening, and now the Muslim League at long last had an opportunity to recreate itself as an effective organization.

Latin American history in the independent period had always been dominated by caudillos (military dictators), based upon landed oligarchies, foreign investors and the use of military power. But by the 1930s the social structures of the more advanced countries had changed, providing the social basis for dictatorships based upon the new urban working classes, sometimes on the peasantry and or the army. The caudillos were now committed against both the landed oligarchies and foreign interests.

In Brazil a military coup brought to power a former governor of a southern state, Getulio Vargas, who established a popular dictatorship that lasted some 15 years. He strongly promoted industrialization (transport, paper, chemicals, steel), public works and some measure of popular welfare (an advanced labor code, educational and medical programs). In Mexico, Lázaro Cárdenas became president in 1936 and created a new political order, based upon organized workers, peasants and other groups. He nationalized the mainly foreign-owned railways in 1937, expelled foreigners and seized their assets and redistributed twice as much land as all the preceding administrations to some three-quarters of a million families. Finally, in Argentina the effects of slump had been a relatively rapid rate of industrialization; by 1943 more Argentinians worked in urban industry than in agriculture and herding. An army colonel, Juan Perón, with the strong support of the powerful trade union federation, built himself an immense base of popular support among the urban working class which not only frustrated an attempt by the army to arrest him in 1945, but also swept him to overwhelming power in 1946.

Jiang Jieshi would have liked to emulate the Latin Americans in China. But his rule depended

Life in Bombay Working-class Districts

There were more than 150,000 people employed in Bombay's cotton mills by the early 1920s. Most of them (more than 80 percent) had been born in distant villages, and would have been recruited as millhands by intermediaries known as "jobbers", men whose leadership and control of labor within the mills depended on the patronage they extended outside them.

Most workers lived within 15 minutes walking distance of their mills in three wards to the north of the old "native town" of Bombay. This working-class district, known to its inhabitants as *Girangaon* – "the mill village" – was dominated by ramshackle, jerry-built *chawls*, or blocks of small tenements with shared lavatories and washing places. Here perhaps as many as one-third of the residents lived in single rooms occupied also by six or more others. There were also boarding houses for single men (called *khanavalis*), which were sometimes organized by jobbers.

▼ Colonial rule and commercial development brought about the rapid growth of some Indian cities. Urbanization was a force for social change, though it could also reinforce caste identity, because these ties gave newcomers some security in the new environment of the town. Immigrants often retained links with their villages, sending back remittances from their earnings.

▶ Social patterns and beliefs were transplanted to the city. Astrologers (like these) remained important in the lives of Bombay's millhands, for it was still important to find the auspicious times for major events in the family and the life cycle of individuals.

▶▼ The textile industry employed large numbers in the production and processing of cotton as well as in its manufacture, though usually in less well paid and secure jobs. Between the wars big cotton growers in other parts of India set up new mills.

Their rural connections were significant for millhands, and workers sent about a quarter of their earnings back to their villages. At the same time a mill manager said that "The millowners generally depend to break a strike upon workers who had lost connections with the land, as these people have no home to return to and hence are the worst sufferers at such times". Far from showing themselves less "committed" to factory work and quick to desert it, as observers supposed, workers who could fall back upon their villages were often the most resilient in maintaining industrial action.

The streets of Girangaon were the center of the leisure and the politics of the working class. The great majority of workers, asked in a contemporary survey to give "an account of their leisure activities… would not be specific and said they pass time roaming, which they consider a mode of relaxation". The street corners offered a meeting place, and liquor shops drew their customers, and gymnasiums their members, from particular neighborhoods, each of them with its own *dada* or local boss. Gymnasiums were an important focus of working-class culture. Leadership of a gymnasium was sometimes the basis of a *dada*'s eminence. Young men who became skilled at fighting through training at gymnasiums frequently provided a basis for community action. Neighborhood connections indeed greatly influenced the possibilities of industrial collective action, partly because workers' ability to stay out on strike depended upon the material resources of the neighborhood, and especially on their ability to command credit with shopkeepers and others. Public morality in particular urban neighborhoods could easily be mobilized against strike-breakers; and the balance of power on the streets – between different *dadas* – closely determined the possibilities for and outcomes of strikes. As unions organized they frequently dealt with *dadas* in order either to contain their hostility or

to negotiate their support. Workers were, generally, more effective politically outside the gates of the mills.

The growth of Bombay's industries has continued to draw in labor from villages outside the city and from farther afield. The social differentiation of the villages has tended to be reproduced in the city. Workers in more secure and better paid jobs are more likely to come from landowning families than those who are daily paid, casual wage laborers. The latter are recruited especially from "lower caste", landless groups. The employment in Bombay of large numbers from other parts of India, and increasing competition for jobs have given rise to a political party, the *Shiv Sena*, which aggressively promotes the interests of local "sons of the soil".

FERIENFAHRTEN RUND UM AFRIKA
DEUTSCHE AFRIKA-LINIEN

upon his army and his warlord allies, not a popular mass base. He nearly succeeded in liquidating the tiny forces of the communist party, but the fragment which survived the rigors of the Long March of 1934–35 to reach the remote base of Yunan was able to exploit the opportunity of the Japanese invasion to fuse the social issue with the national question, backed by independent military power. The communists came to inherit the mantle of Chinese nationalism.

Africa, by comparison with these turbulent events, remained relatively at peace, although strikes were now part of the force of opposition. For the white farmers who survived the slump, there was a short "Indian summer" of being idle rich, circulating between club, pools, dance rooms, races, polo and bridge.

Outside the charmed circle, tax systems continued to drive Africans off the land in search of work and into segregated colonies, rife with overcrowding, insanitary conditions and venereal disease, and where half the babies died below the age of one. There were protests, strikes, and even riots, but in nationalist terms they were more promises for the future than challenges in the present. In South Africa industrialization was already creating the need for a settled and more skilled black labor force, and for a time apartheid looked as though it might be reversed. But the postwar victory of the National Party (1948) ended that prospect.

Women in Africa, Asia and Latin America
The incorporation of Latin America, Asia and Africa into world markets, the continuing transformation of peasant economies by commercial agriculture and industrial production and the shifts in population to urban centers necessarily affected the organization and nature of the

household and relations between individuals within households. One common result was a deterioration in women's status in society.

The changes in sub-Saharan Africa were particularly significant as the acceleration toward a cash-oriented production system proceeded. In earlier periods gender relations had been based on a series of rights and obligations afforded to men and women in the context of production primarily for their own subsistence. Although there existed a wide range of property and other social relations in different African societies, it was common to find a system whereby women had customary rights to the use of specified fields, and control over the destination and distribution of their produce. These rights were complemented by obligations to work on the husband's fields, and to provide (some) staple foods for household consumption. Marriage contracts under such circumstances did not imply the subordination of women; marriage frequently implied specified individual rights and obligations, and required both husband and wife to engage in negotiated exchange of labor and produce for production, consumption and ritual purposes. In other words, far from having a "common" purse, men and women retained separate purses, and women were expected to establish and maintain granaries after marriage.

The privatization of land and the commercialization of agriculture destroyed the context of the existing sexual division of labor. Women's status declined as their access to productive resources became legally and formally mediated through the household head; their work on household land was no longer part of a reciprocal arrangement, but an obligation reflecting dependent status. Women lost control of the products they grew and processed. Cash payments for sales of crops were appropriated by men, who

◄ **A German poster advertising cruises round Africa.** For foreigners, Africa remained the home of the noble savage, living in innocence. Few saw ordinary African life for foreigners lived in segregated enclaves where Africans were only servants. When traces appeared of ancient civilizations – the Ghana empire, the Benin bronzes or the original Zimbabwe – whites denied that it was possible Africans could have created them and attributed them to foreign invaders.

► **Malian women mashing millet.** Africans depended overwhelmingly on cultivation for their livelihood, with staples including sago, millet, cassava and, later on, maize. The majority lived in villages, loosely associated in tribal groups and far from any cities or modern facilities. In parts of the continent, people migrated quite often between cultivating areas. Only in colonial enclaves was modern commerce and export-oriented farming developed.

▼ **A village in West Africa in the late 1930s.** African village life was composed of extended kinship groups, sons and their families sharing a compound with their parents, cultivating as a group. In West Africa women were important in both agriculture and trading. Elsewhere women were dependent upon men and upon their monopoly of the chief source of wealth: the ownership of cattle.

were legally responsible for the payment of taxes to the colonial authorities. While few would argue that women had equal status with men in the precolonial period, the evidence suggests that women's status deteriorated when the traditional basis of the sexual division of labor was transformed.

In Latin America, as in many parts of Asia, religion played a major role in circumscribing the role of women, and influenced the ways in which changes in the relations of production affected women's status. In Latin America it was the religion of the conquistadors (the Spanish conquerors of Latin America and their descendants) which emphasized the reproductive and domestic role of women and created an ideology which insisted that the women's production should be invisible.

During the interwar period, when large-scale urbanization began to accelerate throughout the continent, the sexual division of the urban labor force replicated that within the domestic sphere. New industries, especially chemicals and metal-based industries, solely recruited male workers who formed the basis of the organized working class. Women were confined to the traditional less skilled, lower-paid industries producing cheap consumption goods and to a variety of service

jobs – laundry, domestic servants, food preparation – which mirrored their role within the household. As the demand for clerical and administrative jobs grew within the state bureaucracy and nascent industry, it was men who were recruited as secretaries and clerks, reflecting in part the unequal access of women even to basic education.

In Asia religious tradition interacted with the changing social structure to reinforce gender codes which legitimized the subordinate social status woman.

The commercialization of agriculture and the beginnings of industrialization in many parts of Africa, Asia and Latin America thus had a profound effect on the position of women. It remains true, however, that women, particularly from the educated classes, were organizing to redress some of the more tangible inequalities, particularly in campaigning for women's suffrage, education and property rights. That these movements in Asia and Africa became interlaced with the nationalist and anti-colonial struggles does not detract from the reality that women did begin to organize against their increasing subordination, often in ways that prefigured some of the later feminist agendas in the West.

THE
GLAMOR
YEARS

Time Chart

	1930	1931	1932	1933	1934	1935	1936	1937
Film	• Apr: Opening of *The Blue Angel*, (directed by Josef von Sternberg) starring Marlene Dietrich • *L'Age d'Or*, surrealist film, directed by Luis Bunuel (Sp) • 11 Dec: *All Quiet on the Western Front* (directed by Lewis Milestone) banned in Germany	• 6 Feb: Release of *City Lights*, starring Charlie Chaplin (USA)	• 3-color technicolor first used in Walt Disney's *Flowers and Trees* (USA) • Swimming star Johnny Weissmuller starred in his first Tarzan movie (USA) • Release of *42nd Street*, choreography by Busby Berkeley • Film debut of Shirley Temple, at the age of 3 (USA)	• Release of *King Kong* (directed by M Cooper) (USA) • 12 Aug: Release of *The Power and the Glory*, directed by William Howard and starring Spencer Tracy, introducing a new narrative style (USA)	• First use of 3-color technicolor for a live action film, *La Cucharacha* (USA) • 10 Jan: D Fairbanks and M Pickford began divorce proceedings (USA)	• First use of stereo sound in cinema, for *Napoleon Bonaparte* • *Mutiny on the Bounty*, starring Charles Laughton and Clark Gable (USA) • *Anna Karenina*, starring Greta Garbo (dir C Browne)	• Release of *Modern Times*, directed by Charlie Chaplin (USA) • Release of *Things to Come*, directed by Alexander Korda (USA)	• Release of *Snow White* cartoon by Walt Disney (USA) • *A Day at the Races*, starring the Marx brothers (USA) • 7 Jun: Death of Jean Harlow at the age of 26 (USA)
Media	• Baird television, first factory-made set, marketed in UK • 31 Mar: First television program with perfectly synchronized sight and sound broadcast by BBC (UK)	• 23 Dec: First regular television broadcasts began in USA	• 13 Aug: Marconi successfully tested first shortwave radio in Rome (It) • 21 Dec: First Christmas broadcast by a reigning monarch, George VI (UK)	• Frequency modulation (FM) radio transmission perfected by Edwin Armstrong (USA) • 24 Dec: Church bells from Bethlehem broadcast simultaneously throughout world		• Penguin Books published their first ten paperback titles (UK)	• 11 Dec: Abdication of King Edward VIII broadcast (UK)	• First magnetic tape recorder marketed by AEG/Telefunken (Ger)
Music	• *On The Sunny Side of the Street*, written by Fats Waller and sold to Jimmie McHugh	• 3 Mar: *The Star Spangled Banner* adopted as US national anthem • 23 Nov: Bing Crosby recorded *Where the Blue of the Night*, later his signature tune (USA) • Dec: Stereo sound recording patented by A. Blumlein (USA)	• *Brother, Can You Spare a Dime?* written by Jay Gourlay (USA) • *I Got Rhythm*, written by George Gershwin, in Girl Crazy • *Creole Rhapsody* began to win a serious reputation for Duke Ellington (USA)	• Dance craze for "Nira" – in honor of the US National Recovery Administration (NRA) • Stereo 78rpm disks produced by EMI, but not sold	• Opening of *Anything Goes*, a musical with music by Cole Porter (USA)	• Benny Goodman band, with black and white musicians, popularized swing (USA) • *Porgy and Bess*, with music by George Gershwin, featured *Summertime* (USA) • Feb: Meeting of Coleman Hawkins and Django Reinhardt in Paris to mark the founding of *Jazz Hot* journal (USA)	• First popular music chart published by Billboard magazine (USA) • *Pennies from Heaven*, written by Arthur Johnston (USA)	• Death of blues singer Bessie Smith in a car crash (USA)
Fashion and Design	• French architects, decorators and designers formed the Union des Artistes Modernes as an exhibiting society (Fr) • Completion of architect William Van Alen's art deco Chrysler Building in New York (USA) • Noel Coward's wardrobe for *Private Lives* designed by Capt. Edward Molyneux (UK)	• Fashion Group of America founded (USA) • Inauguration of Empire State Building, New York (USA)	• Crease-resistant process for fabric announced by Tootal Broadhurst (UK) • The styles created by fashion designer Adrian for Joan Crawford in *Letty Lynton* were widely copied (USA) • Industrial designer Norman Bel Geddes' illustrated book *Horizons* helped to spread Modernist ideas in design (USA)	• Italian Triennale design exhibitions held in Milan for the first time (It) • Bauhaus design school closed (Ger) • Council for Art and Industry formed (UK) • Fashion designer Elsa Schiaparelli reintroduced broad-shoulders to the female silhouette (Fr) • May: Opening of Chicago World's Fair	• First mass-produced streamlined car, the Chrysler Airflow, launched in USA • Completion of America's first streamlined train, "City of Salina" • Alexey Brodovitch appointed art director of *Harper's Bazaar* magazine (USA) • Apr: First public fashion show in USSR	• Artek furniture company set up by architect Alvar Aalto (Fin) • Two-piece bathing suits modeled in *Vogue* magazine	• Surrealists Elsa Schiaparelli and Salvador Dali created a shoe-shaped hat • Fiat 500, designed by Dante Giacosa, released as Italy's "people's car" • Ferdinand Porsche designed the Volkswagen (Ger)	• Opening of the Paris World's Fair (Fr) • Diana Vreeland became fashion editor of *Harper's Bazaar* magazine (USA)
Sport	• Jul: First Soccer World Cup held • Jul: Cricketer Donald Bradman (Aus) scored a record 309 runs in one day in a Test Match (UK) • Aug: First British Empire (later Commonwealth) Games held (Can)	• Feb: First television coverage of a baseball match (Jap)	• Feb: Winter Olympics held at Lake Placid (USA) • Jul-Aug: Summer Olympic Games held in Los Angeles (USA) • Jul: India competed in its first cricket Test Match	• Jan: Bodyline crisis during MCC cricket tour of Australia • German Jews banned from taking part in 1936 Olympics	• First European athletic championship held, in Turin, for men only (It) • Aug: Fourth Women's World Games held, in London (UK) • US Masters golf tournament first staged (USA)	• 25 May: Jesse Owens (USA) broke five athletic world records in one day • 3 Sep: Malcolm Campbell (UK) became the first man to exceed 300mph (500km/h) in his car Bluebird	• Baseball Hall of Fame opened (USA) • Feb: Winter Olympics held in Garmisch-Partenkirchen (Ger) • Aug: Summer Olympic Games held in Berlin (Ger); Jesse Owens (USA) won four gold medals	
Misc.	• Introduction of sliced bread and packaged frozen foods (USA)		• Aviator Charles Lindbergh's baby son kidnapped and murdered (USA)	• Prohibition ends (USA) • Mar: FD Roosevelt became US president	• Opening of world's first launderette (USA)	• Monopoly game introduced by Parker Bros (USA)	• Dale Carnegie published his bestseller, *How to Win Friends and Influence People* (USA)	

1938	1939
	• Release of *Gone with the Wind*, starring Clark Gable and Vivien Leigh (USA) • 29 Mar: Clark Gable and Carole Lombard wed (USA) • Aug: Release of *The Wizard of Oz*, starring Judy Garland (USA)
• 31 May: First television games show broadcast (UK) • 30 Oct: Broadcast of *The War of the Worlds* by Orson Welles convinced US public of a Martian invasion	
• Crooner Frank Sinatra's radio debut (USA) • 16 Jan: Benny Goodman gave the first jazz concert at New York's Carnegie Hall (USA)	• Frank Sinatra's second record *All or Nothing at All* sold 1 million copies
• Neiman-Marcus Awards founded for service to fashion (USA) • Norman Hartnell appointed dressmaker to the British royal family • Edith Head became chief costume designer at Paramount Pictures (USA)	• Nylon first manufactured, by Du Pont (USA) • Apr: Opening of New York World's Fair, the first at which industrial design took prominence over decorative (USA)
• Jul: All Wimbledon tennis titles won by US players	• Little League baseball launched, for boys and girls aged 9-18 (USA) • 29 Jul: Jenny Kammersgaad (Den) became first person to swim the Baltic Sea
	• Beginning of World War II, as Germany invaded Poland; France and Britain declared war

"The cinema has thawed out people's brains."

JEAN COCTEAU, 1930

"HER SIN WAS NO GREATER THAN HIS
but
SHE WAS A WOMAN
If the world permits the husband to philander – why not the wife? Here is a frank, outspoken and daring drama that exposes the hypocrisy of modern marriage."

HOLLYWOOD FILM POSTER, 1930

"Rayon is like the times we live in – gay, colorful, luminous...it is so pliable to work with and so luxurious in appearance...[and] launders to perfection."

ELSA SCHIAPARELLI, 1930

"If you are losing your leisure, look out! You may be losing your soul."

LOGAN PEARSALL SMITH, 1931

"One night of heaven in her arms! Snatched from the Hell of War!
COMRADES in the clouds! ENEMIES on the ground! facing danger together – for a lovely woman's smile! A man's picture, that women will love!"

HOLLYWOOD FILM POSTER, 1933

"Fortunately, in her kindness and patience, Nature has never put the fatal question as to the meaning of their lives into the mouths of most people. And where no one asks, no one needs to answer."

C.G. JUNG, 1934

"What I want to see is a mass-produced car costing virtually the same as a motor-cycle."

ADOLPH HITLER, 1934

"While the world is divided between kingdoms, republics and dictatorships and Ethiopian statesmen weigh the problem of threatened Italo-Ethiopian war, Schiaparelli has launched both royalist and republican clothes."

ASSOCIATED PRESS, 1935

"Mechanical splendor, the bolder the better, the crueller the more chic!"

HARPERS BAZAAR, 1935

The 1930s were the golden age of design as an ideal for improving the quality of life for people at every level of society. The art of the industrial designer was taken seriously, and in the United States, at least, design was consciously promoted to encourage the country out of the Depression: the modernistic displays at the World's Fairs of Chicago and New York, in 1934 and 1939 respectively, were emblematic of this.

Elsewhere, the idea of the people's car – the Volkswagen in Germany, designed by Ferdinand Porsche, and its equivalents built by Citroën in France and Fiat in Italy exemplified the desire to bring the benefits of good design to all the people. During the Nazi period, however, German design lost most of the impetus that had been built up under the Bauhaus (which was closed in 1933); whereas other countries were pushing ahead with modernism and streamlining, Germany reverted to neoclassicism until the 1950s.

US national income

Advertising volume in USA

▲▲ As in the 1920s, the volume of advertising in the United States had remained generally in line with the overall national income. It fell back somewhat during the later 1930s, and declined appreciably after 1935, when business confidence was lower and advertising budgets more carefully scrutinized. It fell further during the war.

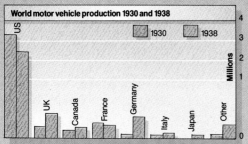

World motor vehicle production 1930 and 1938

▲ The United States remained the chief source of motor-vehicle manufacture during the 1930s, although a dramatic rise was noted in Germany during this period, government support for a rearmament program. The German "people's car", the Volkswagen, however, was not mass-produced until the later 1940s.

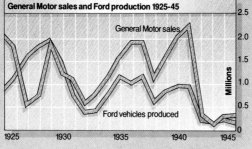

General Motor sales and Ford production 1925-45

▲ During the 1920s General Motors established a sudden lead over their chief rival Ford, as General Motors stressed comfort and style. Both companies were hit by the Depression: Ford's workforce fell from 128,000 in 1929 to 37,000 in 1931. During the war years both companies went over to war work.

◄ In the early 1930s, average personal income fell in real terms by almost half in the United States; while the amount spent on durable goods held up sales of non-durables and services were squeezed. As disposable income (money available after taxation) rose towards the end of the decade sales of non-durables rose.

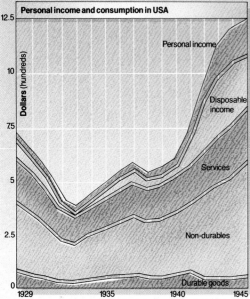

Personal income and consumption in USA

During the late 1920s huge changes had taken place in the way new American technological goods, particularly automobiles, were sold and consumed. Since the early years of production at Henry Ford's Highland Park factory – from 1912 until the mid 1920s – the design of his "Model T" had remained fundamentally unchanged. Ford's manufacturing philosophy involved commitment to standardization, achieved through the use of single-purpose machinery and the production line. Ford's aim was to mass-produce a high-quality, low-price car which the American population, particularly the rural sector, could afford. For the first decade of its implementation this formula proved highly successful, but by the 1920s a second-hand automobile market had developed, while more affluent consumers could pay more for goods that were status symbols as well as useful. Standardization preserved economies of scale in production, but its monolithic application to the appearance of the final product became less and less appropriate – the Model T failed increasingly to provide the degree of novelty and fashionability required by the new American consumers of the 1920s.

The annual model change

General Motors, a composite company that had expanded by absorbing smaller firms such as Cadillac, Chevrolet, Pontiac and Buick, was highly sensitive to the new mood of consumption, and in the mid-1920s instigated a program of product variation and stylistic obsolescence in its automobiles. In 1927 Harley Earl became head of the "Art and Color" section at General Motors. He initiated the idea of the annual model change, which quickly became established within the production and marketing habits of the American automobile industry as a whole.

Ford's reaction to the shrinking market for his product and the growing competition from General Motors was highly dramatic. In 1926 Henry Ford closed down his River Rouge plant for a whole year, designing and tooling up for a new automobile, the Model A, which was launched in 1927. Ford's concession to product styling – by 1931 he had introduced yet another model, the "V8" – demonstrated that the era of flexible mass production, allowing for obsolescence and product styling, had begun.

The lesson learned by Ford was soon instilled into the minds of countless other American manufacturers of technological consumer goods. The buying boom and industrial expansion of the early twenties was followed by an economic recession, already beginning to be felt by 1926. The market for domestic electrical appliances, gas-powered goods and many other "consumer machines" that had only recently appeared,

STREAMLINED STYLE

◄▼ The *Airflow*, from
Chrysler Motors, was the
classic 1930s streamlined
automobile.

became glutted. Goods competed in the market-place with nothing to distinguish one from another. New means were needed to keep them flowing through the cycle from production to sales. The answer lay in the introduction of a new concept: "industrial design". By introducing the idea of visual differentiation manufacturers began to find ways of individualizing their products and increasing their sales.

Introducing a specialist member of the production team responsible for "product styling" was a logical consequence of the expanding use of advertising. Aggressive marketing was a necessary counterpart of large-scale production, and many of the pioneering American industrial designers – among them men such as Norman Bel Geddes, Walter Dorwin Teague, Henry Dreyfuss, Raymond Loewy, Harold Van Doren, Lurelle

Guild, Donald Deskey and George Sakier – came from the world of "commercial art": notably advertising illustration, store design and window dressing.

From the late twenties countless marriages took place between manufacturers and members of this new profession, many of whom set up small New York offices, offering manufacturing companies the benefits of their specialized skills. Designers charged very high fees: Teague received between $12,000 and $24,000 for each of his consultancy jobs, and Van Doren charged $100 a day for his services. They provided a wide range of work including market research, advice on the costs of retooling, and a survey of the competing products available on the market. While designers earned a public reputation for being "arty", much of their work consisted, in reality, of giving advice of a specifically business nature. They were heralded as national heroes by the popular press, their life stories appearing in magazines such as the *New Yorker* and *Life* in the early 1930s.

The requirement behind the emergence of the industrial designer was founded in the fact that if two competing products were similar in terms of their utility value and price, the one with the more pleasing appearance was more likely to be bought first. Until the early 1920s, the refrigerator was little more than a mechanized ice-box that looked like a wooden safe. The innovations that occurred in the 1920s, through the efforts of General Electric and Frigidaire (a division of General Motors) focused on producing the all-steel electric refrigerator. By the end of the decade this new product was widely available, but sold more on the basis of its technological novelty than on its appearance. Visually it still recalled objects from the past. As with the Model T car, the market for refrigerators quickly became saturated. By the end of the decade the need to make the refrigerator more desirable had grown urgent as competition intensified between the major manufacturers – Frigidaire, General Electric, Sears Roebuck and Westinghouse. The answer lay in employing design.

Streamlining

In 1933 General Electric launched a new, "streamlined" refrigerator, designed by Henry Dreyfuss, which instantly made its competitors look old-fashioned. Westinghouse employed Donald Dohner as an inhouse designer for its whole range of electrical consumer goods. By the middle of the decade Raymond Loewy's design team had provided Sears Roebuck with a number of annual model changes. Its 1935, 1936 and 1937 models were all subtly different from each other, each subsequent design instantly making the previous one obsolescent stylistically. By the mid-1930s nearly all the electrical appliances available on the American market – from the Maytag washing machine to Sunbeam's "Mixmaster" food mixer and Hoover's model 150 vacuum cleaner – had been "styled".

Objects played an increasingly important part in creating and sustaining the social myths of progress, modernity and the beneficence of

technology. Together with the marketing man, the industrial designer became the principal creative force behind their origination, a responsibility that gave him an enormous power in determining the appearance of the consumer society. He provided the main source of imagery in the home, the office and the street. The dominant stylistic idiom was referred to as "streamlining", "streamform" or "streamlined moderne". In architecture and the applied arts, America had developed a popularized version of the faceted, step-formed art deco style that had been in evidence at the 1925 Exhibition of Decorative Arts in Paris. The New York skyscrapers, notably the Chrysler Building and the Empire State Building, proclaimed the style triumphantly to the world. In both automobiles and appliances a style developed that was aggressively "modern" in inspiration and originated in the concept of transport aerodynamics itself, rather than in an abstract notion of design.

Favored by this era's seekers after speed, the "tear-drop" shape, complete with chrome "speed whiskers", epitomized the idea of living with advanced technology, with an eye turned to the future. Before long the style permeated static objects such as irons and gum-dispensers as well as passenger trains and ocean liners. Norman Bel Geddes contributed to the evolution of this dynamic, futuristic style through his models of automobiles, trains, planes and liners of the future – all of which manifested the same curved, bulbous front and tapered rear end. In his design work for the Pennsylvania Railroad Company

Raymond Loewy put a number of highly streamlined designs into production.

The application of streamform to static objects was clearly a stylistic decision, not one based on rational principles or aerodynamics. While historians of streamlining have pointed to its origins in the forms of airships, airplane fuselages, and dolphins, it also clearly owed much to contemporary fine art as well. In their book *Art and the Machine* of 1936, for instance, S. and M. Cheney pointed out its resemblance to forms employed by the French painter Jean Helion and the Romanian sculptor Constantin Brancusi, while Margaret Bourke-White, who used modern machinery as the subject-matter of her photographs, also evolved a similar kind of imagery.

From a manufacturing point of view the curved forms of streamlining were the most appropriate ones for objects made from stamped or pressed metal or from molded plastic. The use of metal and plastic was widespread in the new consumer-goods industries in the 1930s and provided an important justification for the appearance of many of the objects that came off the designers' drawing boards in that decade. Lines of chrome trim were often included for strategic as well as merely decorative purposes, disguising what might otherwise have looked like a concave surface, concealing unattractive joints, or unifying surfaces.

From a theoretical point of view the esthetic embraced by industrial designers in the 1930s in the United States had little in common with the purist, craft-based ideal of "form following function", which inspired the architects and designers associated with the European Modern Movement such as the Bauhaus group in Germany which had flourished in the 1920s. While paying lip-service to this source in their writing, the American designers were really much more conscious of the commercial context of manufacturing than their European counterparts. As a result they adopted a more pragmatic approach towards the esthetic of designed objects.

The all-white "continuous flow" kitchen was as much a product of this period as the bulbous automobile. "Labor-saving" automatic and semi-automatic machines in the kitchen and laundry offered the housewife more free time but the near-obsession with hygiene, also promoted by advertising, required higher standards of housework and meant that there was more, not less, work to do. Her time was simply spent on a new set of choices. Less time spent on housework meant more time spent on shopping trips; increased consumption meant more time spent making important decisions about purchases – decisions that increasingly had to do with appearance and style, not just content and function. By 1939 the industrial designer, product styling, and object obsolescence were intrinsic elements within modern consumption. Ford's democratic, utilitarian philosophy of the high-quality standardized product available to all was a thing of the past, sacrificed to the merchandizing esthetics of turnover and volume sales.

Hollywood glamor

The fashion image most associated with the 1930s – a decade of Depression, unemployment, fascism and the approach of war – is probably the glamorous Hollywood pale satin evening gown, a bias-cut creation slithering to the floor, low-backed and clinging to the thighs. This ambiguous garment did not look very different from a nightdress, and managed to appear both sultry and languid – chic and upper-class in the pages of *Vogue* or trampishly sexual when worn by Jean Harlow. The slinky lines of the early thirties, and the return to a more waisted, full-skirted and puff-sleeved silhouette later in the decade both emanated from Paris, but it was their interpretation .by Hollywood designers such as Adrian and Orry Kelly that ensured their rapid dissemination to a much wider audience. Glamor lingerie, one of the consumer items popularized by the movies in the 1920s, began to be mass produced after the development of synthetic fabrics, notably nylon which was discovered in 1935.

Since the 19th century there had been attempts to manufacture an artificial substitute for silk, the most luxurious fashion fabric. By 1930, rayon was made from pulped wood cellulose; nylon and other synthetics were later developed from chemical products and by 1938 ten percent of apparel fibers in Britain were synthetic. The rich and elegant still wore underwear of real silk, but the availability of artificial substitutes meant that ordinary women could also aspire to a more glamorously attired sexuality and a greater sophistication.

Although sections of the clothing industry remained based in small craft tailoring shops and in the sweatshops of centers such as the Lower East Side in New York City and London's East End there were also major innovations in the mass production of clothes, which further broke down distinctions between skilled tailors, semi-skilled workers in tailoring shops and factory workers and outworkers. Conveyor-belt production was introduced, and the more precise sizing of mass-produced clothes developed. This last was a contradictory development, for the intention was to individualize garments, yet individuals were sorted into groups according to their measurements. It could be seen equally as an index of the expanding possibilities for the expression of a customer's unique personality and as part of the increasing conformity of modern mass society.

Department stores, where clothes could still be altered to fit or were even custom-made, remained the mecca of middle-class customers. The appearance of firms aiming to sell to this market – to men as well as women – was a further development of mass production. Menswear firms with their own factories were able to translate personal measurements into factory-made clothes, while for women "wholesale" or "middle-class couture" firms designed distinctive house styles and took pride in the elegance of their creations. This was the era when it was distinctly possible – but sartorially disastrous – for two identically dressed women to come face to face at a social function.

Women's magazines proliferated during the 1930s and contributed to the greatly increased circulation of fashion images, which could be copied by local dressmakers. Fan magazines and studio publicity also promoted "Hollywood" styles. There was a vogue for movies set in department stores, beauty salons or fashion houses. These films acted as showcases for the latest fashions, which could then be copied *en masse* and retailed through special promotions in the big stores. California developed as a center of the clothing industry, and in particular of sports and casual wear. Backless bathing suits, slacks, halter tops and sweaters – all Parisian couture innovations of the 1920s – were now translated for the beaches and high streets of the whole Western world. Trousers were no longer regarded as eccentric or indecent on women, but were becoming a standard feature of sports and casual wear. In a period when "the career woman" was an acceptable image, women's suits followed the bespoke elegance of those worn by men.

Women's magazines took it upon themselves to instruct and inform women about the latest fashions and changes in style, and also to reinforce ideas about correct wear for different occasions and times of day. This etiquette of dress could now reach virtually all women. The elegant poses of *Vogue* could be subtly adapted for women far down the social scale, and transmitted to women far from metropolitan centers of elegance. This helped to speed up changes of style and break down regional and national stylistic differences. In Germany the Nazis regarded this international style of fashion and glamor as a threat to the purity of Aryan womanhood, and sought to return their womenfolk to a peasant-like style of national dress. Left-wing radicals were also suspicious of the "consumptionism" implied by media fashion promotion, which some saw as drawing women away from a true appreciation of their natural womanly beauty

◄ Marlene Dietrich was one of the great Hollywood icons of beauty in the thirties, representing, with Garbo, the European, more sophisticated and ambiguous (in all senses of the word) side of the celluloid dream.

► Those who could afford to still had their clothes made to measure or bought ready-to-wear fashions at every price level; but home dressmaking also increased in popularity and chic with diffusion of paper patterns via the burgeoning mass market women's magazines.

▼ A fashion show in Berlin in the late 1930s offered a range of international styles.

toward the falsity of the film-star image. "Bohemians", or artistic radicals, of the twenties and thirties endeavored to set themselves apart by disregarding fashion and devising their own uniform of rebellion. The King's Road, Chelsea, in London, was a haunt of artists, whose models and mistresses wore the dirndl skirts and gypsy fashions popularized by "Dorelia", who posed for the British painter Augustus John. These full skirts and sleeves and fitted bodices were soon to become high fashion once more.

As in the 1920s, Parisian *haute couture* had close links with the avant-garde. Chanel now had a rival, Elsa Schiaparelli, who introduced a surrealist element into her designs, with a *trompe l'œil* sweater and a hat made in the shape of a shoe. Fashion began to move away from the speedy modernity of the 1920s; self-conscious

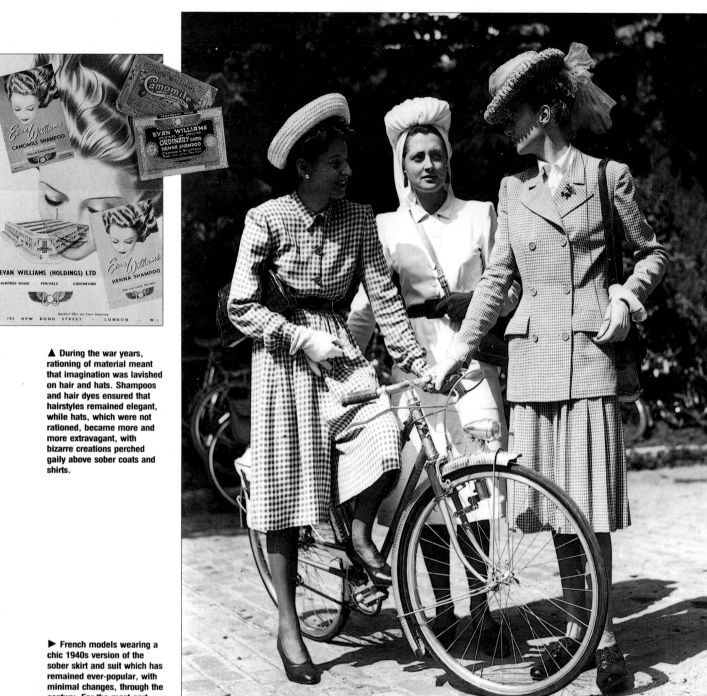

▲ During the war years, rationing of material meant that imagination was lavished on hair and hats. Shampoos and hair dyes ensured that hairstyles remained elegant, while hats, which were not rationed, became more and more extravagant, with bizarre creations perched gaily above sober coats and shirts.

► French models wearing a chic 1940s version of the sober skirt and suit which has remained ever-popular, with minimal changes, through the century. For the most part, elegant clothes were hard to come by in war-ravaged Europe.

femininity was ascendant. In Hollywood, Paris and elsewhere – in the work of the British photographer, Cecil Beaton, for example – one reaction to the Depression and the gathering war clouds was not to adapt dress to sterner political realities, but on the contrary to develop escapist styles and ever more elaborate fantasies of wealth and glamor.

Even Hollywood's big glamor spectaculars, which capitalized on period costume, had an in-direct effect on clothing in fads such as the Dolly Varden hat and even panniered evening skirts; while musicals such as Busby Berkeley's *Gold Diggers of 1933* or *42nd Street* popularized the image of the showgirl, with whom millions of

young women now identified as she lost her aura of "easy virtue".

Even more important than Hollywood's influence on clothes was the way in which the movies popularized cosmetics. In the 18th century and earlier, powder and paint had been freely worn, but for most of the 19th century makeup had been taboo for respectable women. In the European capitals and American cities women had started to wear visible makeup again before World War I. In the 1930s cosmetic ranges proliferated for all classes of women, together with the more subtle and wider range of film-star types. The pioneers of the beauty products that grew into huge business empires – Elizabeth

Arden and Helena Rubinstein being two of the best known – certainly did not regard their products as tainted with immorality. Nor were cosmetics any longer seen as hostile to female emancipation; on the contrary, lipstick, like the cigarette, was a badge of liberation. The use of cosmetics even became a symbol of democracy and class equality, evidence that the culture of consumption gave every woman not only a right to good looks but access to the improvement or even the dramatic transformation of her appearance. Along with the powders, lipsticks and increasingly, the eye shadows and mascaras, came creams and lotions that were promoted as preserving youth and beauty, so that the industry latched on to powerful magical fantasies of unconscious origin: a pot of cream from Yardley or Max Factor became the elixir of eternal youth.

These developments were part of a move away from the idea of equality for women, which had lasted through the 1920s; the return of romanticism seemed to signal a retreat for women into more restricted roles. Max Factor, a Hollywood firm, made much of its connections with the film industry, and the use of film stars in promotions pushed further the idea of distinct types of female beauty. It was no longer simply a case of being a blonde, a brunette or a redhead; qualities of character such as passion, class or independence came to be associated with different types of looks, so that the popular consciousness was peopled with stereotypes of dumb blonde, wicked brunette or fiery redhead. "Dress to your type" became a new command to the ordinary woman, and typologies of various kinds were reproduced in magazines, encouraging women to think of themselves as sporty, fluffy, sultry, artistic, and so on.

The increasing romanticism of thirties' fashion was brutally interrupted by the outbreak of war in 1939. For the second time in less than thirty years women were conscripted into the war effort. Their being at risk, like their menfolk at the front, encouraged a renewed belief in women's equality, but the idea that women achieved equality in wartime and were then pushed back into the home afterward is oversimplified. Women did men's jobs "for the duration", but they did not achieve equal pay. Many women with children spent the war in quiet isolation. Rationing, queues, shortages and the constant anxiety about absent lovers, husbands, brothers and fathers – and the real danger to themselves and their families and friends because of air raids – must challenge the popular view of World War II as a period of glamor and freedom for women. Glamor there was, however, despite the hardship. Paradoxically, women's increased participation in the life of the factory, the forces and the office seemed to lead to a greater emphasis on femininity in moments of leisure, even though fashions certainly adapted to the exigencies of the time. In spite of all the difficulties it seemed more important than ever to look nice in order to keep up morale, so there was a greater emphasis than ever before on face and hairstyle.

With occupied Paris no longer the source of new fashions, the war was the American industry's great chance, but in spite of some highly

The Utility Scheme

For a few years during the war the British people seemed willing to forgo the delights of fashion, novelty and status symbols and accept the idea that mass-produced, standardized high-quality products could provide it with all the items of furniture and clothing that it needed. Shortages of timber and cloth, and the need to use labor to produce war materiel rather than consumer goods set the conditions for the National Government's unprecedented experiment in democratizing design. In 1942 an advisory committee produced specifications for furniture "of good, sound construction in simple but agreeable designs for sale at reasonable prices, and ensuring the maximum economy of raw materials and labor."

Britain's situation was unique: it was more embattled than the United States, but not occupied nor a battleground like most of Europe. An advanced and egalitarian rationing system ensured that scarcity was fairly distributed, while under the Utility scheme well-known designers contributed their work so that elegant clothing and furniture could be produced at low cost and with an economical use of materials. Apart from second-hand and home-made articles, Utility furniture and clothing were the only items on the market during the final years of the war and the immediate postwar years.

The twin criteria of simplicity and quality harked back to the ideals of the British Arts and Crafts movement from the end of the 19th century. The furniture was characterized by a stark simplicity, relieved only by the lightly patterned upholstery fabrics, designed in a limited range of colors by Enid Marx. The public and press (less so the trade) responded enthusiastically to the designs.

The Utility fashion scheme was less thoroughgoing than the furniture project but it provided, nonetheless, the main source of new clothing in wartime Britain. Strict regulations governed their designs, from the use of a minimal amount of cloth to the elimination of all trimmings and decorations and the use of only three buttons on jackets. Like the furniture designs, the success of Utility clothing depended upon the simplicity of its lines and cut, and it too was at first received with much enthusiasm.

Otherwise, it was "make do and mend". The strongest competition for Utility clothing came from the home-made items that housewives produced for their families.

▲ Utility cotton knit underwear was widely felt to be of better quality than the British prewar equivalent; there was more variation in Utility outerwear, to a considerable extent in quality, less so in design.

original designers they did not achieve stylistic dominance of the market, partly because the fashions of the war years were relatively static. The tight-waisted, full-skirted styles that were on their way back in 1938-39 were modified by rationing and the lack of materials. The influence of uniforms led to the widespread popularity of the tailored suit, with broad padded shoulders, revers, and a short narrow skirt. This fashion, which was popularized in films by Joan Crawford, symbolized the career woman. Sensible country fashions such as tweed coats, boots, ankle socks and headscarves came into vogue, while more casual trousers – often called slacks – finally became acceptable.

THE NEW YORK WORLD'S FAIR

Streamlining spawned visions of the future, nowhere more so than at the Big Fair – the New York World's Fair which opened in April 1939.

International expositions had occured regularly since 1851 – the Eiffel Tower had been built for the Universal Exhibition in Paris in 1889 – but "the People's Fair" proclaimed itself "the mightiest exposition ever conceived and built by man." Its director, Grover Whalen, declared that "By giving a clear and orderly interpretation of our own age, the fair will project the average man into the World of Tomorrow." Its major exhibits were the work of America's leading industrial designers – brilliant displays of their ideas of the rationally planned and re-ordered world of the near future. Behind its façade of education and entertainment, the Fair was a gigantic advertisement for American industrial civilization and what was coming to be called the American Way of Life. *Life* magazine called it "A magnificent monument by and to American business". But most of its 45 million visitors treated it as an amusement park.

There was an irony in the Fair's vision of the future. A pavilion dedicated to "Goodwill and Peace" was planned but never built. The Fair's planners hoped that it would make a "forcible contribution to the cause of peace," but this was little in evidence. Albania and Czechoslovakia flew their national flags at half mast to mark the invasion of their countries by Italy and Germany, and no-one collected the prize for an essay competition: a vacation in "gay, colorful Poland". In exhibits by General Motors and American Telegraph & Telephone, the Fair presented communications as central to its vision of the future, but the Fair's managers decided not to broadcast any news of the war in Europe. In the late 1930s Allied governments expected aerial warfare to cause massive devastation. Americans could only imagine the horrors of Total War, conjured up for them most vividly on Halloween 1938, in the panic caused by Orson Welles' radio broadcast of H.G. Wells' *The War of the Worlds*.

▶ The Avenue of the Flags, leading to the Court of Peace at the New York World's Fair.

▶▶ The Fair's most popular exhibit was General Motors' "Futurama", a model of the American cityscape of 1960 as designer Norman Bel Geddes anticipated it (above). *Things to Come*, based on an H.G. Wells novel, was one of the few 1930s films to anticipate the war (below). Images of catastrophe spoke to an anxious paranoia which lay beneath the decade's surface optimism.

▶▼ The two symbols of the Fair, the 200m-tall Trylon and the 60m globe, the Perisphere (bottom). The Trylon, by one account, symbolized "the infinite aspirations of man," while the Perisphere housed the Fair's theme exhibit, human interdependence in Democracity, the city of 2039.

▶ The term "science fiction" was coined in 1929 by Hugo Gernsback, founder of *Amazing Stories* magazine. Comic-strip heroes of the 1930s were creatures from the future: from 1929 onwards Buck Rogers spent most of the 25th century saving the Solar System from the forces of evil. He rapidly provided inspiration for both toy manufacturers and imitators. Superman appeared to battle for "Truth, Justice and the American Way" from 1938, followed a year later by Batman. Flash Gordon first encountered Ming the Merciless in 1934; Ming's oriental appearance hinted at racial fears of "aliens" closer to home.

Datafile

The notion that the audience for popular culture is a passive one – maneuvered into the consumption of useless commodities under an illusion of choice, to provide profits for the few – has been a powerful one. Its roots go back to the 1930s, when evidence of audience manipulation, added to the growth of fascism in Europe, seemed overwhelming. Against this it is possible to discern more independent democratic trends at work in audience responses to popular music. Similarly, it is important to remember the huge variety of individual popular music styles fashioned in the thirties: Billie Holiday, Woody Guthrie, Cole Porter, Lester Young and many others.

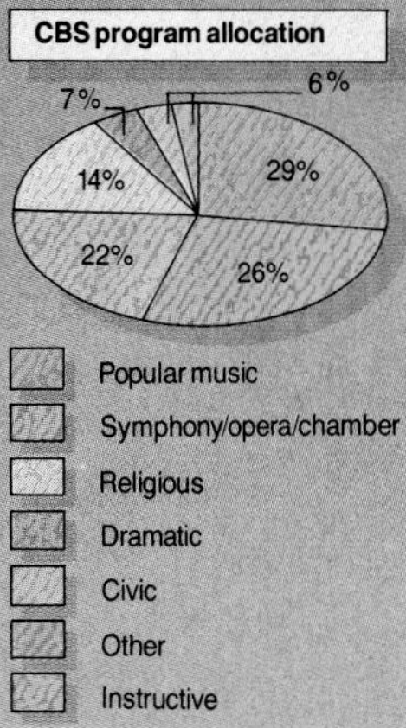

CBS program allocation

6%
7%
14%
29%
22%
26%

- Popular music
- Symphony/opera/chamber
- Religious
- Dramatic
- Civic
- Other
- Instructive

Victor record sales

Millions

60
50
40
30
20
10
0

1930   1935   1940

▲ By 1930 the number of Americans with access to a radio had reached an estimated 60 million, almost half the country's population. And one third of the programs they received consisted of popular dance-band music. These figures, presented by CBS to Congress in 1930, follow a pattern repeated by networks and local stations. The balance between popular and classical music shows radio's desire to live up to its requirements as a public service, while giving the public what they wanted.

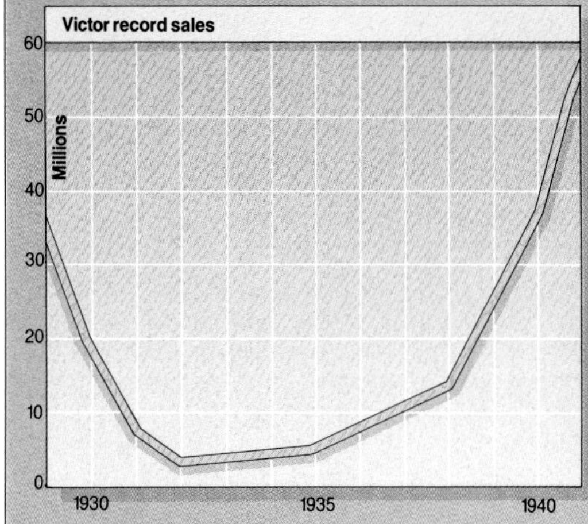

▲ The destructive effects of the Depression on record sales are clearly evident in Victor's sales figures. Even back in 1905 the company had sold more records than in 1932 – and sales hit rock bottom in 1933 at $5.5 million, as compared to $105 million in 1921. In Victor's case its new strength in radio saw it through.

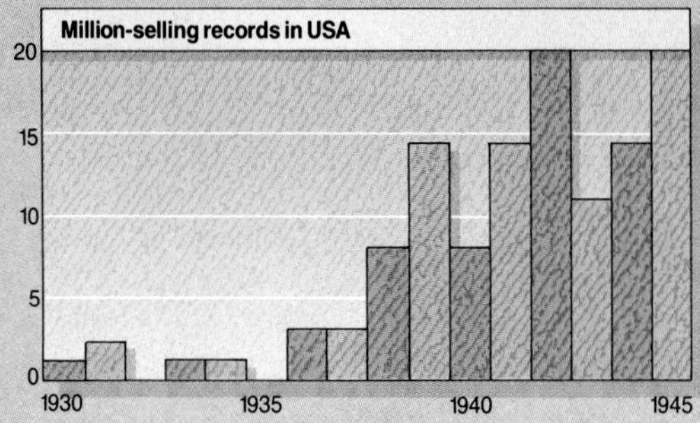

Million-selling records in USA

20
15
10
5

1930   1935   1940   1945

▲ The bleak performance of the record industry during the Depression is well illustrated by its failure, in 1932 and 1935, to achieve any million-sellers, and only four altogether in the six years 1930–35. The recovery was considerably aided by the introduction of a cheap label by the English-owned Decca company.

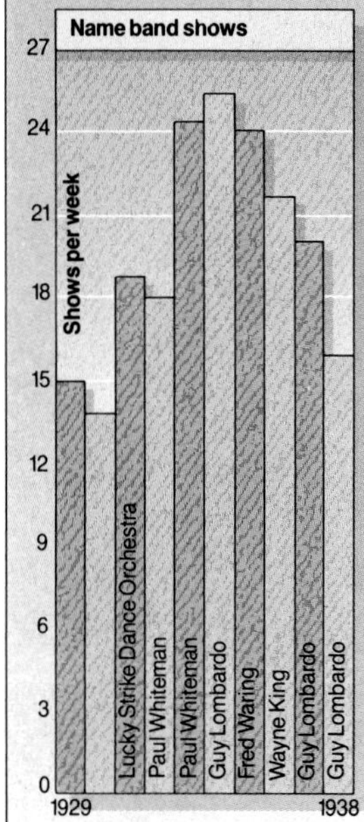

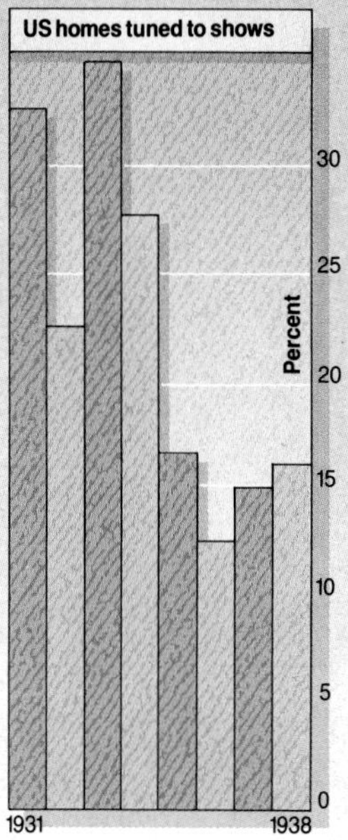

Name band shows

Shows per week

27
24
21
18
15
12
9
6
3
0

1929   Lucky Strike Dance Orchestra   Paul Whiteman   Paul Whiteman   Guy Lombardo   Fred Waring   Wayne King   Guy Lombardo   Guy Lombardo   1938

US homes tuned to shows

Percent

30
25
20
15
10
5
0

1931   1938

◄ The left-hand chart shows network radio's heavy reliance on "name" bands, peaking in 1934–35 with no fewer than 26 weekly shows. In that season Guy Lombardo captured an average 23.5 percent of the listening audience (right-hand chart). The year before a larger percentage had opted for rival Paul Whiteman.

132

On 7 November 1929, nine days after the Wall Street Crash, the song *Happy Days Are Here Again* was registered for copyright. This glaring contrast heralded the escapism of which the music of the next few years is often accused. With a few exceptions (the most famous being *Brother, Can You Spare a Dime?*), the most widely heard music of the 1930s did not relate directly to current problems, and the popular-culture industry seemed insensitive to the problems of its listeners. There was nothing new in this: the music of the 1920s had also celebrated good times, and in that sense thirties' music was a continuation of it. But espousing contemporary music in the twenties had meant taking some kind of stance against established culture; now the onset of the Depression made the music of the time seem to encourage a return to those very values that twenties' music had sought to escape.

For the first half of the decade record sales in the United States dropped steeply, and coast-to-coast radio steadily increased its domination of the entertainment market. Late-night listening became especially popular; tuning in for free to dance bands broadcasting from celebrated night-spots partly compensated for the loss of more costly leisure pursuits. Among the many effects of radio music in the thirties, two stand out: the impact of improved technology on the performance of music, and the creation of a mass audience.

Sweet music

The improvement in the quality of broadcast sound that followed the introduction of the electric microphone in the mid-1920s led to a corresponding rise in the quality of radio receivers. It became possible to discern greater delicacies of instrumental sound and of the singing voice, particularly in the middle range. Songwriters and bandleaders took account of this. It was no longer necessary to limit the size of a band to instruments that could be picked up by the acoustic recording horn, so there was a steady increase in the size of ensembles. Bigger bands, a greater fondness for subtle shades and a higher quality in the middle range meant just one thing: "sweet" music.

Technical changes also had their effect on popular vocal style. The days of declamatory singers such as Al Jolson were all but gone. A whole range of voices previously ruled out for lack of dynamics could now be heard on the air, while the greater clarity of the sung texts increased the importance of lyricists. The microphone's ability to show up not only every flaw in phrasing and enunciation but also each potentially displeasing vocal nuance produced a breed of singers with impeccable diction and with bland, featureless voices. The first singer to respond in full to the microphone's challenge, and to reap its

CROONERS AND SWING

benefits, was one who usually disclaimed having done either: Bing Crosby. So at ease was Crosby with the new technology that he sounded as if he had been "overheard" by it. Crosby's relaxed, intimate style further enhanced the process by which an individual listener could make a private experience out of an ever more widely available musical event. The key elements in this were the characteristic personal timbre – the "grain" – of his voice, his tendency to "talk" a song (coupled with excellent breath control), and his ability to derive effective drama by under-dramatization.

The creation of a mass audience by the networked programs provided the first major opportunity for the manipulation of public taste. In this scheme of things, sweet music had two functions. The first was to create revenue, both for the music industry through its copyright organization, the American Society of Composers, Authors, and Publishers (ASCAP), and for the companies who sponsored the programs. ASCAP had developed an effective system of ensuring that the music of those it represented (Tin Pan Alley) dominated the airwaves. Marketing these songs as standardized products, so they did not attract the critical attention of high-culture opinion-makers, assured large profits.

The second function was less obvious. The peddling of sweet music to a nation whose daily life was often bitter was more than a mere encouragement to escapism. It suited commercial interests for people to soothe the rough edges of their lives with music rather than use it

to sharpen their complaints. The music's synchronized control reinforced a shaken sense of order by echoing and embodying that order in its full but conventional harmonies and regular, mechanical rhythm. One day, it suggested, if everyone was compliant, life could be as "full" as these sounds.

Nevertheless, jazz had brought changes in some of the ways that life was perceived. The rhythmic emancipation of ragtime and jazz was built into almost all of the music which followed them, even music that reached a much wider audience than jazz itself. It was most apparent when a number broke into a jazzy section. Then the music's clothing was being shed, and its structural framework revealed. The essential element in the framework was rhythm, in which neither the regular nor the offbeat was dominant; what was important was the suggestion of interplay between the two. Black music itself was developing this to a sophisticated level, but even in "sweet" music it was sufficient to suggest that there were all kinds of alternatives to regular rhythm.

As the United States pulled out of the Depression, a more vigorous style of band music began to be widely heard. Reviving fortunes for the record industry – in particular Decca's introduction of a cheap (35-cent) record – played a part, but radio was preeminently responsible. One crucial element, however, was new: the beginnings of a youth audience. When band leader Benny Goodman won popular acclaim in Los Angeles

▼ "Sweet" music, as purveyed by bands such as Glenn Miller Swingers, introduced greater subleties of sound, but its bland unobtrusiveness could meet with ambivalent responses. Critic George Simon cited the reason for his favoring one particular group was that, when it accompanied your dinner, "you could hear a mashed potato drop".

and thus inaugurated the "swing" era in July 1935, his audience were in their teens and early twenties. *Let's Dance*, the show on which Goodman's band appeared, was broadcast too late for the younger audience on the East Coast, but fell right into the mid-evening listening slot of the young West Coast audience, who turned out in force to hear the band live.

Goodman's hugely popular music was not new. It operated on principles borrowed from the Fletcher Henderson band of the late twenties and early thirties. Swing took the form of simplified melodies, using riffs, or short, rhythmically interesting melodic fragments: a propulsive, even meter, call and response between brass and wind sections; and a swinging relationship between rhythm and melody. Swing echoed the familiar pattern: a challenge to the status quo, based on approaches and techniques derived from black music; partial absorption into the white mainstream; conflict with the cultural establishment; eventual compromise. In the case of swing, the conflict took the form not of moral or esthetic condemnation but of a turning by some bands to classically-derived techniques and traditions. This process was clearest in the music of Glenn Miller, whose band led the popularity polls in the early 1940s. Miller's trademark was the sonority of his wind section, achieved by using saxophones topped by a clarinet. The discipline and precision needed to realize his sound were equally important, whether the effect was romantic, up-tempo or even improvised. As a result of these processes, the music did not threaten the mainstream; but for all that, when Glenn Miller's music is compared with that of Paul Whiteman, we can see just how far the black influence on white America had advanced.

Like ragtime and jazz before it, swing was first and foremost a music for dancing; and once again that dancing – "jitterbugging" – was derived from black America. It was also much *closer* to black America. Taken to extremes (as they often were) the physical demands of such dancing confirmed the more youthful fans as the principal

▲ With its high levels of energy discharge, the jitterbug provided unprecedented opportunities for inventiveness. Though more abandoned than previous white dances, it still left many blacks unimpressed.

► The powerful, highly organized Erskine Hawkins Orchestra was very popular at black dances, especially in New York. Hawkins based his band's sound on the interplay of brass and reeds as pioneered by Fletcher Henderson and Don Redman. In 1938 the arrival of Count Basie's Orchestra from Kansas City revealed the possibilities on offer when a blues-soaked, riff-based sound was fronted by outstanding soloists.

Broadway Musicals

"Give My Regards to Broadway" – George M. Cohan's 1904 song, in the show *Little Johnny Jones*, already reflected the New York theater district's preeminence in the musical stage. Behind it lay a formidable concentration of money. As Tin Pan Alley was the commercial heart of the popular song industry, Broadway was the financial center of the musical – and the closeness of the two ensured the monopoly. Impresarios vied with each other for control – by the mid-twenties the Shubert brothers were said to own half the available seats on the Great White Way. In such a high-risk business quality product was essential, and producers looked to the most sophisticated songwriters of the day for their material, often linking them with professional librettists wise in the necessary stagecraft.

One result of the musical's increasing maturity was the large output of songs which later became "evergreens". The 1930s stage in particular

yielded a rich crop: *Smoke Gets in Your Eyes* (Jerome Kern/Otto Harbach), *Embraceable You* (George and Ira Gershwin), *I Get a Kick Out Of You* (Cole Porter). But many of these songs were well known only to those who were better educated and more affluent than the average radio "fan". Such songs were often judged to lack the necessary immediate appeal to succeed in the aggressive promotion system and received little radio coverage.

This highly accomplished body of song was the product of a convergence of classically-derived harmony, Afro-American concepts of rhythm, the formal structures of earlier popular song and a solo/accompaniment performance convention. The need for effective drama in the musical had enhanced the status of the lyric, and the best lyricists (Lorenz Hart and Oscar Hammerstein among them) drew on the rhythms, cadences and patterns of American speech in ways which themselves *generated* music.

consumers. Radio music in the home, while still the main source of family entertainment, did not satisfy the social and physical requirements of the new dance craze. By the forties, wartime dance halls, throbbing with life as no fantasy nightspot of the Depression had done, became focal points of activity. The reviving record industry, through its new outlet, the jukebox, also encouraged the consumption of music outside the home.

Records and jukeboxes were gradually increasing the familiarity of both whites and blacks with each other's bands, but the mainstream was still not ready to accept black music on its own terms. Perhaps only Duke Ellington was able to "cross over" without sacrificing the essential nature of his music to commercialism. Dances were still largely segregated. Most were for whites only, and featured white bands. It was rare for a white band to play for a black dance – but then, few white bands could have satisfied the black dancers. In the bands themselves, efforts to increase integration had not made much progress. An important gesture was Goodman's inclusion in his band of black musicians Teddy Wilson and Lionel Hampton, on the prompting of impresario John Hammond. Nevertheless, too many black musicians had been exposed to the trauma of racial insult while performing with white bands for this to kindle any enthusiasm.

▲ Bing Crosby provided the anthem for the poor of 1930s America in a song that derived from a musical.

Datafile

The Depression hit Hollywood in 1931. Sound had protected it from the immediate effects of the crash, but attendances and profits dropped sharply in 1932, and took most of the decade to recover. The war years were the industry's most successful. The eight major companies remained in stable control of the industry, and the type of product was standardized and regulated by the Production Code, written in 1930.

▼ Angels with Dirty Faces was a typical late 1930s major studio production, with one big star, James Cagney, and two lesser ones, Pat O'Brien and Humphrey Bogart. The film's budget of $400,000 had $200,000 added to it for overheads and depreciation.

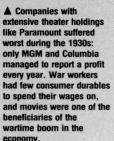

Hollywood profits and box office receipts

Film production budget

Angels with Dirty Faces

- Studio overheads
- Director, producer & production salaries
- Lead – James Cagney
- Other actors
- Sets & studio plant
- Story and writers
- Other costs

▲ Companies with extensive theater holdings like Paramount suffered worst during the 1930s: only MGM and Columbia managed to report a profit every year. War workers had few consumer durables to spend their wages on, and movies were one of the beneficiaries of the wartime boom in the economy.

▼ The Academy of Motion Picture Arts and Sciences was set up by the major Hollywood companies in 1927 to counter attempts to unionize the studios. It became best known, however, for its annual awards, nicknamed Oscars, which became increasingly coveted as badges of success and approval within the industry.

Academy Awards for Best Film of the Year		
1928	Wings	Paramount
1929	The Broadway Melody	MGM
1930	All Quiet on the Western Front	Universal
1931	Cimarron	RKO
1932	Grand Hotel	MGM
1933	Cavalcade	Fox
1934	It Happened One Night	Columbia
1935	Mutiny on the Bounty	MGM
1936	The Great Ziegfeld	MGM
1937	The Life of Emile Zola	Warner
1938	You Can't Take it With You	Columbia
1939	Gone With the Wind	MGM
1940	Rebecca	United Artists
1941	How Green Was My Valley	Fox
1942	Mrs Miniver	MGM
1943	Casablanca	Warner
1944	Going My Way	Paramount
1945	The Lost Weekend	Paramount

▼ Sound sharply increased the average movie budget, and brought about a fall in the numbers of films produced. The Depression brought about a change in American exhibition practice: double-bills became the norm, and independent companies appeared to make the cheap B-feature for the second half of the bill. In Britain production was boosted by low-budget movies, made to meet government requirements about the number of British-made films to be shown in British cinemas.

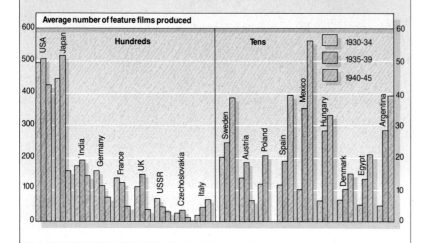

Average number of feature films produced

By the time of the Wall Street Crash in 1929 Hollywood had switched over entirely to "talkies", but even six months later no more than half of the 22,624 movie theaters in the United States had been wired for sound. The conversion cost theaters $300 million, and encouraged a boom mentality that carried the industry over the earliest years of the Depression. The years 1929–31 saw a series of ambitious merger proposals, but the novelty of sound did not have a permanent effect on the box-office and by 1931 the industry was enduring the full rigors of the Depression. Audiences declined. Theaters closed. In 1933, unable to pay their short-term bank debts, RKO and Universal went into receivership, and Paramount was declared bankrupt.

The dominance of the Big Five

These maneuverings of high finance left all the major companies under the control of the largest institutions of American finance capital, but they had relatively little direct effect on the movie-going public. Even during its bankruptcy Paramount promised theater-owners an uninterrupted flow of productions, and underlying the spectacular bids and paper collapses was a gradual process of consolidation. Five companies dominated the industry, maintaining their power by controlling its most profitable sector, first-run exhibition in the cities. As access to this market was vital to the profitability of any but the smallest feature film, this also gave them control of production. Apart from a handful of prestigious independent producers such as Samuel Goldwyn, releasing films through United Artists, the production of big-budget A-features was almost entirely controlled by the "Big Five" – Fox, Paramount, Loew's, RKO and Warner Bros. Smaller firms, including Columbia and Universal, put most of their effort into the production of lower-budget movies, which would play the later-run "neighborhood" theaters as the second or B-feature of a double-bill.

As distributors, the major companies controlled the remainder of the exhibition market by regulating theaters' access to films. By delaying a film's release to cheaper venues and encouraging as many people as possible to see it at a higher-run theater the system maximized distributors' profits. For similar reasons they insisted on selling films in blocks of between five and 50 films; an exhibitor wanting the new Will Rogers or Shirley Temple movie would find himself having to rent half a dozen other less appealing Fox productions in order to get it.

Although the distributors claimed that these arrangements were necessary for them to supply the smaller theaters economically, independent exhibitors continually fought against the majors'

THE STUDIO SYSTEM

control of the movie marketplace. Hollywood publicity concentrated public attention on the glamor of its stars and their purported lifestyles, and on the apparent competition between the studios, but the industry's crucial economic struggles took place between the major companies and the independent exhibitors seeking to break their consolidated power. The Crash, which so publicly discredited big business, gave the independents their best opportunity. The "business of the movies" was conducted very much in the public arena, and their very popularity made the industry particularly vulnerable to criticism of its financial methods as well as its products. For both the film industry's trade association, the Motion Picture Producers and Distributors of America (MPPDA) and its critics in the early years of the Depression, movie morals and the movie business seemed inseparable.

▼ First-run theaters in city centers, such as the Fox Theater in St Louis, kept more than half the money spent on cinema attendance.

Morals at the movies

Few Americans understood the economic causes of the Crash, but there was a widespread view that the Depression was a result not so much of the unstable economic expansion of the Jazz Age as of its hedonism. The movies themselves participated in this anxious reexamination of recent history, but often in a way that rendered them more liable to moral condemnation. Many of their stories of gangsters and "fallen women" were set in the twenties. Stern moral conclusions suggested that the wages of sin seldom bought happy endings, reinforcing a lesson broadcast widely elsewhere; but the movies were accused of representing only too graphically the behavior they claimed to condemn.

Accusations that the movies were subverting the young struck a chord among those looking for moral scapegoats for the Depression. Protestant

The Making of a Gangster Movie

January 1938: Warner Bros announced they had bought Roland Brown's story, *Angels with Dirty Faces*, for $12,500, as one of the three movies starring James Cagney that they would make this year. Head of Production Hal Wallis assigned the film to associate producer Sam Bischoff, who would supervise the film's development through scripting and shooting.

February–March: Studio writers John Wexley and Warren Duff prepared a screenplay, knowing Cagney and Pat O'Brien would star.

April: Production Code Administrator Joseph Breen vetted the script and suggested major changes in its treatment of crime. Because of the success of a recent film starring the *Dead End Kids* Hal Wallis told his writers to include them in the script.

May: Breen approved the final script draft. Other major parts were cast from players under contract to the studio. Art director Robert Haas began designing sets, in consultation with director Michael Curtiz and cameraman Sol Polito.

June: Studio Production Manager Tenny Wright budgeted *Angels With Dirty Faces* at $600,000 – about average for a Warner Bros A–feature. Curtiz, the studio's star director of action pictures, began shooting.

August: Curtiz completed shooting, eight days over schedule and slightly over budget. During shooting, editor Owen Marks had assembled a "rough cut" version of the film for Wallis, who supervised the final cut.

September: Max Steiner's musical score was added. The film was copyrighted and its advertising campaign planned. "Sneak previews" were held to test audience reaction and make final adjustments to the editing.

November: *Angels With Dirty Faces* opened in Warner Bros' premier Los Angeles and New York theaters to enthusiastic reviews and the best business of the year.

church leaders and educational groups grew increasingly vocal in their attacks on the majors' monopoly during the early 1930s, demanding stricter film censorship, enforced by the federal government if necessary. Underlying their concern was the anxiety on the part of the white Protestant elite that their cultural authority, particularly over the immigrant working class, was being surrendered to a mass medium that did not reflect their values and, even worse, was apparently largely owned by "aliens" (a euphemism for Jews).

The industry responded to this pressure by introducing a stricter system of self-regulation in the form of the Production Code. Written in 1930, it was brought into operation with increasing strictness during the following four years, but its implementation failed to keep pace with the ever more vehement demands for a wide-ranging reform of the industry. The extreme popularity of gangster movies, Universal's horror films and Mae West's bawdy comedies increased demands for government supervision of so important a social influence, and provoked repeated charges that the moral guidelines of the Hays Code were a sham and Hays himself only a fixer employed to disguise the industry's misdemeanors. Wide-

spread publicity was given in 1933 to the Payne Fund Studies into the influence of motion pictures on the nation's youth, and it became increasingly evident that some more drastic defense than the code against the threat of legislative control was necessary.

The Legion of Decency campaign launched by the Roman Catholic Church in 1934 provided the industry with an opportunity for a suitably public act of atonement and distracted public attention from more drastic proposals to reform the industry's business practices and break the majors' control over exhibition. In fact the stricter enforcement of the Code after 1934 became an instrument for the preservation of their power. As Hays had long argued, once the "organized industry" demonstrated that it could make morally acceptable movies without federal supervision, it could convincingly assert the general benefits resulting from its monopoly on decency.

To some extent each company, or studio, sought to establish a corporate identity in its productions, but only MGM and Warners really succeeded in imposing a consistent style on their output: MGM by the lavishness of its sets, costumes and lighting, Warners by the frenetic pace at which it told its stories. It was not a coincidence

▶ The MPPDA's Production Code stated: "No picture shall be produced which will lower the moral standards of those who see it. Hence the sympathy of the audience shall never be thrown to the side of crime, wrong-doing, evil or sin. Correct standards of life, subject only to the requirements of drama and entertainment, shall be presented." Reformers argued that the blatant sexuality of stars such as Jean Harlow and Marlene Dietrich and the bawdy wisecracking of Mae West, seen here, did little to promote "correct thinking". What they most feared was that girls would imitate the stars' mannerisms and behavior. As one of Will Hays' advisors put it: "The very man who will guffaw at Mae West's performance as a reminder of the ribald days of his past will resent her effect upon the young, when his daughter imitates the Mae West wiggle before her boyfriends and mouths, 'Come up and see me sometime' ".

that these were the only two studios whose management structure and personnel remained constant throughout the decade. At Warner Bros, the flamboyant Jack Warner ran the studio administration, but the Warners' style was dictated by the studio's head of production, Hal Wallis, and his attention to pacing and detail in editing. The keynote to MGM's lavishness (the opposite of Warners' notorious parsimony) was similarly provided not so much by studio head Louis B. Mayer as by his head of production, Irving Thalberg, whose influence on the studio's style continued to be felt long after his early death in 1936.

With other studios, *aficionados* might notice the *art moderne* emphasis in RKO's set designs (in Van Nest Polglase's sets for the Fred Astaire and Ginger Rogers musicals, for example), or the "European" style of comedy at Paramount, but such consistencies, which came from studios

employing particular writing, camera or design teams, were more likely to be observed by industry professionals than by most of the audience, who were drawn to movies above all by their best-known stars.

With each of the major studios producing more than fifty feature films per year, no company could afford to specialize in any particular genre or type of production. Warners' crime films are remembered for the performances of James Cagney and Edward G. Robinson, but every studio made films about gangsters in the early 1930s, just as each studio had a comedy team spreading harmless anarchy similar to that of the Marx Brothers at Paramount. Musicals and romantic melodramas were also staple products, while most Westerns were B-movies made by small "Poverty Row" companies such as Monogram and Republic.

To provide a comprehensive service to its ex-

▼ Watched by some of the production crew, Fred Astaire and Ginger Rogers dance the Piccolino and (below) "Cheek to Cheek" in *Top Hat*. As well as inaugurating new dance crazes, movie musicals showed their audiences the latest fashions in clothes and decor. Fred and Ginger's dancing was as streamlined as their sets; as they glided across RKO's lavish *art moderne* sets, they were filmed by a mobile camera that followed their every move. Between takes, the scratches had to be removed from the high-gloss bakelite floor.

hibitors, a studio also needed to keep a stable of stars representing each of the most prominent types. Competition between stars was exaggerated by studio publicity and fan magazines, which delighted as much in inventing feuds between female stars of similar appeal ("Now it's Garbo vs. Dietrich", ran one headline) as they did in devising new romantic permutations among Hollywood's leading figures. For dedicated fans, whom the industry presumed were overwhelmingly women, the movie world extended beyond the films themselves into magazines, gossip columns and news stories. Only in Washington were there more reporters than in Hollywood. The studios ensured that their stars stayed as prominently before the public eye as possible, but they were also constantly engaged in private struggles to keep stars powerless to shape their own careers. Actors and actresses were tied to their studio by long-term contracts with harsh

penalty clauses, and only the most popular were able to choose their roles or suggest script changes.

Movies told similar stories over and over again, with minor variations on recurring themes. By far the most persistent story element was romantic love – nine out of every ten movies used it either as the main plot device or in a prominent subplot, while the endless publicity chatter of dalliance among the stars built Hollywood into the "capital of romance". If there was one thing movies traded more energetically than romance, it was "entertainment", a commodity that advertised itself, even during the Depression, as existing outside politics and economics. Movies seldom engaged in direct commentary on current affairs; the commercial failure of films dealing directly with the Depression, such as King Vidor's *Our Daily Bread*, demonstrated industry wisdom that politics was "box-office poison", and even for the pro-Roosevelt Warner Bros overt rhetoric was only rarely included as in the display of the President's face and the New Deal's Blue Eagle symbol in Busby Berkeley's musical finale to *Footlight Parade*. In making films from headline news stories Warners looked more often to the crime and human interest pages of the newspapers for inspiration.

The comedies of Frank Capra, the most successful director of the later 1930s, on the other hand, were populist fantasies of goodwill that explicitly recognized the realities of the Depression, but moved rapidly away from them to propose solutions based on a rediscovery of neighborliness, charity and industriousness. If movies rarely depicted the social and economic realities of the Depression, they did offer a series of psychological parallels in their emotionally heightened accounts of the impact of adversity on families and relationships. In the early years of the Depression, when confidence in the businessman as national hero was at its lowest ebb, there was a notable absence of strong fatherfigures in movies. Without a firm patriarchal presence, it seemed, younger brothers might run riot and become hoboes or gangsters, while wives and daughters could be tempted into worse sins, which might bring on the destruction of the family itself. The chaotic state of movie families reflected the economic chaos and the fears of political chaos in the nation.

The aspect of social instability most closely

▼ Warner Bros musicals were as elaborate but less ethereal than RKO's. Busby Berkeley's troupe of almost identical chorines waving their limbs in synchrony (in *Gold Diggers of 1933*) was among the most dehumanized versions of female sexuality Hollywood produced.

attended to was, not surprisingly, that implied by Hollywood's representation of women. In 1933 the top box-office star in the nation was Mae West, the most frequent target of movie reformers and the extreme, parodic, embodiment of an independent female sexuality. In 1934 she was replaced by four-year-old Shirley Temple – a shift in public values not accounted for simply by the imposition of the Production Code. Temple frequently played an orphan in search of a family, and the discovery or rediscovery of a father was always more important than was the absence of her mother. Temple represented the female as helpless child in need of male protection, and in exchange she offered the boundless resources of love as a form of charity given to the emotionally needy, capable of reuniting or constituting families. The plots of her films conformed to romantic stereotypes in which men were frequently required to prove their emotional or moral worth in order to win her, yet neither producers nor audiences could acknowledge any sexual dimension to Temple's appeal (she and her studio, Twentieth Century–Fox, sued the British novelist Graham Greene for making that suggestion in a review of *Wee Willie Winkie*). The threat posed by West or Jean Harlow was replaced in mid-decade by a representation of women that had rendered their sexuality literally unspeakable.

Elsewhere, in the "screwball" comedies of Capra and others, women, however beautiful, were always zany, unpredictable, irresponsible and in need of an authoritative man who would bring them under control. Almost always this man advertised his responsibility as a middle-class virtue, and in the movies, as elsewhere in the late 1930s, there was a celebration of the culture of the middle classes as being more truly American than any other. Many of the male stars who had risen to prominence in the early 1930s had tended to be easily identifiable in class terms – aristocrats like

▲ Between 1934 and 1938 Shirley Temple's popularity was phenomenal. An industry developed around the promotion of her image as America's perfect child: dolls, coloring books, dresses, and even child beauty parlors. By 1940 older girl-children – Judy Garland, Deanna Durbin – replaced her as the site of Hollywood's fantasies of sexual innocence.

William Powell or urban workers like James Cagney or Edward G. Robinson. The new heroic archetypes of the second half of the decade – Henry Fonda, James Stewart – advertised the virtues of the small-town American middle class in their bearing and manners as well as in the stories in which they appeared.

While the early years of the decade tended to look back only at the events of the immediate past, the later 1930s, in the wave of nationalism which swept a nervous world, witnessed a much more conscious exploration of history for cultural heroes. The search for the roots of American virtue looked to a rural past from which great figures might emerge: the later 1930s saw a wave of books and films relating Abraham Lincoln's journey from log cabin to White House; historical biographies sold in large numbers, and historical fiction celebrating the survival of an American spirit through adversity – such as Margaret Mitchell's *Gone With the Wind* and Walter Edmonds' *Drums Along the Mohawk* – sold even better.

From the mid-1930s onward both the movie industry and other cultural entrepreneurs – such as the publishers of *Reader's Digest* – were finding new ways of marketing works aimed at a culturally aspirant middle class that wanted "European" sophistication without surrendering their small-town virtues of democracy and industriousness. Adaptations of the less intellectually arduous literary classics such as *Little Women* or *A Midsummer Night's Dream* were part of Hays' campaign to persuade the public of the movies' moral virtue. The success of MGM's series of operettas featuring Nelson Eddy and Jeanette Macdonald and Warners' biographies of 19th-century liberal humanitarians showed that by 1935 such films could be sold to a public looking beyond its immediate concerns less for escape than for confirmation that it had survived the Depression with its social and moral rectitude intact.

National Film Traditions

The influence of American culture in other countries was not always welcome. In the 1930s Japan was the most prolific filmmaking country in the world, producing 400 to 600 features a year. Like Hollywood, Japanese cinema had its established genres. The most popular were historical films, swordfight action dramas appealing largely, like Westerns, to male audiences. *Gendai-geki*, films set in modern Japan, included comedies, films about the lower middle class, and home dramas, which dealt with family problems. Like the Japanese, the German and Italian governments restricted the import of foreign films, but they produced their propaganda in newsreels and radio. Their feature films tended instead to express the feeling of their cultures about entertainment, social relationships and individual emotions. Under Mussolini the Italian industry produced far more Italian "pink" films – sentimental comedies and romantic melodramas, – than "black" or truly Fascist films. Similarly, the German film industry produced far more drawing-room comedies and operettas than Nazi propaganda.

◀ The Japanese drama *A Brother and His Sister* (1939).

Nationalism in the cinema

The United States, the largest consumer economy in the world despite the Depression, remained immune to cultural incursions from abroad, and had no difficulty in following a policy of cultural as well as political isolationism. Elsewhere the commercial power of exported American culture, both of Hollywood and of the consumer goods it celebrated and advertised, was regarded as a threat. In response, governments round the world encouraged cultural nationalism in resistance to the invasions of American-dominated international culture.

An example was Italy, where from 1930 the Fascist regime had built up the film industry; in 1937 Mussolini opened the Cinecitta studio complex. Like that of Germany, the Italian propaganda machine used radio and newsreels more overtly than feature films. Under Fascism the Italian industry produced far more "pink" films – sentimental comedies and romantic melodramas – than "black", or truly Fascist films. Italian "white telephone" films, like Hollywood movies, articulated a consensus shared between producers and audiences about entertainment, social relationships and individual emotions. But in common with German drawing-room comedies and operettas and Japanese period dramas and *shomin-geki* (comedies or melodramas of middle-class life), these films expressed that consensus in terms of a specifically national idiom.

The British approach, at least in the important area of documentary filmmaking, was more pragmatic, as the middle-class image offered by the BBC during the 1930s as a "national" culture found its niche. It was documentary filmmakers who exerted the strongest influence on the style

Now in 70 mm. wide screen and full stereophonic sound!

DAVID O. SELZNICK'S PRODUCTION OF MARGARET MITCHELL'S
"GONE WITH THE WIND"

CLARK GABLE
VIVIEN LEIGH
LESLIE HOWARD
OLIVIA de HAVILLAND

Winner of Ten Academy Awards

A SELZNICK INTERNATIONAL PICTURE • VICTOR FLEMING • SIDNEY HOWARD • METRO-GOLDWYN-MAYER INC.
IN 70mm. WIDE SCREEN • STEREOPHONIC SOUND • METROCOLOR

It is worth notice that when we think of Hollywood we tend to think of its worst movie product, or of the typical. But when we think of books or magazines, plays or paintings, we recall only the distinguished; we have forgotten the malodorous. An audience of the gigantic size of Hollywood's means that, unlike book publishers or magazine editors or play producers, Hollywood must appeal to mentalities ranging from six to sixty, from stevedores to seminary students, from barmaids to dowagers. Hollywood is geared to a mass market, yet it cannot employ the methods of mass production. Each picture is a different picture and presents unique demands; those who say that movies are merely variations of Boy meets Girl, Boy loses Girl, Boy gets Girl would not suggest that symphonies are merely rearrangements of the same notes.

LEO ROSTEN, 1940

ERROL FLYNN FRED MacMURRAY

Presented by WARNER BROS.

DIVE BOMBER

IN TECHNICOLOR

▲ The US office of War Information wanted movies like *Dive Bomber* (1941) "to arouse the emotions of the apathetic, and direct the energies of the frustrated into the war effort". Hollywood's version of the war was criticized for its "escapism" and lack of substance; the majority of movies explicitly about the war were espionage stories, reworking classic crime themes by substituting enemy agents for gangsters. However great the espionage threat in movie after movie, the FBI always got their man in time. One critic complained, "They present the war in absurdly romantic terms and their entertainment value is impaired by the conflict in the mind of the audience between the hard facts of real war and its glamorous embellishments on the screen".

of British propaganda. Under the leadership of John Grierson, documentary film practice in Britain during the decade acquired a more clearly articulated esthetic than was the case in the United States, where the dominant force was the *March of Time* newsreels. Grierson, like John Reith a Scots Calvinist critical of "the scarlet women . . . and the high falsehood" of Hollywood, saw documentary as an instrument of education: "We want to see [citizens] given what they are not getting now: a service of information on the immediate needs and services of the state [and] a living sense of what is going on." In practice, with its pervasive images of the conditions produced by the Depression, documentary became the form through which the sympathetic British middle class looked at those worse off.

Nationalist propaganda was latent in the very notion of resistance to American cultural influence, and there was widespread antipathy to Hollywood's "superficiality" among European intellectuals. This did nothing to hinder the emergence of more extreme forms of nationalism. In all the countries of Europe, bourgeois guardians of "traditional national values" linked American and indigenous working-class culture together through their "vulgarity". The appeal of Hollywood to the working classes was taken as evidence of their need for "education" in the superiority of their own traditions. Cultural nationalists throughout the 1930s attempted to restrict the flow of American cultural imports, protested about Hollywood's misrepresentation of their national culture, and sought to create and disseminate a rival cultural idiom. Such attempts were most effective where cultural nationalists exerted most institutional power; in Britain the monopolistic BBC presented its own version of national culture more effectively than the British cinema, which was in economic thrall to Hollywood, while in Japan the film industry, which enjoyed sufficient economic protection as well as cultural distance from American forms, developed genres of its own.

The shadow of war

As the clouds of approaching global war gathered, there began the dissemination in certain countries of propaganda which intensified the cultural nationalism of the decade, although the cultural struggle, for those on all sides, was to remain directed against the American institutions of Hollywood and Madison Avenue, whose presumptuous brashness was unacceptable to the maturer cultures of Europe and Japan.

Allied governments in the late 1930s doubted the likely effectiveness of wartime propaganda, in part because of their expectations of the massive devastation and irreparable destruction of civilian morale which bombing would cause. Few films of the 1930s anticipated the war, since to take an overt political stance would inevitably lead to bans in European markets and loss of revenue. *Things to Come*, a British example, based on the H.G. Wells novel and designed and directed by William Cameron Menzies in 1935, presented some of the few images of the anticipated catastrophe and its streamlined aftermath. However, it spoke more to an anxious paranoia, elsewhere reflected in the panic caused by Orson Welles' 1938 radio broadcast of another H.G. Wells novel, *The War of the Worlds*, than it did to the realities of the Blitz.

The Japanese film industry did deal in military allusion, but proceeded cautiously and projected a strong nationalism. "National policy" films, in

Soviet and Nazi Cinema

Among the nations that would fight World War II, only the Soviets had a cinema dedicated completely to the war effort, with all its production geared "to help in the moral, political and military defeat of Fascism". Such unembarrassed propaganda was possible in the Soviet Union, where the media openly operated as instruments of the state. Audiences recognized the appropriateness of Eisenstein's *Alexander Nevsky* – which depicted the peoples of 13th-century Russia repelling the invading Teutonic Knights – being withdrawn after the signing of the Nazi–Soviet Pact in 1939, and reissued after the German invasion of 1941.

The Nazis confined most of their wartime propaganda to *Die Deutsche Wochenschau*, an extended weekly newsreel. During the early war years newsreels emphasized the speed and power of Blitzkrieg to demoralize potential opponents, as well as boosting morale at home. Some wartime fiction films contained overt propaganda messages and, like other belligerents, the Nazis put history to propaganda service. Postwar investigation suggested that only 20 percent of Nazi feature films were directly propagandist, and took this as confirmation of Goebbels' proclaimed strategy of filling cinemas with entertainment features, and carrying propaganda in the newsreels that accompanied them. Subsequent analysis, however, has been less prepared to make such a clear distinction between propaganda and entertainment – even light-hearted items can be seen as reinforcing the political status quo.

▶▶ Riefenstahl's *Triumph of the Will* (1936).

▶ Leni Riefenstahl directing *Olympia* (1936).

the main avoided glorifying the war, but their representations were nevertheless subject to careful state control: "Do not distort military orders. Do not make light of military matters. Do not exaggerate horror in scenes dealing with war. Avoid scenes of close fighting. Do nothing to lower the morale or destroy the fighting spirit of conscripted men and their families. Avoid scenes of corruption and excessive merriment. Eliminate tendencies toward individualism as expressed in American and European pictures. Develop the Japanese national philosophy, especially the beauty of the peculiarly indigenous family system and the spirit of complete sacrifice for the nation. Because young men and women, especially modern women, are being Occidentalized, re-educate the people through films toward true Japanese emotions. Banish insincere thoughts and words from the screen: deepen the respect toward fathers and elder brothers." (Home Ministry Instructions, 1937–38) . . . "National movies of healthy entertainment value with themes showing persons ready to serve are hoped for. Comedians and vaudeville satirists will be restricted if they overdo their comedy. Films showing industrial and food production, particularly the life in farming villages, should be presented. Scripts will be censored before production, and will be rewritten until they fully satisfy the Censorship Office of the Home Ministry." (Home Ministry Instructions, 1939).

For America, the war, like the movies, was a different proposition. The president and the people shared the perception that British propaganda had persuaded the United States into World War I, and remembered with discomfort the unfulfilled postwar promises of "the war to end all wars". Moreover, this war would be a foreign war, its dangers remote, its sacrifices far less frequent than its temporary inconveniences.

The sleeping giant was stung at last, however, into action, and joined the Allied combatants. Working with the US government's office of War Information (OWI), one of Hollywood's wartime roles was to wake the United States up fully to the end of its period of international isolation.

But in early 1943 *Casablanca*, like many other Hollywood movies, deliberately set out to convince American audiences that World War II had required and did require the nation's committed entry into world affairs. "If it's December 1941 in Casablanca", Humphrey Bogart asks Dooley Wilson, "what time is it in New York? I bet they're asleep in New York. I bet they're asleep all over America.

Bogart's character rehearsed a heroic role constantly reenacted in American culture: the man drawn reluctantly into a conflict he cannot avoid unless he compromises his principles. His renunciation of the character played by Ingrid Bergman completes the pattern in which characters sacrifice their personal desires for a greater cause.

MICKEY MOUSE

Historian Warren Susman has suggested that "Mickey Mouse may be more important to an understanding of the 1930s than Franklin Roosevelt." His creator, Walt Disney, was a fantasist on a grand scale. Dominating American film animation from 1930, Disney built an empire on the periphery of Hollywood. He then built a magical kingdom, Disneyland, and at the time of his death had begun to build a better world in the wilderness of the Florida swamps. His grandiose schemes survived him, because his fantasies of innocence were rooted in commercial reality: whatever else they might signify, his dreams were saleable commodities.

Disney's career in animation began in 1923 with *Alice in Cartoonland*, a series of films mixing cartoons and live action. His most enduring creation was Mickey (originally Mortimer) Mouse, the leading character in the first sound cartoon, *Steamboat Willie*, in 1928. Disney won every Oscar for cartoon shorts from 1932 to 1939, as well as special Academy Awards for creating Mickey and for *Snow White and the Seven Dwarfs*, released in 1937.

The Disney films created an idealized world, out of time and free from responsibility, where the impossible could happen harmlessly and without consequence. There was, nevertheless, an underlying moral order to this world, which would always assert itself at the end of Disney's narratives. Nevertheless, Disney's world of fun and fantasy also contained images of terror and evil: families are separated, and children seldom have their real mothers.

Increasingly the company's output was aimed at "the child in all of us" – more cynically, at the young families of the postwar baby boom. The Disneyland television series began in 1954, and a year later the world's first theme park opened in Anaheim, California, with Mickey as its host. When *Snow White and the Seven Dwarfs* was re-released in 1987, it took $45 million at the American box-office.

▶ The world's most famous mouse, and perhaps the most widely recognized image in the world, Mickey Mouse has for 60 years been a figure of international signficance. The early Mickey, designed by animator Ub Iwerks, was neither really mouse nor human, but always remorselessly cheerful and optimistic. It was a characteristic he shared with all Disney's cartoon creations except the irascible Donald Duck. As the thirties progressed, Mickey acquired a wider emotional repertoire, but became respectable, even bland. The studio needed Donald to provide the anarchy Mickey could no longer supply.

▼ Disneyland, the world's first theme park, might equally have been called Waltopia. Disney said of it, "I don't want the public to see the world they live in while they're in Disneyland, I want them to feel they're in another world."

▶ Mickey in a variety of the guises he had appeared in by the time of his 50th birthday including his first sound role as *Steamboat Willie*, and his costume for the *Sorcerer's Apprentice* sequence of *Fantasia*, Disney's second full-length animated feature.

► Technical innovation – what he would later call "imagineering" – was a prominent component of the Disney operation; in 1932, the studio made the first three-color Technicolor film, *Flowers and Trees*. Later in the decade the studio developed the multiplane camera, which created the effect of depth in the animated image.

► Uncle Walt and Uncle Mickey, the two life-size hosts of Disneyland. Disney's business philosophy, "dream, diversify – and never miss an angle," created the most successful merchandising operations and provided a stable base for the company's other activities, including his most extravagant fantasy, Disney World.

SCIENCE AS THE FINAL FRONTIER

Although life in the 20th century has depended increasingly on the application of the products of scientific research, that activity is too technical and specialized to be appreciated fully by untrained people. Hence what the lay public perceives as science is in fact a mixture of engineering, medicine and magic. This last is not a matter of invoking supernatural agencies; any phenomenon which appears strange or wonderful, however natural its causes, conveys the effect of magic.

In this sense the exploration, or conquest, of space is not merely the last great frontier for humanity; it is an unending source of magic. This can be conveyed in unexpected ways; thus the planetaria, with their projectors resembling gargantuan ants, reproduce the night sky indoors and change its configuration at will. Magic is also reflected in imaginative literature; and here the theme of space travel has dominated "science fiction" from its beginnings at the turn of the century.

The early, primitive attempts at taking the human imagination into space were inevitably the endeavors of visionaries. As in the earlier case of flying, it was the military who provided the resources whereby these visions could become practical realities. Strange and complex bargains could be struck, as between the German rocket specialist Wernher von Braun and first the Nazis and then the Americans. The distinction between space rockets and ballistic missiles carrying hydrogen bombs was a fine one; and hence the dream of the conquest of space turned into the nightmare of Armageddon on Earth. The magic of space was blackened; the suspicion of military motives could never be lifted from this field.

But astronomy has managed to retain its innocence as a source of wonder and edification. When the astronomers and cosmologists argued about the origins of the Universe, or about the first split-second of its existence after the supposed big bang, they still attracted a large public who were not at all deterred by their lack of technical comprehension.

▲▶ The mad scientist, creating a robot capable of simulating a human being but subject to his evil will, has been a recurrent nightmare figure of the 20th century. He appeared in an early but definitive version in Fritz Lang's film *Metropolis* (1926).

▶ The threat from outer space has been domesticated in various ways. The appearance of Halley's Comet in 1910, so often the harbinger of bad tidings, was laughed away as a ghoul from a child's story. By the 1930s comics flourished, in which an intergalactic struggle between good and evil took up imagery once popular in the cowboy genre.

◀ One of the most popular
television science fiction
series has been *Star Trek*,
created in the late 1950s, but
still popular 30 years later.
Here space is used as a
field in which the values of
modern Western man can be
presented as of a genuinely
universal validity — a morality
play for our time. Unlike later
science fiction films, the
gadgetry is of little importance
to the story.

▲ In the 1970s the US space
agency NASA developed its
own vision of life in space in
the future. The fantastic space
stations that were proposed
differed from science fiction
only in that they were officially
sponsored by an organization
that might genuinely aspire to
build them.

◀ The planetarium, as here
at the Adler Planetarium in
Chicago, aims to combine a
genuine educational function
with a large element of
show business. Once the
imagination of a young
audience has been captured
with dreams of the stars, the
future of science is assured.

Datafile

During the 1930s the major spectator sports – soccer, baseball, cricket – won some of their largest audiences. Even the outbreak of war did little to avert enthusiasm for spectator sports in belligerent countries. Sport offered its participants a way out of poverty, gave the spectators an escape from the daily grind, and, through gambling, held out the hope of instant riches for little effort.

The popularity of mass sport, and enthusiasm for international competition, meant that political conflicts could easily spill over into the sporting arena, and the metaphors of sport provided a comprehensible expression of national ideology – whether it be the Aryan myth in Nazi Germany, the British ideal of gentlemanly fair play, or the American vision of equality or opportunity. Even Soviet Russia gave an important role to sport, reorganizing it within trade-union-based sporting societies.

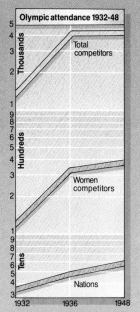
Olympic attendance 1932-48

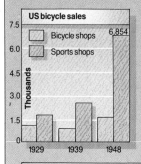
US bicycle sales

◀ **The Depression hit sport less severely than most other industries in the United States. The emphasis on war production, which cut the numbers of cars being built, may have served to promote the sale of bicycles. Similarly, in Britain, sales of bicycles rose sharply during the Depression.**

▲ **The 1936 Berlin Olympics were more successful, in terms of athletes participating, than those held four years previously in Los Angeles. The Los Angeles Games were a lavish extravaganza that made a profit of more than $1 million. The outbreak of war meant that no further Games were held until 1948, in London.**

Year	Winners	Runners-up	Venue
1930	Uruguay	Argentina	Uruguay
1934	Italy	Czechoslovakia	Italy
1938	Italy	Hungary	France
1950	Uruguay	Brazil	Brazil
1954	West Germany	Hungary	Switzerland
1958	Brazil	Sweden	Sweden
1962	Brazil	Czechoslovakia	Chile
1966	England	West Germany	England
1970	Brazil	Italy	Mexico
1974	West Germany	Holland	West Germany
1978	Argentina	Holland	Argentina
1982	Italy	West Germany	Spain
1986	Argentina	West Germany	Mexico
1990	West Germany	Argentina	Italy

World Cup winners 1930–90

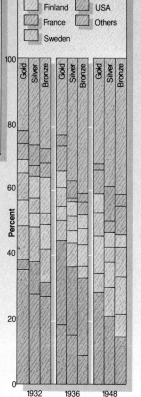
Olympic medals

UK, Italy, Hungary, Germany, Finland, USA, France, Others, Sweden

▲ **The World Cup became Association Football's showpiece competition between the world's top national professional teams. The trophy was named for Jules Rimet, the president of the international football association (FIFA) from 1921. Only 13 countries took part in the first competition, deterred by the difficulty of traveling to Uruguay during the Depression years. The second World Cup, held in Italy, was used by Mussolini as an instrument of Fascist propaganda.**

▶ **The striking success of United States athletes at the Los Angeles Games, and of German athletes at the Berlin Games four years later, initiated the tendency for the host country to achieve disproportionately good results. Games were planned to be held in Finland in 1940, but these were cancelled owing to the outbreak of war. The 1948 Games were held under difficult conditions in war-ravaged London, with minimal preparation time and rationing of many vital materials.**

The Depression left an uneven pattern of poverty and prosperity. Like the rest of the service sector and the mass entertainment industry, spectator sports expanded during the Depression, as those who could afford it grasped the alternative vision of fun and the "good life" that sport provided. In Britain it was the "golden age" of soccer and cricket attendances, and in the United States baseball, football and basketball were flourishing businesses.

Professional football was still organized for the working class rather than by them. Like baseball and other sports, soccer (Association football) provided working-class men and boys with the fantasy of escape from hardship and poverty. By the 1930s it was played almost exclusively by men with working-class origins. Soccer was also used by entrepreneurs to cultivate legalized gambling, institutionalized in the football pools. By the mid-1930s more than sixteen times as many people gambled on football in Britain as watched it, attracted by the potential jackpot win. As early as 1931 there was one pools win of £345,000. By 1938 the annual turnover was close to £40 million.

The football pools' jackpot was one of the dreamlike scenarios sport provided for working-class people in the 1930s. The poverty of the Depression induced people to look to sport to transport them from the ghetto: poor people under capitalism believed that sport, like other forms of popular culture, might change their rags to riches.

In the United States boxing became a route out of poverty for some blacks. Inspired by the supremacy of Joe Louis, world heavyweight champion from 1937 to 1949, blacks began to dominate professional boxing, though prize-winners' purses remained relatively small until after 1945.

Throughout Europe and in North America participation sports remained rigidly class-specific: skiing, climbing, tennis, sailing, yachting and motor-racing remained middle- and upper-class sports. New working-class hobbies and recreations developed as a direct result of unemployment and enforced leisure. An open-air and fitness movement developed, symptomatic attempts to escape from the industrial environment. Working-class people took to cycling, camping, hiking and rambling. The fear of Fascism provoked concern about national fitness and unity through sport, and governments actively encouraged young working-class people to take up sport and exercise. In France the *auberges de jeunesse* expanded under the Popular Front government

SPORT AND NATIONALISM

(1936–39), which encouraged outdoor activities through the Office of Sport and Leisure Time. One historian has even suggested that the most enduring legacy of the French Popular Front "was probably the paid holiday to the sea".

The expansion of women's sport was still slow, but there was some relaxation of attitudes about women's physical abilities and an increasing interest in, and demand for, opportunities to participate. Girls were playing sports in schools, thanks to the development of the women's physical education professions in Europe and North America. In 1930 the Women's League of Health and Beauty was founded in London with 16 members – by 1939 there were 166,000 members, centers in Canada, Australia and New Zealand, and representatives in Hong Kong, Denmark and the United States.

Alternatives to conventional sport

There was still opposition, on both moral and biological grounds, to women competing in vigorous sports. Sports heroines such as the Americans Mildred "Babe" Diedrikson and "the world's fastest woman", Helen Stevens, who disavowed conventional images of femininity, were exploited and ridiculed by the press, who treated them as freaks. Female athletes began to match the attainments of their male counterparts, yet sought to preserve the feminine qualities of their style. There was however, no stigma attached to women's participation in the Workers' Sports

Association, which maintained a philosophy of democracy and openly encouraged female athletes. By 1930 Workers' Sports Associations were flourishing in most parts of Europe and many areas of North and South America and Asia, with a total membership of over four million. Opposed to both national and sexual chauvinism and to elitism in sport, the Workers' Sports Movement was a massive internationalist working-class organization. In 1932 it organized the second Workers' Olympics, which took place in Vienna with over 100,000 competitors from 26 countries. The third Workers' Olympics was scheduled to take place in Barcelona in 1936, in opposition to the Nazi Olympics in Berlin, but the Spanish Civil War began on the morning of the opening ceremony. When they returned home, however, many worker athletes were banned from their national associations, whereas those who took part in the Nazi Olympics were hailed as national heroes.

The Nazi Olympics

The 1936 Olympics were the first Games to be televised, although only to 160,000 people in and around Berlin. They became a stage for the incitement of nationalism and ritualistic struggle of one nation against another. In August 1936, *The Times* editorialized on the "failure" of the British team and the relative success of other countries: only three years after the Berlin Games Britain and Germany were at war again.

▼ Governments were quick to encourage the passion for health and fitness that arose during the 1930s, in response to the enforced leisure of the Depression years. United by sport into huge national teams, men and women could be fit and ready when the struggle over Fascism broke into war. Here a group of hardy swimmers enjoy a midwinter dip in London's Serpentine.

"To the spectators at Berlin, Owens was not only a great athlete – he was athletics."

"Heroic" performance and achievement in sport has fueled the notion that individual merit is more important than national affiliation. The case of the black American athlete Jesse Owens, seen as the perfect counterbalance to Nazi propaganda, argues against this.

The conspicuous success of a black athlete dealt a serious blow to Hitler's philosophy of the natural supremacy of the Aryan race. Outside Nazi Germany, Owens' victories were celebrated as evidence that sport provided a setting for equality of opportunity and an avenue for social mobility. Owens was heralded as symbolic proof of the openness of American culture, in which ability, not color, was the sole criterion for success.

For many people the 1936 Berlin Olympics are regarded, mistakenly, as the first example of the serious intrusion of politics into sport. The Olympic Games of the modern era have consistently offered a platform for national political gesturing in various guises. The Nazi doctrines enshrined

▶ "Babe" Diedrikson was one of the most versatile female athletes in the history of sport. She broke the world javelin record at the age of sixteen. Two years later, in 1932, she competed in eight events in two and a half hours at the US Championships, winning five of them. At the Los Angeles Olympics she won two gold medals and one silver. In 1934 she took up golf; from 1940 to 1954 she was one of the foremost amateur and professional golfers on the women's circuit. She was voted Athlete of the Year five times in a career that included not only athletics and golf but also baseball, basketball, tennis, swimming, diving and billiards.

▲▶ The rhetoric that greeted Owens' Berlin success embodied nationalist sentiments and notions of cultural supremacy. Germany and Japan used sport as a means of national expression and political propaganda with unprecedented success. Germany had a long tradition of state intervention in sport with national scheme of physical fitness designed to promote German unity. In Nazi Germany sport was again contrived to promote and reinforce communal solidarity. The pageants, rallies and festivals of the 1930s were massive extravaganzas, including marching, gymnastics and eurythmics, carefully planned so that the emotional involvement had an intoxicating effect, barely different to the ceremonial of the Olympics. And the Olympic posters reflected Nazi ideas of the super-race.

in the 1936 Games merely presented an extreme version of the Eurocentric roots of most modern sport. Despite international concern about the Games, the official British Olympic Association report on Berlin suggested that there was only one real incident to mar the Games: the withdrawal of the whole Peruvian team following a dispute in the soccer tournament. The writers of the report concluded that the Berlin Olympiad "Was surely one of the greatest sports festivals of all time, having made its magnificent contribution towards a fitter youth and more peaceful international relations."

The diplomatic language of the British report and the optimism of these sentiments presented a familiar paradox: idealist sentiments were being expressed that sport could rise above politics, at a time when sport was undeniably politicized.

International conflict expressed in sport was not limited to the quadrennial Olympic Games. The soccer matches played between England and

Germany in 1935 and 1938 became propaganda events for both sides; the British ambassador to Berlin saw England's victory in 1938 as a triumph for British prestige, not least, apparently, because the England team gave the Nazi salute before the game began. The 1932–33 cricket tour of Australia by the British national team, the Marylebone Cricket Club (MCC) produced its own diplomatic controversy: the so-called "bodyline" series seemed to challenge the essence of the game of cricket. During the Test Match series, the MCC team adopted a particular bowling strategy – one that threatened physical injury – to minimize the effectiveness of the Australian batsman Donald Bradman. The series was almost halted when the strategy was labeled "unsportsmanlike" by the governing body of cricket in Australia, the Australian Board of Control. The MCC captain, Douglas Jardine, and one of the bowlers, Harold Larwood, were castigated for "dangerous" bowling. After diplomatic talks between the two countries, the tour continued but with "undiminished bitterness" and the conflict between the ideals of fair play and the search for effective tactics remained unresolved.

Throughout World War II, cricket at the highest level was encouraged by the British government to boost national morale, although international contacts – as in most other sports – ceased until the return of peace. Similarly, professional football continued, although subject to restrictions on traveling and on the size of the crowds, and occasionally endangered by air raids. In all sports, teams were weakened by players entering the armed forces, but spectator enthusiasm was undiminished.

▲ After his success at the Berlin Olympics, winning gold in the 100m, the 200m, the long jump (seen here) and the 4x1000m relay, black American athlete Jesse Owens' extraordinary talents were exploited for profit: he became a sideshow attraction, racing for money against horses and motorcycles in sleazy hippodromes in Mexico and Reno.

The only things that will produce the class performers is numbers, time and extreme specialization ... But would the production of one 25ft long jumper, one 52ft weight putter, or one 230ft javelin thrower really demonstrate anything of national importance?... The criterion of an Olympic victory must not be exaggerated.

HAROLD ABRAHAMS, 1936

BIOGRAPHIES

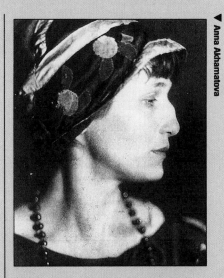

Aalto, Alvar 1898–1976

Finnish architect, city planner and furniture designer. His mature work was informal and personal – with an imaginative use of free forms, indigenous materials and the ability to "fit" buildings to their sites. The Saynatsalo town hall, set in a forest clearing, is his masterpiece. Three commissions undertaken in 1927–28 established his international reputation, especially his use of wood and construction of spatially complex interiors in the library at Viipuri.

Akhmatova, Anna 1889–1966

Russian poet. Writing from 1900, in 1910 Akhmatova, her husband Gumilev, and Mandelstam founded Acmeism, eschewing the Symbolists' fuzzy mysticism for concrete clarity. Her first collection, *Evening* (1912) dealt mostly with the pain of love. After the execution in 1921 of her first husband, she was increasingly oppressed; her son, and later husbands, were interned, and she was banned from publishing from 1923 to 1940, and 1946 to 1956. She remained a prolific poet, acknowledged as great; works like *Poem Without a Hero* (1940–62), dealing powerfully with the dilemma of being a poet in such times, and *Requiem* (1963), exemplify the responsibility she felt of bearing witness to the truth.

Alfvén, Hannes Olof Gösta 1908–

Swedish theoretical physicist. After graduating in physics at the University of Uppsala (1934), he held professorships in the Royal Institute of Technology, Stockholm (1940–73). In 1967 he was appointed visiting professor in the University of California, San Diego. Much of his research was concerned with plasma, neutral gases which contain a high concentration of positive and negative ions in equilibrium. His interest was twofold: in the plasma that exists in the far reaches of the Universe and in the contained artificially produced plasma which is potentially a source of fusion energy, largely free of the radiation hazards of fission processes. In 1942 he predicted that magnetohydrodynamic waves must exist in plasma; the existence of such so-called Alfvén waves was subsequently demonstrated experimentally. In 1970 Alfvén shared the Nobel Prize for Physics with L.E.F. Néel.

Ashton, Frederick 1904–88

British choreographer. After studying dance under Massine, Ashton worked in the Ballet Rambert company (1926–33); Marie Rambert encouraged him as a choreographer; his first piece, *The Tragedy of Fashion*, was produced in 1926. In 1933 Ashton, a fine character dancer and mime, joined the Vic-Wells (later Royal) Ballet, as dancer and principal choreographer. *Symphonic Variations* (1946) is perhaps his masterwork; he choreographed many innovative and popular pieces, including *La Fille*

Mal Gardée (1960), and *Marguerite and Armand* (1963) for Fonteyn and Nureyev. Director of the Royal Ballet (1963–70), from 1970 on, he choreographed exclusively, save the occasional dancing appearance, as in his 1971 film, *Tales of Beatrix Potter*. Ashton brought lyricism and wit to classical dance, and taught dancers how to work with their minds as well as their bodies.

Astaire, Fred 1899–1987

US actor, dancer and choreographer. After a successful stage career with his sister Adele, he turned to films in 1933. His partnership with Ginger Rogers lasted through 10 films, including *Roberta* and *Top Hat* (both 1935), *Swing Time* (1936) and *Carefree* (1938). His sophisticated, yet apparently casual style was based on matchless technique and elaborate rehearsal and preparation. Later partners included Rita Hayworth, Eleanor Powell and Cyd Charisse. He also had a light, charming, singing voice.

Auden, Wystan Hugh 1907–73

British US poet. Auden's first poem was published in 1924. In 1925 he went up to Oxford to read natural sciences; he changed to English, and became leader of the group of poets, influenced by Marx and Freud, who dominated the literary scene in 1930s Britain. He collaborated with Christopher Isherwood on several plays, including *The Ascent of F6* (1936). He visited Spain during the Civil War and China in 1938, and in 1939 emigrated with Isherwood to the USA. He was a guest professor at many US colleges. *The Double Man* (1941), heralds his reconversion to Christianity. Auden published three long poems, *For the Time Being* (1944), *The Sea and The Mirror*, in the same volume, and *The Age of Anxiety*, which won the 1947 Pulitzer Prize, and collaborated with his companion Chester Kallman on libretti, including Stravinsky's *The Rake's Progress* (1951). As a Christian, Auden repudiated many of his earlier leftwing poems. In 1972 he moved back to Oxford. Auden's poetry is by turn cynical, satirical, dogmatic and didactic; he was much admired by later poets such as Joseph Brodsky and Derek Walcott.

Balfour, Arthur 1873–1957

British industrialist. During his early employment by Seebohm and Dieckstahl of Sheffield, sellers of crucible steel, a few years' rewarding experience in the US presaged the activity in overseas trading for which his own firm was later famous. Returning to Sheffield in 1897, in 1899 he became managing director of the company, which, as one of the first two in Sheffield to develop high-speed steel, prospered and became Arthur Balfour and Company, Ltd., in 1915. Balfour served on many committees and councils, and was a British delegate at the League of Nations economic conference in 1927. Chairman of the Industry and

Trade Commission (1924–9) and of the Advisory Council for Scientific and Industrial Research (1937–46), he was also a member of the Economic Advisory Council. A champion of Sheffield and its industry, Balfour also successfully promoted overseas trade in his business and as a national policy. He received several honors, and was created Baron Riverdale of Sheffield in 1935.

Balthus 1908–

French painter. His parents were both painters, and among family friends were Bonnard and Derain, who told him he should paint. He also knew Rilke, who influenced him most, and who published a book of Balthus' drawings in 1921. In 1924 Balthus moved to Paris, and, self-taught, painted childhood themes, explored Impressionism, and then discovered his own style, based on Italian Renaissance painters like Masaccio and on oriental art – *La Rue* (1934) is an example. He had a strong moral vision, and sought, like the Surrealists, profoundly significant subject-matter. Works such as *Nu jouant avec un chat* (1954) and *Japonaise à la table rouge* (1976) demonstrate the tender eroticism found in many of his figure paintings, especially those of pubescent girls; he painted many fine landscapes (see *Bouquet of Roses on a Window Sill*, 1958) and portraits, notably of Derain (1936) and Miró (1938). His sketches reveal a matchless draftsmanship.

Basie, Count 1904–84

US jazz pianist and organist. With Bennie Moten's band from 1929 to 1933, he began forming Kansas City groups, taking with him several fellow members, from 1934. By late 1936 he had moved to New York, gained a record contract and enlarged to a 12-piece. His style relied on a uniquely cohesive rhythm section which functioned like a sextet. Through the forties the line-up changed a lot and the band shrank to an octet, but in 1952 he established a 16-piece and in 1954 made the first of many European tours; his music remained a formative influence on most big bands throughout the 20th century.

Beadle, George Wells 1903–89

US biologist, pioneer of biochemical genetics. After graduating in 1925 he did postdoctoral work on maize genetics at Cornell before working (1935) on the genetics of eye color in the fruit fly. As professor of biology at Stanford University (1937–46) he collaborated with the microbiologist E.L. Tatum in research on the biochemical genetics of the bread fungus *Neurospora crassa*, using X-rays to produce mutations. Tests on these led to formulation of the "one gene/one enzyme" concept, which postulates that the role of a gene is to control synthesis of a specific enzyme. In 1958 Beadle and Tatum shared a Nobel prize with J. Lederberg, pioneer of bacterial genetics.

▲ Léon Blum

▲ Jorge Luis Borges

▲ Wernher von Braun

Beaton, Cecil 1904–80

British photographer and stage designer. His decorative portraits of celebrities were his most important work. He worked as a staff photographer on *Vogue* and *Vanity Fair* in the twenties and continued his portrait work, using elaborate backgrounds that subordinated the sitter to an overall pattern. He was a war photographer in World War II. Many of his portraits are published in *The Book of Beauty*, *Persona Grata* and *It Gives Me Great Pleasure*.

Bergman, Ingrid 1915–82

Swedish film actress. Her radiant vitality brought rapid success in Swedish films and in 1939 she went to Hollywood. She was enormously popular until 1949 when her private life shattered the wholesome image her studio had pushed hard. It was 1956 before America welcomed her back in *Anastasia*. Credits include *Casablanca* and *For Whom the Bell Tolls* (both 1943), *Gaslight* (1944), *Notorious* (1946), *Joan of Arc* (1948), *Murder on the Orient Express* (1974) and *Autumn Sonata* (1978).

Berkeley, Busby 1895–1976

US choreographer and film director. One of Broadway's leading dance directors, his film break came when Warners hired him to choreograph *42nd Street* (1933). Lavish, erotic, vulgar, his set-pieces for massed girls delighted audiences, and his inventive camera shots – from above, below, diagonal or traveling – and rhythmical cutting multiplied the pleasure. Credits include *The Gold Diggers of 1933*, *Fashions of 1934* and *Dames* (1934).

Berlin, Irving 1888–1989

US song writer. In a long career which spanned the jazz age through to the fifties, he wrote over 800 songs. Graduating from street singer and singing waiter to song plugger, he began writing lyrics and later his own music. He wrote for Broadway revues, musical comedies – his most popular was *Annie Get Your Gun* (1946) – and the film scores for his stage successes, notably *Top Hat* (1935), *Easter Parade* (1948) and *Call Me Madam* (1953). Among his standards are *Alexander's Ragtime Band*, *God Bless America*, *There's No Business Like Show Business* and *White Christmas*.

Bethe, Hans Albrecht 1906–

German-US physicist, noted for contributions to the theory of nuclear reactions and the production of energy in stars. After graduating in physics at the Universities of Frankfurt and Munich, he did research work in Frankfurt, Stuttgart, Cambridge and Rome. In 1932 he was appointed assistant professor at Tübingen, but in 1933, when the Nazis came to power, he left for England, working in Manchester and Bristol. In 1935 he moved to Cornell University in the USA, where he remained

as professor of theoretical physics. During the war he was seconded to the Radiation Laboratory of MIT, to work on microwave radar, and to Los Alamos to work on the atomic bomb project. His main research was concerned with nuclear reactions, developing Bohr's theory of the compound nucleus. This interest led him to consider the source of stellar energy and he concluded that this is basically the result of the condensation of four hydrogen nuclei to form one helium nucleus, with emission of fusion energy. With R.A. Alpher and G. Gamow he formulated in 1948 a theory of the distribution of the chemical elements consistent with the "big bang" theory of the origin of the Universe and the abundance of helium in it. In 1967 Bethe was awarded the Nobel Prize for Physics.

Blum, Léon 1872–1950

French prime minister. In 1919, Blum was elected to parliament as a Socialist. He rebuilt the party after the 1920 split with the Communists, and came to power in 1936 as head of the Popular Front coalition. France's first Socialist premier, he introduced radical measures, including a 40-hour week, paid holidays and collective bargaining and the nationalization of the Bank of France and the defense industries. Preparations for war against Germany were begun, but a policy of nonintervention in the Spanish Civil War alienated Communist coalition members. Blum resigned in 1937, after he had been refused emergency powers to deal with economic problems. He served again as prime minister for a brief period in 1938. He was arrested in 1940 and tried in 1942 by the Vichy government on charges of neglecting France's interests, but defended himself so effectively that the trial was abandoned. He was then imprisoned in a concentration camp from 1943 to 1945. Returning to politics after the war, in 1946 he secured a US loan for the reconstruction of France. In the same year he briefly headed a caretaker government, and was vice-premier for a short time in 1948. He then became France's chief representative to UNESCO.

Bonhoeffer, Dietrich 1906–45

German Protestant theologian. In 1931 Bonhoeffer was appointed to a lectureship at the University of Berlin. From 1933 he became a leading Protestant critic of the Nazi regime, and worked in the resistance movement. As an active member of the conspiracy against Hitler in 1943 he was arrested, imprisoned and hanged in 1945. Bonhoeffer's work influenced both ecclesiastics and academics and he has been admired for his willingness to confront controversial issues. In *The Cost Of Disciplesihp* (1937) he attacked "cheap grace", that which costs nothing in sacrifice to its followers, in the belief that real grace and the suffering it involves gives truth to life. His best known book, *Letters and*

Papers From Prison (1972) calls for a "religionless" Christianity which should be aimed at the mature modern man and reject the traditional religious predispositions. It also advocated a Christianity directed at man not in weakness but rather when he is strong. These views have subsequently given rise to much debate.

Borges, Jorge Luis 1899–1986

Argentinean writer. A lover of English language and literature from childhood, he traveled Europe from 1914 to 1921, encountering the Spanish *Grupo Ultra*, who believed in "pure" poetry, not dependent on context. He later judged his first three collections too Ultraist, but they contain the metaphysical games and questions of time and identity which characterize his mature work. From 1925 Borges wrote pieces for a Sunday newspaper, and magazine stories. He was becoming more and more blind. In 1946 Perón dismissed him from his librarianship, but in 1959 he was restored, and made Director of the National Library until 1973. Borges's stories were jewel-like in their clarity and vision, as in *Fictions* (1944) and *The Aleph and other Stories* (1949).

Bourke-White, Margaret 1906–71

US photographer. One of the first to create photo essays, she became an industrial and architectural photographer in 1927. By 1929 she had been snapped up for *Fortune*. In 1936 she was one of the first four staff photographers on the new *Life* magazine and covered World War II. Thereafter her assignments included the partition of India, unrest in South Africa and the Korean War.

Bradman, Don 1908–

Australian cricketer. The greatest batsman ever, he set an unequaled Test record with an average of 99.94 runs per innings. His perfect eye and timing were acquired early. He scored 334 runs in a Test innings in 1930, during his first English tour, a record which no Australian has equaled, and he scored 19 Test centuries against England from 1928 to 1948. In later years he was involved with cricket administration in Australia.

Braun, Wernher von 1912–77

German-US pioneer of rocket propulsion. After studying engineering in Zurich and Berlin, he began rocket research for the German army in 1932, initially with solid fuel propellant but within two years using liquid fuel. In 1938 he was appointed technical director of the German rocket research establishment at Peenemünde on the Baltic. He there developed the highly destructive V2 rockets. Afterward he and his team surrendered to the American forces. He then played a leading role in the American space program which ultimately succeeded in landing men on the Moon. He resigned from NASA in 1972.

Butenandt, Adolf Frederick Johann 1903–

German biochemist. After studying at Marburg and Göttingen, he was professor of organic chemistry in Danzig before being appointed director (1936–72) of the Kaiser Wilhelm Institute for Biochemistry, Berlin-Dahlem (postwar, Max Planck Institute for Biochemistry, Munich). His research was mainly on the chemistry of sex hormones. He isolated oestrone in 1929 and androsterone in 1931, followed by progesterone in 1934. Later he worked on insect hormones, including ecdysone, which controls the molting process. He also did research on the physiologically extremely active sex attractants of insects, the pheromones. He was awarded a Nobel prize in 1939 but the German government forbade him to accept it.

Calder, Alexander 1898–1976

US sculptor. A graduate in mechanical engineering, and a fine draftsman, Calder's first job was illustrating the National Police Gazette. He produced, over a period around 1926, when he visited Paris, a *Circus*, of small figures made of miscellaneous materials, like used corks. He also made portraits out of wire, and exhibited them in 1927 in New York. In 1931 he moved to Paris, where he began to produce the seminal hanging thin, flat shapes, which Duchamp named "mobiles". Through these, Calder gained international fame, winning the 1952 Venice Biennale Sculpture Prize. Calder's sense of play was paramount; he never called himself an artist, but his work touched millions.

Camus, Albert 1913–60

French writer. Son of an Algerian farmworker and a charwoman, Camus' academic career – he read philosophy – was arrested by TB. In 1936 he wrote: "People think only in images. If you want to be a philosopher, write novels." *L'Etranger* (1942) followed by *Le Mythe de Sisyphe*, brought him instant fame. Camus joined the Resistance in 1942, editing its journal. *La Peste* (1947) uses a plague-stricken Algerian town as an analogy of occupied France. Camus quarreled with Sartre after denouncing Communism in *L'Homme Révolté* (1951). He also rejected Christianity; but *La Chute* (1956), reveals a painful self-doubt with comic irony. Camus' writing was in the Absurd tradition, pinpointing the futility of life in view of death; he also celebrates intense pleasure of living – and he ratifies the Absurd paradox with the possibility of a nobility of spirit, a stubborn creativity which seems either blind, or immune, to circumstance.

Cardenas, Lazuro 1895–1970

Mexican politician and social reformer. Cardenas rose to the rank of general in the Mexican revolutionary army before becoming governor of his native Michoacan (1928–32). He was

instrumental in forming the Partido Nacionál Revolucionário (1929), of which he became chairman. As president of Mexico (1934–40) he was known for his introduction of social reforms. He inaugurated a successful six-year plan of agrarian reforms to distribute land to the peasants, establish credit systems and form communal village holdings (*ejidos*). He also extended education, established confederations to prepresent both peasants and workers, and nationalized foreign-owned industries, most notably oil properties. Stepping down as president in 1940, he continued in public and political life but with diminishing influence.

Carnegie, Dale 1888–1955

United States author and teacher of public speaking. An active member of debating clubs at school and college, Carnegie became a salesman and an actor before he began to teach public speaking at the YMCA. A successful response and large attendances led to the publication of pamphlets, eventually collected in book form in *Public Speaking: A Practical Course for Business Men* (1926). The publication of *Little Known Facts About Well Known People* (1934) led to a radio series of the same name, but his most successful book was *How to Win Friends and Influence People* (1936). In this Carnegie presented common-sense advice for overcoming handicaps in order to become successful, emphasizing the importance of a positive attitude. He achieved great popularity in a success-orientated American society.

Carothers, Wallace Hume 1896–1937

US industrial chemist. In 1928 he became head of the organic chemistry department of the giant chemicals company Du Pont. Charged with investigating substances of high molecular weight, he produced neoprene (1932), one of the first satisfactory synthetic rubbers. He then proceeded to study the fiber-forming properties of polymers based on esters and amides. Finding the first unpromising, he concentrated on polyamides. This experimentation led to the discovery of nylon, a highly successful synthetic fiber first marketed in 1938, the year after Carothers' suicide. This development was to revolutionize technology and social artifacts.

Chadwick, James 1891–1974

British physicist. A Manchester University physics graduate, he continued there to do research on radioactivity under Ernest Rutherford. In 1913 a scholarship took him to the Technische Hochschule, Berlin, to work with H.W. Geiger. There he was interned for the duration of the war. Afterward he rejoined Rutherford, now director of the Cavendish Laboratory, Cambridge; Chadwick was appointed assistant director in 1923. In 1932 he proved the existence of the neutron, a hitherto

unknown particle with approximately the mass of a proton but without charge. He was professor of physics at Liverpool University (1935–48) and was closely involved in the British contribution to the development of the atomic bomb.

Chain, Ernst Boris 1906–79

German-born biochemist. Chain, a Jew, emigrated to England in 1933, after graduating in Berlin. After working briefly in Cambridge, he joined Florey in Oxford in 1935. He worked for a time on the antibacterial enzyme lysozyme, and then in 1939 embarked on a joint project with Florey to make a general study of the antagonisms between microorganisms. Fortuitously, this included penicillin, abandoned by Fleming, its discoverer. By May 1940 its unique properties had been demonstrated. After the war Chain became director of the International Research Center for Chemical Microbiology in Rome (1948–61). In 1954 he became associated with the Beecham Group and collaborated with them in developing a range of semisynthetic penicillins. In 1961 he returned to England as professor of biochemistry at Imperial College, London (1961–73). In 1945 he had shared a Nobel prize with Fleming and Florey.

Chamberlain, Neville 1869–1940

British prime minister. Director general of national service in 1916 and 1917, in 1918 Chamberlain was elected to parliament as a Conservative. He served as Postmaster General (1922–23), Paymaster General (1923), health minister (1923, 1924–29, 1931), Chancellor of the Exchequer (1923–24, 1931–37), and finally prime minister (1937–40). As a minister he introduced social reforms, but his premiership was largely concerned with foreign policy. He ceded control of naval bases in Eire, pursued a policy of nonintervention in the Spanish Civil War, and one of appeasement towards the Axis nations. He dropped the sanctions which had been introduced against Italy after its occupation of Ethiopia, and in 1938 approved at Munich the German occupation of western Czechoslovakia, meanwhile increasing the pace of British rearmament. In 1939, Hitler occupied all of Czechoslovakia, and Chamberlain reversed his policy. He introduced conscription, and promised armed assistance to Poland, Romania and Greece. He declared war on Germany in 1939. After the British defeat in the 1940 Norwegian campaign, Chamberlain resigned. He then joined Churchill's cabinet, as Lord President of the Council.

Chevalier, Maurice 1888–1972

French entertainer and actor. He specialized in Gallic roguery: charm, swagger and joie de vivre. Partnering Mistinguett at the *Folies-Bergère* in 1909 was his break and after 1918 he starred on the halls, earning international fame. His Hollywood career began in 1929, and he won popularity in

romantic comedies like *The Love Parade* (1929), *One Hour with You* and *Love Me Tonight* (both 1932). Filming in Europe from 1935 to the late fifties, he returned to entertaining, but made a brilliantly successful Hollywood comeback in *Gigi* (1958).

Christie, Agatha 1890–1976

British detective novelist. Her international popularity was based on ingenious plotting, the brilliant use of suspense and misdirection and an excellent ear for dialog. Her chief detectives are Hercule Poirot and Miss Marple, and she wrote 67 novels, among them *The Murder of Roger Ackroyd* (1926), *Murder on the Orient Express* (1934) and *Ten Little Niggers* (1939). She also wrote several plays (including the long-running *Mousetrap*, 1952), six pseudonymous novels and an autobiography.

Churchill, Winston 1874–1965

British prime minister. After a period as a soldier and war correspondent, Churchill entered parliament as a Conservative in 1900. In 1904 he broke away over tariff reform to join the opposition Liberal party, and in 1906 was appointed Colonies Undersecretary, going on to become President of the Board of Trade in 1908 and Home Secretary in 1910. In 1911 he moved to the Admiralty, but resigned in 1915 after the failure of the Dardanelles expedition. Elected to parliament as an Independent in 1916, he served as munitions minister during 1917 and 1918. He rejoined the Conservative party in 1924, and was involved in breaking the General Strike of 1926. He was war secretary (1918–21), colonial secretary (1921–22), and Chancellor of the Exchequer (1924–29). As a backbencher from 1929 to 1939 he campaigned against Indian independence and constantly warned against the appeasement of Nazi Germany. Returning to the Admiralty in 1939, he became prime minister in 1940. During World War II Churchill's outstanding leadership qualities, oratorical skills and determination rallied and inspired the British people. He worked tirelessly to forge closer wartime alliances between Britain, the United States and the Soviet Union, holding meetings with both Roosevelt and Stalin. After the war he campaigned vigorously against Soviet power. Surprisingly defeated in the 1945 postwar election, he was reelected in 1951 at the age of 77, and resigned in 1955.

Cockcroft, John Douglas 1897–1967

British physicist. After a year at Manchester University, and war service, he read mathematics at Cambridge. In 1924 he joined Rutherford's team of atomic physicists at the Cavendish Laboratory. It was there that, with Walton, he succeeded in splitting atoms of lithium and boron by bombardment with protons (1932). For this they were jointly awarded a Nobel prize in 1951. Later he was associated with the development of radar

and other aspects of air defense, concurrently serving as Jacksonian Professor of Natural Philosophy at Cambridge (1939–46). After the war he was successively director of the Canadian Atomic Energy Commission (1944–46); director of the UK Atomic Energy Research Establishment, Harwell (1946–58); and master of Churchill College, Cambridge (1959–67).

Cooper, Gary 1901–61

US film actor. One of Hollywood's most popular stars, his laconic style and lanky looks appealed to men and women: he was the strong, silent man of adventure and romance. He went to California with hopes of a career in cartooning and drifted into extra work in 1925. His break came quickly, as replacement second lead in *The Winning of Barbara Worth* (1926). In the thirties Capra and Hawks extended his range into comedy. Credits include *The Virginian* (1929), *A Farewell to Arms* (1932), *Mr Deeds Goes to Town* (1936) and *High Noon* (1952).

Coward, Noel 1899–1973

British actor, director, librettist and playwright. He was an excellent actor, taking the lead in many of his plays, memorably *The Vortex* (1924) and *Private Lives* (1930). His comedies won admirers and detractors in the twenties and thirties: sophisticated, technically brilliant and frequently defying moral convention. *Hay Fever* (1925) and *Blithe Spirit* (1941) are among his most accomplished works. In 1942 he wrote, produced, co-directed and starred in the wartime sea drama *In Which We Serve*.

Crawford, Joan 1904–77

US film actress. She was the most durable Hollywood star. Not particularly pretty or sexy, she had glamor; no brilliant actress, she worked hard. Mostly she was ambitious and adaptable: a flapper to rival Bow in the twenties; working girl in the thirties; melodramatist in the forties; mature femme fatale in the fifties; and horror star in the sixties. Credits include *Our Dancing Daughters* (1928), *The Women* (1939), *Mildred Pierce* (1945), *Johnny Guitar* (1954) and *Whatever Happened to Baby Jane?* (1962).

Crosby, Bing 1904–77

US vocalist. Signed by Paul Whiteman in 1927 as one of the Rhythm Boys, it was with the trio's booking at the Coconut Grove that his solo career took off. A nationwide CBS hookup in 1931 caused him to lose his voice and find fame: his unique sound was attributed to nodules on the vocal cords. The relaxed, casual style was much imitated. He made many films – musical romances in the thirties, "Road" movies in the forties and later took some dramatic roles. With over 2600 records released (among them 22 million-sellers), by 1975 he had sold over 400 million discs.

Dam, Carl Peter Henrik 1895–1976

Danish biochemist. He graduated in the Copenhagen Polytechnic Institute in 1920 and, after training in veterinary medicine and teaching in the Institute's School of Agriculture and Veterinary Medicine, became a lecturer in the Physiological Laboratory of Copenhagen University. He worked in the Institute of Biochemistry (1929–41) and spent several years lecturing and doing research in the USA before returning in 1946 to become professor of biochemistry at the Polytechnic. At the time of the invasion of Denmark he was in the USA: he returned to Denmark in 1956 to join the Danish Fat Research Institute. In 1929 he had observed that chicks on low-fat diets develop hemorrhages and their blood fails to clot normally. At first he thought that this was a form of scurvy, but later he identified it with a then unknown vitamin which he called Vitamin K (Ger.=*Koagulation*). This he showed to be present in many plants and also in certain animal organs, notably the liver, and valuable in reducing bleeding or preventing hemorrhage. Although he prepared highly active concentrates of Vitamin K, he failed to isolate it in pure form. This was achieved in 1939 by the American biochemist E. Doisy, with whom he shared a Nobel prize in 1943.

de Valera, Eamon 1882–1975

Founder and prime minister of Eire (Republic of Ireland). In 1916 de Valera was a commander of the Irish Volunteers in the unsuccessful Easter Rising in Dublin, and was imprisoned until 1917, when he was elected president of the separatist party Sinn Fein ("We ourselves"). He was voted into parliament at the 1918 elections when Sinn Fein won three-quarters of the Irish seats, but was then imprisoned again. He escaped to the United States and in 1919 was elected president of the Irish Republic. Returning to Ireland toward the end of the Anglo-Irish War of 1919–21, he unsuccessfully opposed the partition of Ireland, and created a self-governing dominion of the British Empire in the south. In the ensuing civil war (1922–23), he fought for the Republicans against the Free Staters, who, on coming to power, imprisoned him. Released in 1924, he broke away from Sinn Fein, and in 1926 founded the alternative republican party Fianna Fail ("Soldiers of destiny"), and reentered the Dail. Head of government in 1932, he refused to pay land annuities to Britain, and started an economic war that lasted until 1938. In 1937 he created the state of Eire, and claimed sovereignty over all Ireland. In 1939, he outlawed the Irish Republican Army (IRA). During World War II he remained neutral. He was defeated in the 1948 elections, when a coalition renamed the state the Republic of Ireland. He was prime minister again from 1951 to 1954 and from 1957 to 1959, and president from 1959 to 1973.

▲ Babe Didrikson

▲ Duke Ellington

▲ William Faulkner

Didrikson (Zaharias), Babe 1914–56

US sportswoman. She excelled in basketball, baseball, softball, swimming, figure skating, track and field events and as a golfer. A member of the women's All-America basketball team in 1930–1, in the 1932 Olympics she won gold medals in the 80m hurdles and javelin. From 1934 she concentrated on golf, winning the US Women's Amateur in 1946 and 17 championships in 1947, including the British Ladies' Amateur, the first American to do so. Turning professional for the second time in 1948, she earned more than any other woman golfer in 1948–51, taking the US Women's Open in 1948, 1950 and 1954.

Dietrich, Marlene 1901–92

German-born film actress and entertainer. Joseph von Sternberg's *The Blue Angel* (1930) brought prominence. Signed to Paramount, she made six of her first seven films with Sternberg, most notably *Shanghai Express* (1932) and *The Scarlet Empress* (1934), indulgent pieces with her as a sexual icon, alluring in fur and feathers or drag. In 1935 the partnership ended, and her best later work was with Borzage, Lubitsch, Wilder and Lang.

Disney, Walt 1901–66

US film animator, producer and executive. In 1928, with Ub Iwerks, his artist-collaborator, he created Mickey Mouse. Other characters followed – Minnie Mouse, Donald Duck, Goofy and Pluto – and the *Silly Symphony* series, matching action to pre-recorded sound. A leader in the technical field, he was using Technicolor by the mid-thirties, developed a multiplane camera which improved perspective and action shots, and produced the first feature-length cartoon, *Snow White and the Seven Dwarfs*, in 1937. In 1950 he made his first pure live-action film, *Treasure Island*. In 1954 he opened the Disneyland park in California.

Domagk, Gerhard 1895–1964

German industrial chemist, discoverer of the sulfonamide drugs. A graduate, in medicine, from the University of Kiel, he worked first as a pathologist. In 1927 he became director of research in experimental pathology and bacteriology in the new company I.G. Farbenindustrie, seeking chemical agents capable of destroying infective bacteria within the body. In 1932 he discovered that Prontosil Red, a dye developed by I.G., could control streptococcal infections in mice. This was published in 1935, and it was soon discovered elsewhere that the antibacterial activity resided not in the whole molecule but in a moiety known as sulfanilamide. As this had been known of since 1908 (although its antibacterial activity was unsuspected) I.G. were unable to patent the discovery. The Nazis would not let him accept the 1939 Nobel Prize; in 1947 he received it.

Dorsey, Tommy 1905–56

US jazz bandleader and trombonist. Work with, among others, Paul Whiteman preceded the shortlived Dorsey Brothers orchestra, formed with Jimmy Dorsey (1934). He took over Joe Haymes's band, buying star talent throughout the thirties. An ambitious perfectionist, he created a versatile, disciplined swing orchestra, and made a series of hits, including *I'm Getting Sentimental Over You* and *The Sunny Side of the Street*.

Eames, Charles 1907–78

US designer and architect. His most famous work is a series of molded plywood chairs created in the thirties and forties, some of them with Eero Saarinen. Exhibited successfully at New York's Museum of Modern Art in 1946, his plywood chairs were later mass-produced by the Herman Miller Furniture Co. Subsequent designs used plastic reinforced with glass-fiber and wire mesh.

Egas Moniz, Antonio 1874–1955

Portuguese neurologist, statesman, and founder of modern psychosurgery. Appointed to the newly created chair of neurology at the University of Lisbon (1911–44), Egas Moniz introduced and developed cerebral angiography. This involved injecting dyes that were opaque to X-rays into the arteries in order to make the blood vessels of the brain visible, a technique used in the diagnosis of brain tumors. He devised prefrontal leukotomy (1935), the severing of the nerve fibres between the prefrontal lobes in order to relieve severe emotional tension in psychiatric patients. Egas Moniz advocated it only as a last resort. He received the Nobel Prize for Physiology or Medicine (1949). He was also a successful politician during and after World War I.

Ellington, Duke 1899–1974

US jazz composer, arranger and pianist. With his embryonic sextet, The Washingtons, formed in 1924, his extraordinary career took off. Using ten (later most commonly 15) pieces, he appeared at New York's Cotton Club, toured regularly in the USA and worldwide. No one else has been creatively involved in so many stages of jazz development. He wrote extended pieces and simple ballads, and his song-writing had the universality to produce numerous standards.

Faulkner, William 1897–1962

US novelist. Mississippi-born Faulkner traveled the world early, but remained a Southern writer. After the publication of a book of poems, he met Sherwood Anderson, and turned to fiction with *Soldier's Pay* (1926). His most productive years, 1929–36, saw the issue of his first stream-of-consciousness novel *The Sound and the Fury*, the superb *As I Lay Dying* and *Light in August*, and *Sanctuary* (1931), which shocked the public and brought him fame. As a Hollywood script-writer until the 1950s, he scripted *The Big Sleep* (1946) among other films; his reputation declined during this time, until winning the 1950 Nobel Prize revived it. Faulkner was a brilliant innovator, playing with narrative time and using multiple perspective. His influence has been far-reaching.

Fermi, Enrico 1901–54

Italian-US physicist. After graduating at Pisa, he did postgraduate research in Germany and Holland, returning to Italy to be professor of theoretical physics in Rome (1927). There his brilliant papers established for him an international reputation. In 1938 he was awarded a Nobel prize and left Fascist Italy for Columbia University, New York. There he built an atomic pile in 1941, but it was too small to become self-sustaining. He then moved with his research group to Chicago and there, on 2 December 1942, set in train a self-sustained atomic reaction that could be started and stopped at will: the Atomic Age had begun. From 1943 he took part in the Manhattan Project for the production of atomic bombs. After the war he resumed his research at Chicago, working mainly on radioactivity.

Ferrari, Enzo 1898–1988

Italian automobile manufacturer. A test driver in 1919, he joined Alfa Romeo in 1920, racing for them until he formed an agency in 1929, which from 1930 to 1932 was in reality Alfa's works team. In 1939 he set up a company to make racing cars, but war halted production. His first postwar cars were racers, one forming the basis of his earliest road car, the 166 Inter (1947). The successful 250 Europa series (1954) suggested a commitment to road cars, but his heart was in racing and that has shaped the company's technical and commercial development ever since.

Fitzgerald, Ella 1918–

US jazz vocalist. For 45 years America's greatest interpreter of popular song, she is best known for the songbook recordings of Gershwin, Mercer, Kern, Porter, Berlin and Ellington she began in the late fifties. High-speed scat improvizations on numbers like *Lady Be Good* and *Flying Home* were equally brilliant. She sang with Chick Webb's band from the mid-thirties, leading for two years before going solo in 1941. From the forties her international reputation grew as she honed an increasingly cabaret-style performance.

Florey, Howard Walter 1898–1968

Australian-born physician. After qualifying in Adelaide in 1921 he went to Oxford as a Rhodes Scholar and then held a succession of medical appointments in Britain, finally as professor of pathology in Oxford (1934–62) subsequently becoming provost of The Queen's College, Oxford.

▼ Howard Walter Florey

▼ Francisco Franco

▼ Martha Graham

Early in his career Florey took an interest in the antibacterial enzyme lysozyme, discovered by Fleming in 1922. This led him in 1939 to undertake, with E.B. Chain, a general study of antimicrobial substances. Fortuitously, one of those they selected was penicillin. By May 1940 the unique chemotherapeutic properties of this substance had been demonstrated, but manufacture in wartime Britain was impossible. With his colleague N.G. Heatley he went to the USA and was instrumental in getting government agencies and industrial firms to launch a crash program to produce penicillin for all military casualties. In 1943 he went to North Africa to demonstrate the use of penicillin to army doctors there. He shared a Nobel prize with Fleming and Chain in 1945 and was president of the Royal Society (1960–65). He became a Life Peer in 1965.

Ford, John 1895–1973
US film director. An instinctive artist, his work has a folk quality, the Westerns in particular demonstrating a nostalgia for America's past which draws on evocative musical scoring and images of men within landscape. A director since 1917, two silents merit attention: *The Iron Horse* (1924) – the film that inspired a new wave of popular Westerns – and *Four Sons* (1928). His reputation rests on films such as *The Lost Patrol* (1934), *Stagecoach* (1939), *The Grapes of Wrath* (1940), *How Green Was My Valley* (1941), *They Were Expendable* (1945), *My Darling Clementine* (1946), *She Wore a Yellow Ribbon* (1949), *The Quiet Man* (1952), *The Searchers* (1956) and *The Man Who Shot Liberty Valance* (1962).

Franco, Francisco 1892–1975
Spanish dictator. An army officer, in 1927 Franco was appointed head of the military academy at Zaragoza. In 1931, the monarchy was replaced with a republic, and Franco was successively appointed to posts in the Balearic Islands and Morocco. In 1933 the center-right came to power, and in 1935 Franco became the army's chief of staff. However, after the radical Popular Front had gained a majority in 1936, he was demoted and posted to the Canary Islands. Anticipating revolt, he went to Morocco, from where he launched an attack on Spain; this was the beginning of the Civil War. He obtained aid from the Fascist governments of Italy and Germany, and was declared commander-in-chief and head of state. In 1937 the Falange and Carlist parties were merged, creating the State party, and in 1939 the republicans were finally defeated. A single-party state was established, and a short time later, Spain joined the anti-Comintern pact. Franco remained neutral in World War II, although he was openly sympathetic to the Axis nations. Afterwards the West at first ostracized, then gradually rehabilitated Spain as the Cold War progressed. In 1947 the monarchy was restored, with Franco as

effective regent. In 1953, he permitted the establishment of US bases on Spanish soil in return for economic aid, and in 1955, Spain obtained membership of the United Nations Organization. Economic problems improved, and the country became more liberal, although there was some unrest. In 1969 Franco named Prince Juan Carlos as his successor. He resigned as premier in 1975, remaining party leader, head of state and commander-in-chief.

Gable, Clark 1901–60
US film actor. His name spelt sex appeal – he was a man's man and a woman's dreamboat. The thirties were his great decade: his third wife's death (1942), active service in World War II and age seemed to take the edge off later work. Signed by MGM in 1931, he played mostly brutes and gangsters, in films like *Possessed* (1931) and *Red Dust* (1932), before *It Happened One Night* (1934) softened the image. *Gone With the Wind* (1939) brought his most important role, but his best performance was his last: *The Misfits* (1961).

Garbo, Greta 1905–90
Swedish film actress. The protegée of Mauritz Stiller, she was part of the deal when he signed with MGM. Her first film, *The Torrent* (1926), took them and the public by storm. Among her other silents, those made with John Gilbert did particularly well, and after sound her greatest roles were *Queen Christina* (1933) and *Camille* (1936). She retired in 1941. She always protected her private life jealously.

Goebbels, P. Joseph 1897–1945
Nazi politician. Goebbels joined the Nazi party in 1925, and became head of the Berlin branch in 1926. In 1929 he was made responsible for party propaganda and in 1930 elected to the Reichstag. He was heavily involved in the Nazis' rise to power, and in 1933 was made government minister for propaganda. He controlled the media and used his position to justify policies like the persecution of the Jews. In 1944 he aroused the public appetite for war, and became minister for total war. He committed suicide in 1945.

Goldmark, Peter Carl 1906–77
Hungarian-US physicist. A physics graduate from the University of Vienna, in 1944 he became director of engineering research and development for CBS, and its vice-president in 1956. In 1940 he produced the first practicable color television system. However, this was a photomechanical system and proved not to lie on the main line of development. He therefore turned to all-electronic systems and in 1946 received the Zworykin Award for the development and utilization of electronic television. In 1948 he invented the long-playing (LP) microgroove record.

Göring, Hermann 1893–1946
German industrialist and Nazi leader. Göring met Hitler and joined the Nazi party in 1922. He fled Germany after the unsuccessful Munich putsch in 1923, returning in 1927, when he cultivated contacts in German industry, and re-established contact with Hitler. Elected to the Reichstag in 1928, he became its president in 1932. In 1933 he became interior minister for Prussia, organizing the local Gestapo and establishing concentration camps. Rapidly promoted in the Nazi party, by 1935 he was Commander of the Luftwaffe and the most important man in Germany after Hitler. In 1936 he was made minister of economic affairs and became responsible for the four-year plan of the war economy, directing industry and re-arming Germany. From 1937 onwards he amassed a large fortune through the Reichwerke- Hermann Göring, the state-owned giant mining and industrial enterprise created by Hitler. In 1939 he chaired the Council for the Defense of the Reich, playing a major role in the preparation for war, and was named as Hitler's successor. In 1940 he took control of economic policy. During World War II he became very rich by plundering Jewish communities. His fall from grace began after the Luftwaffe's defeat in the Battle of Britain of 1940, and ended in his expulsion from the Nazi party in 1945. After Hitler's suicide Göring surrendered to the Americans, was found guilty of war crimes at Nuremberg but poisoned himself two hours before he was due to be executed.

Graham, Martha 1894–1991
US choreographer and founder of "modern dance". Graham attended the Denishawn dance school, where she explored ethnic and primitive dance. Her dance debut was in 1920. In 1923 she joined the Greenwich Village Follies and from 1924 taught dance, and began to choreograph. Her social and feminist conscience showed in her work, such as *Revolt* (1927). As a performer, Graham was intense, graceful, and dramatic. In 1929 she founded her own school and company; the members were all women, until 1938. She has created a dance form which is disciplined, but radically different from classical ballet – the spine is flexible, movement comes from the solar plexus, gravity is an ally, "floorwork" is important, and the "contraction" of the body, in and back, at the solar plexus, is a basic element. Graham's technique is taught widely, and companies like the London Contemporary Dance Company are based on it. In content, Graham explored myth, ethnic and ancient dance, but with vigor and certainty, as in *Appalachian Spring* (1944), *Cave of the Heart* (1946), and *Clytemnestra* (1958). Fusion of dance and design, and three-dimensional sets, are central. She also used Japanese mime and Absurd themes.

▲ Haile Selassie

▲ Jean Harlow

▲ Barbara Hepworth

Granit, Ragnar Arthur 1900–91

Swedish neurophysiologist. He graduated in medicine at Helsinki University, Finland and was appointed professor of physiology there in 1937. In 1940 he moved to Stockholm as professor of neurophysiology (declining an invitation from Harvard) and subsequently became director of the department of neurophysiology in the Medical Nobel Institute (1945–47). Early in his career he became interested in the visual process, approaching its study initially through psychology, but soon turning to physiology. Using electro-physiological methods he demonstrated that the retina contains three different types of cones differentiated by their spectral sensitivity. From 1947 he turned his attention to the different nerves serving the muscular system and their relationship to the spinal cord. In 1967 he shared a Nobel prize with two other pioneers in the physiology of vision, H.K. Hartline and G. Wald.

Haile Selassie 1892–1975

Ethiopian emperor. A member of the Ethiopian nobility, in 1916 he was instrumental in deposing Lij Yasu; when Zaudita became empress in 1917 he was regent and heir apparent. A progressive, in 1923 he gained membership for Ethiopia of the League of Nations. He became king in 1928, and emperor in 1930, taking the name Haile Selassie. In 1931 he introduced a new constitution, concentrating power in himself and making parliament redundant. In pursuit of centralization, he strengthened the police and abolished feudal taxation. After Italy invaded Ethiopia in 1935, Haile Selassie went into exile in 1936, addressing the League of Nations conference in the same year. In 1941, Ethiopia was liberated with British assistance, and he resumed his position. He westernized Ethiopia, and extended educational facilities. Internationally, he aligned himself with the United States, and in 1963 was a founder member of the Organization for African Unity. He was deposed by a military coup in 1974, after mismanagement during the previous year's famine, and eventually replaced by a Marxist, Major Mengistu.

Hansson, Per Albin 1885–1946

Swedish Social Democratic politician and prime minister. Joined the Social Democratic Youth Association in 1903 and edited its newspaper, *Fram* (1905–09). He joined the Social Democratic party (SPD), and in 1918 was elected to the Riksdag (parliament) serving as minister for defense (1918–26). In 1925 Hansson became leader of the party, campaigning successfully for lower military expenditure but opposing total disarmament. He served on the government's Public Debt Commission (1929–32). In 1932 he became prime minister and formed a coalition with the Agrarian party which allowed him to pass legislation covering such areas as public works construction, agricultural support, pensions, unemployment insurance, financial expansion and tax to finance these programs. His measures were largely successful. Wages recovered by 1936 and unemployment had fallen sharply by 1939. The growing European crisis after 1936 caused Hansson to expand Sweden's defenses and to reject a nonaggression pact with Germany. He formed a coalition government after war broke out and maintained Sweden's neutrality. Hansson formed his last SPD government in 1945.

Harlow, Jean 1911–37

American film actress. Born Harlean Carpenter, she eloped from her native Kansas City with a millionaire at the age of 16 and became a film extra in Hollywood. Frank Capra's *Platinum Blonde* in 1932 established her as the archetypal Blonde Bombshell of that decade; brassy, wise-cracking, ineluctably female. After a brief period playing the "man's woman" opposite Clark Gable in films such as *Red Dust* (1932) and *China Seas* (1935), she died of a cerebral edema at the age of 26.

Hart, Lorenz 1895–1943

US song lyricist. During his 25-year collaboration with Richard Rodgers, they produced about 1000 songs. Among them are *My Heart Stood Still* (1927), *With a Song in My Heart* (1929), *Lover* (1933), *Blue Moon* (1934), *My Funny Valentine* (1937), *Falling in Love with Love* (1938) and *Bewitched, Bothered and Bewildered* (1940). In contrast to Rodgers, his attitude towards work remained that of the determined non-professional, but his lyrics were as well crafted as serious poetry.

Hawks, Howard 1896–1977

US film director, screenwriter and producer. A professional craftsman and untricksy storyteller, involved in every aspect of his films and working in every genre, he made some of Hollywood's best films. Credits include *Scarface* (1932), *Bringing Up Baby* (1938), *Ball of Fire* (1942), *The Big Sleep* (1946), *Red River* (1948), *Gentlemen Prefer Blondes* (1953) and *Rio Bravo* (1959).

Hayek, Friedrich August von 1899–1992

Austrian economist. Studied law, psychology and economics at the University of Vienna, then at New York University (1923–4). He was the first director of the Austrian Institute for Economic Science (1927). From 1931 to 1950 he was Tooke Professor at the London School of Economics. In *Price and Production* (1931) Hayek argued that in a boom rising prices cause a fall in real wages and increased capital investment in equipment to replace labor. As the demand for capital goods rises faster than supply, interest rates rise, investment falls and the economy turns down. The converse occurs in a slump. This directly opposed the Keynesian viewpoint. Involved in the major economic debates during the 1930s concerning monetary, business cycle and capital theories, he also argued against government intervention in modern economies, as politically undesirable and ultimately ineffective. After the war he took up psychology and social, political and legal philosophy, holding professorships at Chicago (1950), Freiburg (1962), and Salzburg (1969). Awarded the Nobel Prize for Economics (1974), he continued publishing in the 1980s.

Hepworth, Barbara 1903–75

British sculptor. Hepworth studied sculpture in London and Italy (1920–26), meeting Henry Moore, who was to be a close friend for 20 years. Working in a classical style, she exhibited first in 1928 with her first husband, the sculptor John Skeaping. In 1931 she produced *Pierced Form*, the first work in which she explored interior and exterior space by piercing. In 1933 she joined the Abstraction-Création group and Unit One; she was now developing space with the use of strings and of color. By 1935 her work was fully abstract. In 1944, inspired by the Cornish landscape she had made her home, she produced *The Wave*, a beautifully shaped hollow ovoid. The Greek landscape inspired her to such works as *Curved Form (Dolphin)* (1955). By now internationally known, she started bronze casting. In 1963 she made *Single Form* as the UN Dag Hammarskjold Memorial, in New York. Always moved by landscape, especially in relation to human figures, Hepworth, in the tradition of Brancusi, was a mistress of forms, organic and abstract, always making manifest a spiritual essence.

Hicks, John Richard 1904–89

British economist. Graduated from Oxford (1925), lectured at the London School of Economics (1926–35), became a fellow of Cambridge University (1935–8) and then took up a professorship at Manchester University (1938). In 1946 he moved to a fellowship at Nuffield College, Oxford, becoming professor in 1952 and retiring in 1965. Knighted in 1964, he was joint winner (with Kenneth Arrow) of the Nobel Prize for Economics in 1972. His major works include *A Reconsideration of the Theory of Value* (1934) which introduced an indifference theory to explain consumer behavior as opposed to the traditional marginal utility theory. His celebrated IS-LM analysis appearing in *Mr Keynes and the "Classics"* (1937), was Hicks's method of illustrating why Keynes differed from the "Classical" economists in his approach. This innovative apparatus is now an established means of purveying economic arguments and its versatility is such that differences between Keynesian and monetarist policies may be explained by differing interpretations within the IS-LM framework.

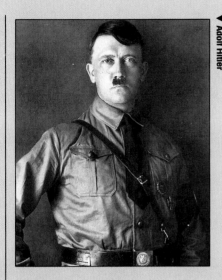
▲ Adolf Hitler

▲ Dorothy Hodgkin

▲ Howard Hughes

Himmler, Heinrich 1900–45

German politician. Himmler joined the Nazi party in 1923, and in 1928 became its deputy propaganda officer. In 1929 he took charge of the SS, originally Hitler's bodyguard, which by 1933 numbered 50,000. After Hitler came to power in 1933, Himmler was appointed head of the Gestapo (secret police) in Bavaria, and by 1934 he controlled the organization nationwide. In the same year, he drew up a list of Hitler's opponents in the SA (stormtroopers) and had them murdered by the SS. From 1936 he commanded all police forces. Using the SS and the Gestapo, he set up 17 concentration and extermination camps. In 1943 during World War II, he became minister of the interior, and in 1944 head of the German home forces and effective second in command. Toward the end of the war, Himmler, believing Hitler was lost, secretly proposed surrender to the Allies. Captured, he committed suicide before he was identified.

Hitler, Adolf 1889–1945

Austrian-born dictator and leader of Germany. By 1920 Hitler had come to dominate the German Workers' party, which he re-christened the National Socialist German Workers' (Nazi) party, becoming its leader in 1921. In 1923 he inspired their unsuccessful coup in Munich. Although in 1932 he failed to win the presidency of the Weimar Republic from Hindenburg, in 1933 he became chancellor. When the Reichstag burned down, the Communists were falsely blamed and soon afterwards Hitler assumed dictatorial powers. He ordered the establishment of the Gestapo (secret police) and concentration camps for political opponents. A magnetic orator, he preached a doctrine of German racial supremacy, and blamed Germany's problems on the Jews, who were ruthlessly persecuted, most until they died in extermination camps. He rebuilt the armed forces, leading to economic recovery and raised morale. In 1934, he had potential enemies in the SA (storm-troopers) massacred, and in the same year he succeeded Hindenburg and took the title *Führer*. He then set about the complete restoration of national pride by avenging the Treaty of Versailles. In 1936, Germany occupied the demilitarized Rhineland, and made a pact with Italy, and in 1937, with Japan. In 1938, Hitler's troops invaded Austria, and occupied German-populated areas of Czechoslovakia. Hitler declared that he had no more territorial ambitions, but then occupied the rest of Czechoslovakia, and, after signing a nonaggression pact with Stalin, invaded Poland, bringing Britain and France into the war. In 1940, he invaded Denmark, Holland, Norway, Belgium and France, and reached the peak of his popularity in Germany. In 1941, Germany attacked the British in North Africa, supporting Mussolini, and turned on Russia, reaching, but not taking, Moscow. In 1942,

Rommel's forces invaded Egypt but lost to Montgomery at El Alamein, and during 1942–43 the Allies drove them out of Africa. On the Eastern front, the Russians began gradually to repulse Hitler's troops. By 1944, members of the military had begun to plot against Hitler, and tried to kill him. Germany was now invaded from both sides, and on 30 April 1945, Hitler committed suicide.

Hodgkin, Dorothy Mary Crowfoot 1910–

British chemist, distinguished for elucidating the structure of large biological molecules. After studying chemistry at Oxford (1928–32), she spent two years at Cambridge working wth J.D. Bernal on the structure of sterols. In 1934 she returned to Oxford to work in the sub- department of crystallography, eventually as Wolfson research professor (1960–77). In 1941 she began an investigation, with the aid of X-ray crystallography, of the structure of penicillin, then the subject of intensive research in Oxford. Progress was slow because computational methods were then very laborious but a complete structural analysis was completed in 1945, confirming a result achieved by purely chemical methods. In 1956 she and her group elucidated the structure of vitamin B12. Now assisted by computer technology, in 1972 she announced the structure of insulin. In 1964 she received the Nobel Prize for Chemistry.

Holiday, Billie 1915–59

US jazz vocalist and composer. The greatest jazz singer of the thirties, her small, bell-like voice was ecstatic, sensual and vulnerable. She first recorded with Benny Goodman, hitting real form with Buck Clayton, Lester Young and Teddy Wilson in 1935. Segregationism on tour for the Glaser organization (1935–39) forced her to go solo but heroin devoured her talent and she ceased to trust her audiences. By 1952 (two cures on) she was working the clubs and recording again; public interest in her life kept the career alive till 1957 but heroin finally killed her.

Hoover, Herbert Clark 1874–1964

Republican US president. He studied mining engineering and his subsequent career in mining involved traveling around the world and amassing great wealth. In 1914, Hoover was appointed head of Allied Relief in London, and head of the Commission for Relief in Belgium. He served as secretary of commerce under Harding and Coolidge. As chairman both of the Colorado River commission and of the St Lawrence Waterways commission, he brought about the construction of the Hoover Dam and the St Lawrence Seaway. In 1928 Hoover was elected president, entering the White House at a time of great prosperity. However, he soon had to face the "Great Depression". He failed to cope with this crisis, believing the slump to be temporary and mistakenly adhering to accepted

economic strategy. Federal expenditure on public works was restrained to avoid a budget deficit. In addition, no effective system of hardship relief was developed, owing to his belief in the responsibility of regional governments and private charities. As the Depression spread to Europe Hoover postponed international debt payments in 1931 and established the Reconstruction Finance Corporation, though he still refused to undertake a major program of public works, or to give direct relief to the unemployed. The presidential election of 1932 brought a decisive defeat by Franklin D. Roosevelt. After World War II, Hoover was involved in famine-relief work in Europe.

Hope, Bob 1903–

British-born film actor and entertainer. Fast gags and topical wisecracks brought success on film, TV specials and worldwide tours, making him possibly the richest ever entertainer. He began in vaudeville, and became a radio star. His film break came in *The Big Broadcast* of 1938, and *The Cat and the Canary* (1939) was his first hit. The hugely popular "Road" series, with Crosby and Lamour, began in 1940. Of the rest, *The Paleface* (1948), probably rates best.

Hopper, Edward 1882–1967

US painter. After studying under Robert Henri at the New York School of Art, Hopper visited Europe three times (1906–10), without absorbing any influence. He was a commercial artist until his first one-man show in 1920. His style did not change throughout his life, and epitomized, especially, small-town and rural America. He used dramatic but mellow lighting effects, and large, solid masses – see *House by the Railroad* (1925). His work also conveys a sense of human loneliness, as in *Nighthawks* (1942), in which the figures seemed as estranged from one another as from the architecture that dwarfs them.

Hughes, Howard 1905–76

US millionaire, businessman, film producer and director, and aviator. He inherited his father's tool company at the age of 18 and two years later moved to Hollywood, producing films such as *Hells Angels* (1930) and *Scarface* (1932). Hughes left Hollywood suddenly in 1932 to work as a pilot, then formed the Hughes Aircraft Company and turned to designing, building and flying aircraft. Between 1935 and 1938 he broke most of the world's air speed records. He abruptly returned to Hollywood, producing his best- known film *The Outlaw* in 1943. He built a large business empire including RKO Picture Corporation, and continued his involvement in aviation, designing for and controlling Trans World Airlines. In 1950 he became a recluse and controlled his vast business interests from secluded hotel rooms.

Jiang Jieshi ▲

Pyotr Kapitsa ▲

Gene Kelly with Judy Garland ▲

Jansky, Karl Guthe 1905–50

US physicist, pioneer of radio astronomy. He graduated in physics at Wisconsin in 1928 and then joined Bell Telephone. One of his assignments was to investigate the sources of the "static" which interferes with short-wave radio reception. Using a directional aerial he identified one constant source as lying in the direction of Sagittarius and suggested in 1932 that this corresponded with some source of radio emission in that constellation. Surprisingly – for the use of radio waves could be useful in astronomy because, unlike light, they penetrate interstellar dust – this observation aroused little interest. For all practical purposes radio astronomy is a postwar field of research. However, Jansky's name is commemorated in the international unit used to measure the power received at a radio telescope from a cosmic source.

Jiang Jieshi 1887–1975

Chinese politician, leader of the Nationalist party, and soldier. Jiang fought in the overthrow of the Manchu dynasty, and then during 1913–16 against the would-be dictator, President Yuan Shikai. In 1918, he associated himself with the Nationalists (Guomindang), and in 1925, took control of the Nationalist Army. In collaboration with the Communist Party in 1926 he undertook a campaign against the Northern Warlords, achieving victory in 1928 by taking Beijing. Jiang then headed a new government at Nanjing. Meanwhile, in 1927, he purged the party of leftwingers, and began a civil war against the Communists which was suspended only during 1937–46 to make common cause against the Japanese. By 1946, the party was riddled with corruption and the army demoralized, and in 1949, Jiang was finally defeated by the Red Army of China. He fled to Taiwan (then Formosa), and formed a government in exile. He at first enjoyed US support, and so was able to begin the modernization of Taiwan's economy, but relations cooled with the rapprochement between China and the US in the 1970s.

Johnson, Amy 1903–41

British airwoman. She became interested in flying while working as a secretary in London. She caught the public imagination when, with no long-distance experience, she made an unsuccessful attempt to break the record for a light-aeroplane solo flight to Australia in May 1930; her time to Karachi (6 days) was a record. Later she established other flight records, including Siberia to Tokyo (1931); London to Cape Town (1932); and London to the Cape return (1936).

Kapitsa, Pyotr Leonidovich 1894–1984

Russian physicist. He graduated in electrical engineering in 1918 at Petrograd (Leningrad) Polytechnic and in 1921, sent by the Soviet

government to buy scientific equipment, went to the Cavendish Laboratory, Cambridge, where he remained for 13 years and worked with Rutherford. He investigated the electrical properties of metals in high magnetic fields and at very low temperatures, showing much experimental ingenuity in achieving both conditions. He discovered the phenomenon of superfluidity (complete loss of viscosity) in liquid helium. In 1934 he visited the USSR and was forbidden to return to Cambridge, though the Soviet government negotiated a deal with the Cavendish to enable his equipment to be sent to Moscow. During the war he worked on the mass production of oxygen for steel-making. This brought him into conflict with the notorious Beria, head of the KGB. He was dismissed, but later rehabilitated, and did important research in high-temperature physics (plasma) and lightning. Very belatedly, at the age of 84, he was awarded a Nobel prize for his valuable early research on extremely low temperatures.

Kelly, Gene 1912–

US dancer, actor, choreographer and director. Master of an athletic, spontaneous style, he succeeded Astaire as Hollywood's leading dancer and as a choreographer revitalized film dance. He worked his way to Broadway, starred in *Pal Joey* (1940) and choreographed a Broadway show (1941) before his screen debut in 1942. His first outing as choreographer came in *Cover Girl* (1944); other star/choreo roles include *Anchors Aweigh* (1945), *On the Town* (1949), *An American in Paris* (1951) and *Singin' in the Rain* (1952); for the two latter he was director as well as star.

Keynes, John Maynard 1883–1946

English economist. A Cambridge graduate, he became a member of the "Bloomsbury Group" and lecturer in economics. Treasury advisor in both World Wars, Keynes attended the Paris Peace Conference but resigned, voicing his strong opposition to the draft treaty in *Economic Consequences of the Peace* (1919). He became the leading critic of established economic theory and strongly attacked Churchill's restoration of the gold standard in 1925. The Depression inspired his two great works, *A Treatise on Money* (1930) and *General Theory of Unemployment, Interest and Money* (1936). He argued that full employment was not a natural condition but could be achieved by adopting a cheap money policy and undertaking a program of public investment. His views on a planned economy influenced Roosevelt's New Deal administration. In 1943, he proposed an international clearing union, and, as chief British delegate in the Bretton Woods Agreements, played an important part in the establishment of the International Monetary Fund and the postwar global economy.

Kolff, Willem Johan 1911–

Dutch physician. With a small group of colleagues he succeeded, despite the German occupation of the Netherlands, in devising in 1944 a machine that would take over the function of the kidneys. In this, blood was circulated through a cellophane tube immersed in a water-bath. Toxic constituents of the blood diffused out into the water, while protein and blood cells were returned to the patient's body. The machine could provide only temporary relief while damaged kidneys recovered. It was, nevertheless, the prototype of the dialysis machines of the 1960s by which patients with renal defects could remain active indefinitely with the help of regular dialysis.

Krebs, Hans Adolf 1900–81

German biochemist, notable for his elucidation of metabolic pathways. After studying at several German universities, as was then customary, he graduated in medicine at Hamburg in 1925 and then worked under Otto Warburg in Berlin (1925–30) and at Freiburg. With the rise of the Nazis (1933) he emigrated to England, working first under F. Gowland Hopkins at Cambridge, then at Sheffield and finally (1954) as professor of biochemistry in Oxford. Throughout his career the chemistry of metabolic processes had a particular fascination for him, especially those concerned with the utilization of energy. He is remembered for three main developments. First, the synthesis of urea in the liver. Second, the tricarboxylic acid cycle for the oxidation of pyruvic acid to carbon dioxide and water: this is now generally known as the Krebs Cycle. Third, in association with Hans Kornberg, the glyoxalate cycle, important in fat metabolism. In 1953 he shared a Nobel prize with Fritz Lippmann.

Kuznets, Simon 1901–85

US economist. Born in Russia, he emigrated in 1922 to the US where he received his PhD in economics from Columbia University in 1926. Employed at the National Bureau of Economic Research (1927–61), he began studying national income, which led to his comparative study of economic growth in different countries. Kuznets was also professor of economics at the University of Pennsylvania (1930–54), Johns Hopkins University (1954–60) and Harvard University (1960–71). He was elected president of the American Statistical Association (1949) and the American Economics Association (1954) and in 1971 received the Nobel Prize for Economics. One of his major contributions to economics was the recognition of cycles in economic growth (Kuznets cycles). His investigation for differing periods in the US revealed cycles of 15–20 years duration. Kuznets also demonstrated the inverse relationship between national income per capita and the degree of inequality in the distribution of income.

▲ John Maynard Keynes

▲ Hans Adolf Krebs

▲ Vivien Leigh

Laval, Pierre 1883–1945

French politician. Laval joined the Socialist party in 1903, and in 1914 was elected to the Chamber of Deputies. He advocated compromise in World War I, and so lost his seat in 1919. He left the party in 1920, and began to move gradually to the right. Elected a deputy in 1924 and to the Senate as an independent in 1926, he served in four ministerial posts, and finally, in 1931, as prime minister. He lost the premiership a short time later, but regained it in 1935. He fell from power in 1936, after attempting to appease Mussolini with the Hoare-Laval pact, by which Abyssinia would have been partitioned. He helped to create the Vichy government after the fall of France, and in 1940 became its foreign minister. He was dismissed by Pétain in the same year, however, after the discovery of a plan to take power himself. In 1942, the Germans forcibly installed Laval as effective head of government, and he pursued a policy of open collaboration. In 1944 he fled to Spain, but in 1945 on his return to France was convicted of treason and executed.

Lawrence, Ernest Orlando 1901–58

US physicist. After gaining his doctorate at Yale in 1925 he was on the staff of the University of California, latterly (1936–58) as director of the Radiation Laboratory. A.S. Eddington's suggestion that nuclear reactions might occur within stars at very high energies led Lawrence to explore the possibility of effecting nuclear reactions with high-energy particles generated in the laboratory. With M.S. Livingston he conceived the idea of achieving a very long path within a manageable space by repeatedly accelerating particles along a circular path. This machine they called a cyclotron, and with it a number of radioactive isotopes were prepared. Later a number of synthetic elements were prepared in his Laboratory. In 1961, after his death, element 103 was detected and named Lawrencium (Lw) in his honor. He was awarded a Nobel prize in 1939.

Leigh, Vivien 1913–67

British actress. She was an extraordinarily beautiful woman whose career was largely dominated by her relationship with Laurence Olivier: in the late forties and early fifties they were British theater's leading couple. In films she had her greatest successes in *Gone With the Wind* (1939) and *A Streetcar Named Desire* (1951), the former being her first Hollywood role, the latter revealing previously unseen depth.

Lewis, John Llewellyn 1880–1969

US trade unionist. A coal miner from the age of 15, he rose to become president of the United Mine Workers of America (UMWA) from 1920 to his retirement in 1960. A ruthless leader, he expelled many of his opponents. Lewis built the UMWA

into a large, united force. In 1935 he established and became president of the Committee for Industrial Organization (CIO). The CIO expelled by the ATL became the most powerful labor union in the world. Initially a supporter of Roosevelt, Lewis clashed with the president, and when Roosevelt won the 1940 elections, Lewis resigned as president of the CIO, but continued to lead war-time strikes, contributing to a wave of antilabor legislation. Postwar strikes, at a time when Europe was desperately short of coal, led to the establishment of miners' pension funds but also the federal seizure of the mines. A subsequent strike against the government defied a court order and led to heavy fines for Lewis and his union.

Litvinov, Maksim Maksimovich 1876–1951

Soviet politician. Litvinov joined the Russian Social Democratic Labor party in 1898, and was exiled to Siberia in 1901. He escaped in 1902, and eventually settled in England. In 1903 he sided with the Bolsheviks, and after the October Revolution of 1917, he became Soviet representative in London. He was not formally recognized in this role by the British, and a short time later he was arrested and deported to the Soviet Union, in exchange for the freedom of a British diplomat. In 1921 he was appointed deputy commissar for foreign affairs. In 1924, he gained recognition of the Soviet Union from Britain, and in 1928 signed the Kellogg-Briand pact, condemning the use of force to settle international disputes. He also spoke strongly in favor of disarmament at the preparatory commission of the League of Nations' World Disarmament Conference (1927–30). In 1931, Litvinov became commissar for foreign affairs. He was chief Soviet representative at the World Disarmament Conference (1932) in Geneva, and in 1933 led the Soviet delegation to the World Economic Conference in London. In 1934, he gained official recognition from the US and brought the Soviet Union into the League of Nations. From 1934 to 1938, he campaigned for the military isolation of Germany and Japan, and concluded pacts with France and Czechoslovakia. He was dismissed in 1939, and the Hitler-Stalin nonaggression treaty was signed. Litvinov was rehabilitated after the German invasion, and served as ambassador to the United States during 1941–43. He then became the Soviet deputy commissar for foreign affairs, and retired in 1946.

Loewy, Raymond 1893–1986

French-born industrial designer. Trained as an engineer, he went to New York in 1919. He founded a design company in 1929 and designed many household products to be made by unskilled labour as part of the New Deal. He designed Studebaker cars, Greyhound buses and Lucky Strike cigarette packaging as well as electric

shavers, office machines, soft-drink bottles and radios. In the sixties and seventies he worked in aerospace, designing for Apollo and Skylab. He wrote *The Locomotive (Its Esthetics)* (1937) and *Industrial Design* (1979).

Lombardo, Guy 1902–77

Canadian-born dance-band leader. The conductor of "the sweetest music this side of paradise" formed his band, the Royal Canadians, in Ontario in 1925 and soon won representation by MCA. His first national broadcast was from Chicago in 1927 and from 1929 he was booked each winter for New York's Roosevelt Grill, moving to the Waldorf-Astoria when that closed. For 48 years his broadcasts were part of America's traditional New Year's Eve celebrations. He introduced more than 300 new songs and sold over 100 million records.

Lorenz, Konrad Zacharias 1903–89

Austrian physician, founder of ethology, the science of animal behavior. After graduating in medicine in Vienna he held a succession of posts there, in anatomy and then in psychology. In 1940 he became professor of psychology in the University of Königsberg. After wartime military service, and capture, he returned to Germany and held various posts in ethology, finally (1961) as director of the Max Planck Institute, Seewiesen. In the 1930s his interest moved from human psychology to that of animals. From a study of birds he concluded that their behavior is not entirely flexible but derives from visual images imprinted in the young. He preferred to draw conclusions from studies in the wild rather than in the laboratory. His attempts to relate the behavior of animals to that of humans had a mixed reception. He was awarded a Nobel prize in 1973.

Louis, Joe 1914–81

US boxer. The longest reigning world heavyweight champion (22 June 1937 to 1 March 1949), he defended the title 25 times (with 21 knockouts), and lost it only on his first (brief) retirement. He turned professional in 1934, peaking in the years 1939–42, when he defended the championship seven times during the December 1940 to June 1941 period. He failed to recover the title in 1950 and retired again in 1951.

Lynn, Vera 1919

British vocalist. After residences with pianist Charlie Kunz and Ambrose and His Orchestra, she began her solo career in 1941, launching a radio series, *Sincerely Yours›* Immensely popular with troops worldwide, she was nicknamed the Forces' Sweetheart, and toured extensively; the song *The White Cliffs of Dover* dates from the period. *Auf Wiederschen Sweetheart* (1952), the first big hit of her comeback career, was the first British disc to top the British and US charts.

163

Douglas MacArthur

Harpo, Groucho and Chico Marx

MacArthur, Douglas 1880–1964

US general. MacArthur graduated from West Point Military Academy in 1903, and served with distinction in France during World War I. From 1919 to 1922 he was superintendent of West Point, and from 1922 to 1925 US commander in the Philippines. From 1930 to 1935, now a general, he was chief of staff, and from 1935 to 1937 head of the US military mission in the Philippines, building up their defensive capacity. He retired in 1937, but was recalled in 1941 to head US forces in the Far East. He fought a delaying action against the Japanese in the Philippines, retreated to Australia in 1942, and became Supreme Commander in the Southwest Pacific. After a successful Allied campaign in 1943–44, MacArthur became a five-star general. In 1945, as Supreme Allied Commander, he formally accepted the Japanese surrender in Tokyo. From 1945 to 1951, as the commander of Allied occupation, he was responsible for the demilitarization, democratization, and economic regeneration of Japan. In 1950, he became UN commander in Korea, leading troops against the Communist forces and twice invading the north, but he was relieved of his duties in 1951 when he publicly disagreed with President Truman over policy extending the war into China.

Magritte, René 1898–1967

Belgian painter. Magritte studied fine art in Brussels (1916–18). From 1920 to 1924 he produced work influenced by Cubism and Futurism but in 1925, after de Chirico's *Le Chant d'Amour*, subject matter became vitally important, and he became a Surrealist. 1927 saw his first one-man show, in Brussels; he then lived in Paris, and from 1928 to 1930 used words in his work, exploring word-object relationships. In 1929 he visited Dalí, with whom he shared an intense clarity of execution; but his paintings shocked by incongruity of subject matter, and implied but never expressed intensity of feeling. *The Human Condition* (1933) dealt with the split consciousness humans create by "recreating" the world they are part of. In 1938 Magritte had work in the International Surrealist Exhibition in Paris. He then took on Impressionism (1943–46), and in 1947–48 worked in a violent, grotesque style, before reverting to his previous calm. He was commissioned in the 1950s and 1960s to do many murals. Magritte strongly influenced the Pop artists.

Mannheim, Karl 1893–1947

Hungarian sociologist. Mannheim taught at Frankfurt (1926–33) and the London School of Economics (1933–46). His works include *Ideology and Utopia* (1936) and *Man and Society in an Age of Reconstruction* (1941). His main contribution to his discipline was the creation of a new arena of debate called the "sociology of knowledge". He argued that all social thought was related to the thinker's class; that all social thought was ideological. The implication of such a position was that objective knowledge and science were not possible. Mannheim attempted to surmount this problem by postulating that an independent intellectual class could achieve a disinterested knowledge. However, he eventually rejected his original position. His later work looked at contemporary mass society and the need for social planning.

Marx Brothers, The

US comedy team: brothers Chico (1886–1961); Harpo (1888– 1964); Groucho (1890–1977) and Zeppo (1901–79). All but Zeppo had a separate comic persona and their style was an almost surrealistic blend of slapstick, boisterous vitality, insult, anarchy and logic-chopping. After a tough apprenticeship in vaudeville, they made Broadway in *I'll Say It Is* (1924); then *The Coconuts* (1925) and *Animal Crackers* (1928). The last two were filmed (1929–30) and ten more movies followed. Even weak direction and weaker plots could not lessen their impact in classics such as *Duck Soup* (1933) and *A Night at the Opera* (1935)

Messerschmitt, Wilhelm 1898–1978

German aviation designer and producer. Graduated in engineering and became chief designer and engineer of Bayerische Flugzeugwerke from 1926, and its chairman and director in 1938 when it became Messerschmitt Aircraft Manufacturing Works. It produced the Me 109, which set the world speed record in 1939. Messerschmitt made a variety of aircraft and supplied the Luftwaffe during World War II. Held by the US for two years after the war ended, he was banned from producing aircraft until 1958. In 1968–69 he established, and became honorary chairman of, the Messerschmitt- Bölkaw-Blohm company, also producing satellites and missiles.

Messiaen, Olivier 1908–92

French composer. Messiaen began to compose at seven. In 1919 he entered the Paris Conservatoire, where he won all major prizes. On leaving in 1930, he became principal organist at La Trinité, Paris. In 1936 he began to teach, and was one of a group, *La Jeune France*, dedicated to restoring seriousness and emotional depth to French music. As a prisoner-of-war he wrote *Quartet for the End of Time* (1941). His *Turangalîla-symphonie* (1946–48) is based on the legend of Tristan and Isolde. After the war, he became professor of harmony at the Paris Conservatoire, and in 1966, professor of composition – he has taught many celebrated musicians, including Boulez, Stockhausen, Xenakis and George Benjamin. Always interested in birdsong, in 1953, with *Réveil des Oiseaux*, he began to transcribe it; Messiaen's rhythmic innovations draw on this and ancient Greek and Hindu rhythms, and the work of Stravinsky and Debussy. Even theological works like *Vingt Regards sur l'Enfant Jésus* (1944) contain music taken from birdsong. He developed his own modes and wrote the first total serial work, the *Mode de valeurs et d'intensité* (1949). Messiaen's work is distinguished by a simplicity of spirit, innovative technique, and deep mysticism. He has written *The Technique of My Musical Language* (1947).

Miller, Glenn 1904–44

US jazz trombonist, arranger, composer and band leader. His was the most successful big band ever, producing music which swung harder than any other white band of the time. By 1939 RCA singles and a radio series were confirming his success, and his films, *Sun Valley Serenade* (1941) and *Orchestra Wives* (1942), found a worldwide audience. Drafted into the US Army in 1942, he re-formed his band using several key men from his previous line-up and wowed Britain before being lost in a plane over France in 1944.

Moholy-Nagy, László 1895–1946

Hungarian artist, designer and theorist. Moholy-Nagy, an ex-law student wounded in the Great War, co-founded the MA (="today") group in 1917, and from the following year devoted himself to art. Influenced by Malevich, he used circles, crosses and squares; and in 1922 he produced his first "photograms", images resulting from the exposure to light of photographic paper with objects placed on it. After his first one-man show, Gropius invited him to teach at the Bauhaus, which he did from 1923 to 1928. After a time in Amsterdam, Moholy-Nagy went to London, where he worked on posters, books and films, with a Constructivist group, and developed Space Modulators – arrangements of plexiglass and metal producing fascinating lighting effects when in motion. From 1937 he lived in the USA, first directing the New Bauhaus in Chicago, then opening his own design school. His last book, *Vision and Motion*, was published posthumously. Moholy-Nagy is less important for the quality and stature of his work, more for the impact he had on others; he was a forerunner of Pop, as well as other postwar movements.

Molotov, Vyacheslav 1890–1986

Soviet politician. Molotov joined the Bolshevik party in 1906, and was a member of the military revolutionary committee during the Bolshevik revolution. He joined the central committee in 1921, and the Politburo in 1925, when he also became chairman of the Moscow party committee, and in 1930 was selected as chairman of the Soviet of People's Commissars (premier). In 1939, as commissar for foreign affairs, he negotiated the

Eugenio Montale

Maria Montessori

Benito Mussolini

nonaggression pact with Hitler. In 1941 Stalin replaced Molotov as chairman of the council of ministers, and he then became first deputy chairman. He also joined the state defense committee (war cabinet), helped to form alliances with Britain and the US, and attended all the conferences of Tehran, Yalta, Potsdam, and San Francisco. After the war, he made extensive use of the Soviet veto in the United Nations. He retired as foreign minister in 1949, but then served again in this capacity during 1953–56. In 1956 he was appointed state control minister, but after participating in the attempted coup against Khrushchev in 1957, he was posted to Mongolia. He retired in 1962 and was reinstated in 1984.

Montale, Eugenio 1896–1981
Italian writer. Montale turned to writing after World War I blocked his singing career. His first book of poetry, *Cuttlefish Bones* (1925), is a powerful expression of his deep pessimism – he was opposed to Fascism. After working for a publisher, Montale became director of Florence's Gabinetto Vieusseux Library, dismissed in 1938 by the Fascists. *The Occasions* (1939), is esoterically allusive, as is *Land's End* (1943). As literary editor of the newspaper *Corriere della sera* from 1948, he began to publish his short stories in it, releasing a collection, *The Butterfly of Dinard*, in 1956. In 1966 he published *Auto da Fé*, a critical work, and the superb and poignant *Xenia*, poems in memory of his dead wife. Montale became more prolific in old age, producing volumes of poetry, criticism, stories, and excellent translations from English. Montale changed the face of Italian poetry, and won many awards, including the 1975 Nobel Prize for Literature.

Montessori, Maria 1870–1952
Italian educationalist, and the first woman to qualify as a doctor of medicine in Italy (1894). From 1900 she taught at the University of Rome, becoming professor of anthropology in 1904. She developed the educational system that bears her name, which gained international recognition and has had an immense influence upon nursery and infant education. Her first "children's house" was opened in Rome in 1907. The Montessori method sought to organize the child's environment and provide it with a variety of materials for educational development, including the climbing frame now found in many nursery schools. She emphasized the importance of work rather than play but this work was to be undertaken at the child's own pace and in its own direction. Self-education was a key factor in her strategy and teachers were to remain in the background. Montessori also advocated scientific observation and induction. Her publications include *The Montessori Method* (1912) and *The Secret of Childhood* (1936).

Montgomery, Bernard L. 1887–1976
British general. Mentioned in dispatches during World War I, after the outbreak of World War II Montgomery led the British Third Division in France, and, after the evacuation of Dunkirk, commanded the Southeastern army in England. In 1942, as commander of the British Eighth Army in North Africa, he defeated Rommel's troops at El Alamein. The Axis forces were then driven across North Africa, and surrendered in the following year in Tunisia. Montgomery then led the Eighth Army in the invasions of Sicily and Italy. In 1944, he was given command of the ground troops in the offensive across the English Channel, and a short time later he led the Twenty-first Army Group through Western Europe. He was then made a field marshal. Immediately after the war, he commanded the British army of occupation, and during 1946–48 was chief of the imperial general staff. He then served from 1948 to 1951 as chairman of the commanders-in-chief of the Western alliance, and from 1951 to 1958 as NATO deputy supreme commander in Europe.

Morgenthau, Henry Jr 1891–1967
US politician. In 1934, Morgenthau, then governor of the federal Farm Board, was appointed secretary for the Treasury. He financed Roosevelt's New Deal, and ran the US war economy. He was the principal architect of the International Monetary Fund and the World Bank. He resigned in 1945, after Truman's rejection of the Morgenthau Plan to prevent the re-industrialization of Germany.

Morton, Jelly Roll 1890–1941
US jazz pianist, composer, arranger and vocalist. He explored the limits of the small band and many of his New Orleans stomps and blues are classics. Doing anything from pimping to pool, boxing promotion to running a tailor's shop while playing piano (1906–23), his hour came in 1923 in Chicago: published by the Melrose brothers, recording for Gennett and touring with his own groups. In 1926 he made his greatest recordings, the Red Hot Peppers sessions. By 1928, the big bands were catching on and he was old hat. Self-centered and boastful, he was often thought over-rated.

Mosca, Gaetano 1858–1941
Italian jurist and political theorist. Educated at the University of Palermo, Mosca taught constitutional law there (1885–88) and at Rome (1888–96) and Turin (1896–1908). He was a member of the Chamber of Deputies (1908–1918), and made a senator for life in 1919. With Pareto he is regarded as the founder of the elitist view of society, arguing in his work, especially *The Ruling Class* (1896), that all societies have only two classes of people, the minority who rule and the majority who are ruled, whatever the form of government. The ruling class continues and justifies its

domination by legal and arbitrary means, using not only violence but also the imposition of its ideology. Mosca's theory was sometimes used as a justification for fascism although he opposed both Mussolini and Hitler and favored a liberal stance.

Mussolini, Benito 1883–1945
Italian dictator. In 1914, Mussolini was expelled from the Socialist party for advocating Italian intervention in World War I. He joined the armed forces in 1915 and became a fervent antisocialist. In 1919 he founded the Fascist movement, entered parliament in 1921, and in 1922 his supporters embarked on their March on Rome. The king asked Mussolini to form a government. He became prime minister in a multi-party coalition, but by 1928 had created a single-party state with the Fascist Grand Council in control. Whilst using terror tactics against his opposition and curtailing civil liberties, Mussolini restored self-respect to Italy and began a large program of public works. In 1929 he agreed the Lateran Treaty with the Papacy, by which the latter, in return for the establishment of the Vatican State, considerable compensation and the position of official religion of Italy, abandoned claims to land elsewhere in the country. Mussolini reached the height of his popularity with the invasion of Abyssinia (Ethiopia) in 1935–36; he supported Franco in the Spanish Civil War. In 1936 he formed the Rome-Berlin axis with Hitler, and in 1940 entered World War II, in which Italian troops acted principally as auxiliaries to the Germans. Italy gained control of Albania in 1939, and went on to a series of military débâcles, regularly requiring German assistance. In 1943, the Allies invaded Sicily, and Mussolini was voted out of office by the Grand Council of Fascism, and imprisoned, to be freed by the Germans, who set him up in a puppet Fascist state in the north, where he executed several members of the Grand Council who had voted for his dismissal. The Allies advanced north, and as the Germans withdrew, the partisans began to take control. In 1945, they captured Mussolini disguised as a German soldier, and shot him.

Narayan, R.K. 1906–
Indian novelist. Son of a headmaster, and a teacher himself, Narayan found international acclaim with *Swami and his Friends* (1935), a novel about schoolboys, and through the patronage of Graham Greene. Narayan wrote over a dozen more novels, in elegant English, all social comedies set in the fictitious town of Malgudi. Often, as in *The Guide* (1958) he looks through the surface of Hinduism to a mystical center. *The Sweet Vendor* (1967), his best novel, centers on a man alienated and uprooted by his son's marriage to a non-Hindu. Narayan also wrote autobiography, essays, and produced modern versions of the *Ramayana* (1972) and the *Mahabharata* (1978).

▲ Jesse Owens

▲ Pius XII

▲ Ferdinand Porsche

Néel, Louis Eugène Félix 1904–

French physicist. After graduating at the Ecole Normale Supérieure, Paris, he was appointed professor in the University of Strasbourg (1937–45). He then moved to the University of Grenoble as professor in the faculty of science and was appointed director of the Centre d'Etudes Nucléaires in Grenoble when it was founded in 1956, retiring in 1971. Throughout his long research career he took a particular interest in the magnetic properties of solids. In 1936 he predicted, on theoretical grounds, that there should be a new form of magnetism, antiferromagnetism, in which the properties were determined by nonsymmetrical ordering of the spins of unpaired electrons. Above a certain temperature (the Néel critical temperature) such materials should become paramagnetic: that is, they should acquire magnetic properties when located in a magnetic field, losing them when this is removed. Such materials were made in 1938, confirming Néel's prediction. Together with Hannes Alfvén, he received the 1970 Nobel Prize for Physics.

Nelson, George 1917–

American industrial designer. He graduated from Yale School of Fine Arts in 1931 and after spending the early 1930s in Europe, imported European modernism into America, introducing, for example, Mies van der Rohe to his home country. He founded the magazine *Architectural Forum* and prompted corporate modernism in his office-designs, such as the *Storage Wall* and the *Action Office*. Like so many other leading designers, he has done work for Olivetti, designing their Editor 2 typewriter in 1968.

Neumann, John (János) von 1903–57

Hungarian-US mathematician, pioneer of computer theory. A child prodigy in mathematics, he retained his brilliance as an adult. After studying in Berlin, Zurich and Budapest and developing (1923) the theory of numbers as sets, he went to America in 1930 and was appointed professor of mathematical physics at Princeton (1930–33), where he formulated the von Neumann algebras, the concept of rings of operators, then moving to the newly founded Institute for Advanced Study at Princeton. During World War II he became deeply involved in the development of computers, and formulated the basic von Neumann Concept. This postulates that the two essential features of a computer are a memory in which to store information and a system to transfer memorized information according to a predetermined program. During the war he was consultant on the Manhattan Project. He is remembered also for his contributions to the theory of games. He was perhaps the last of the great mathematicians who were equally at home in both the pure and applied fields.

Northrop, John Howard 1891–1987

US biochemist. A chemistry graduate, Northrop worked from 1925 to 1962 at the Rockefeller Institute, New York. When J.B. Sumner succeeded in crystallizing an enzyme in 1926, showing it to be a protein, Northrop realized that this opened up new vistas in protein chemistry. Proteins could now be manipulated and studied far more easily. By 1930 he had succeeded in crystallizing several other enzymes. In 1946 Northrop shared a Nobel prize with Sumner and W.M. Stanley, the first to crystallize a plant virus.

Ohain, Hans Pabst von 1911–

German aeronautical engineer. Ohain studied aerodynamics at Göttingen, and realizing that the piston engine/propeller system was nearing its limit for high-speed flight, turned his attention to turbines and rockets. In 1936 he joined the Heinkel Company, taking with him a design for a turbo-jet engine. The world's first jet flight – with a Heinkel He 178 – was achieved on 27 August 1939. However, the first production jet aircraft, the Messerschmitt 262, did not appear until 1944. The delay was due partly to a major change in design. Whereas Ohain, like Whittle in Britain, had used centrifugal compressors, the Jumo gas turbine which powered the Me 262 used a multistage axial flow compressor, which proved to be on the main line of development.

Olivetti, Adriano 1901–60

Italian industrialist. Trained as an industrial chemist, he inherited a small typewriter factory and turned it into one of the world's largest producers of office machinery. An ardent anticommunist, he nevertheless pursued a "Christian Socialist" industrial policy, providing employee benefits and allowing for a degree of worker participation in management.

Oppenheimer, Sir Ernest 1880–1957

South African mining magnate; industrialist and financier. Born in Germany, he moved in 1902 to South Africa as a representative for a London firm of diamond merchants. He soon became a leading figure in the diamond industry and in 1917 established the Anglo-American Corporation of South Africa, Ltd. Oppenheimer founded the Consolidated Diamond Mines of South West Africa, Ltd. in 1919, and then gained control of the pre-eminent De Beers Consolidated Mines. He formed the Diamond Corporation, Ltd. in 1930. He also formed a company in Rhodesia to exploit rich copper deposits. His final project was the opening of goldfields in the Orange Free State, South Africa. By 1957 Oppenheimer owned 95 percent of the world's diamond mines. He was mayor of Kimberley (1912–15) and its MP (1924–38). He was knighted in 1921. From 1967 he was chancellor of Cape Town University.

Owens, Jesse 1913–80

US athlete. His record in the long jump, set in 1935, stood for 25 years and he won four gold medals in the 1936 Berlin Olympics – for the 100- and 200-meter runs, the long jump and the US 400-meter relay team – to the fury of Adolf Hitler, who had hoped to demonstrate Aryan superiority. But his most remarkable feat was on 25 May 1935, when he equaled the world record for the 100 yards and broke those for the 220 yards (and 200 meters), the 220-yard (200-meter) low hurdles and long jump. He was belatedly honored in 1976, with the Presidential Medal of Freedom. Owens later made lecture tours; he was an eloquent and charismatic speaker.

Peierls, Rudolf Ernst 1907–

German-British theoretical physicist. After graduating in physics at Berlin University he embarked on a research career just as the advent of quantum mechanics was reshaping the whole basis of theoretical physics. After studying with W.K. Heisenberg in Leipzig and W. Pauli in Zurich he moved to the UK and was appointed professor of mathematical physics in Birmingham (1937–63), Oxford (1963–74) and subsequently Washington, Seattle (1974–77). His early research was largely in solid state physics, but he turned increasingly to atomic physics in the 1930s. In 1940 he was a member of the influential Maud Committee, whose report indicated the feasibility of an atomic bomb. The British government took this up and Peierls became part of an investigative research group, concerned particularly with the separation of uranium isotopes. This became absorbed into the Manhattan Project (1943) which produced the first atomic bomb in 1945.

Piccard, Auguste 1884–1962

French physicist, famous for his exploration of the stratosphere and the ocean depths. After graduating in physics at the Federal College of Technology, Zurich, he taught there (1907–22) until appointed professor of physics at Brussels Polytechnic Institute. Becoming interested in the physics of the upper atmosphere and in the cosmic rays discovered by V.F. Hess in 1911–12 he decided to make direct observations from a manned balloon at great altitudes, a technique profitably used by Hess. In 1931 he made a record ascent of 15,780m (51,775ft) using an air-conditioned gondola. A year later he achieved 16,200m (53,153ft). In 1937 he made a complete reversal in policy by deciding to explore the ocean depths, using an independent self- propelled bathyscaphe. With his son Jacques he descended 3,099m (10,168ft) in 1953, trebling the record set by William Beebe in 1934. Together they built a new bathyscaphe, the *Trieste*, which they sold to the US navy. This reached a depth of 10,910m (35,800ft) in the Mariana Trench in the Pacific in 1960.

▲ Sergey Prokofiev

▲ Leni Riefenstahl

▲ Bill Robinson

Pilsudski, Jozef K. 1867–1935

Polish revolutionary and politician. In 1887, Pilsudski was falsely accused of plotting to assassinate the Russian czar, and was exiled to Siberia. On his return he joined the Polish Socialist party, of which he later became leader. Having failed to overthrow the government during the Russo-Japanese war (1904–05) and the Russian revolution which followed it, he formed the Polish Legion in Austria. Technically under Austro-Hungarian command, he led the legion against the Russians during 1914–16, but then disbanded it, sure that Germany and Austria-Hungary would not grant Polish independence. He was imprisoned 1917–18, and then became provisional head of state of an independent Poland, as well as commander-in-chief of the Polish army. He was promoted to Marshal of Poland in 1919, and defeated a Soviet invasion in 1920. He did not stand in the subsequent general election; he served as chief of staff until 1923. In 1926, during an economic crisis, he staged a military coup. He then served as defense minister (1926–35) and prime minister (1926–28, 1930). From then on he effectively ran the country, and in 1930 had 18 opponents arrested. In 1934, he signed a nonaggression treaty with Hitler, after the French had refused to join forces against Germany, and extended his treaty with the Soviet Union. He later refused to meet Hitler, and rejected his proposals for an anti-Soviet alliance.

Pius XII (Eugenio Pacelli) 1876–1958

Italian Pope. Ordained in 1899, Pacelli rose to become papal nuncio in Germany during the Weimar Republic. He was appointed secretary of state (1929), drafted the Concordat with Hitler (1933), and was elected Pope in 1939. Ineffective in his efforts to prevent the outbreak of World War II, during the war Pius used the Vatican's neutrality to carry out much humanitarian work, especially for prisoners of war and refugees. However, his attitude towards the treatment of Jews in Germany has caused controversy. Critics argue that Pius could have used his influence to prevent persecution whereas others contend, and he believed, that his intervention would have made no difference, or possibly made things worse. After the war he was concerned with the future of Catholicism in communist countries. Pius was a gifted scholar and very spiritual man, but brought little creativity to the papacy.

Porsche, Ferdinand 1875–1951

German automobile designer. He designed cars for Daimler and Auto Union, becoming director of Austro-Daimler Company (1916) and moving to the Daimler Company in Stuttgart (1923). In 1931 Porsche left to establish his own firm designing sports and racing cars. In 1934 he produced a design for Hitler's project, the Volkswagen ("People's Car"). This mass-produced car broke records on the postwar export market. Porsche designed military vehicles during World War II. Imprisoned postwar by the French, he developed and introduced the Porsche sports car (1950).

Porter, Cole 1892–1964

US composer and lyricist. His songs are witty, subtle, civilized, detached: everything he was himself. He had his first Broadway musical in 1916, then military service and a playboy lifestyle kept him busy. But after *Fifty Million Frenchmen* (1929) he was a major force on Broadway. Credits include *The Gay Divorce* (1932), *Kiss Me Kate* (1948), *Can-Can* (1953) and *Silk Stockings* (1955). He also worked in films, and *I Get a Kick Out of You* (1934) is one of his most successful film songs.

Prokofiev, Sergey 1891–1953

Russian composer. By 1902, when he had his first formal music tuition, Prokofiev, a proficient pianist, had written two operas and several piano pieces. He studied at St Petersburg Conservatory (1904–14) under Rimsky-Korsakov. He first played his own work in public in 1908, galvanizing audience and critics, who denounced him as an *enfant terrible*. His First Piano Concerto (1912) nevertheless won the 1914 Rubinstein Prize. In 1914 he was deeply impressed by the *Ballets Russes*, and Stravinsky's *Le Sacre du printemps*. He worked, at first unproductively, with Diaghilev until 1929. Prokofiev's *Classical Symphony*, (1917) brought world fame; in 1918 he moved to the USA, producing another celebrated work, *The Love for Three Oranges* (1919), for the Chicago Opera. In 1922 he returned to Europe, settling in Paris until his return in 1936 to Russia. Here he composed *Romeo and Juliet* (1935) and *Peter and the Wolf* (1936). In 1948, Prokofiev was censured by Zhdanov for writing "anti-democratic" music. The erstwhile iconoclast toed the party line, although he produced further fine work. Prokofiev's music, often Romantic in flavor, and often playful, shocked and engaged audiences in its exploration of deep, atavistic emotions.

Reich, Wilhelm (1897–1957)

Viennese psychoanalyst. Reich joined the Viennese Psychoanalytic Society (1924) and trained under Freud. In *The Function of the Orgasm* (1927) he advocated the need to achieve orgasm to obtain personal fulfillment and asserted that failure to do so would lead to neurosis. He subsequently combined Marxist politics with sexual freedom, founding the German Association for Proletarian Sexual Politics to provide advice on sex and birth-control to the working class. Fleeing from Germany (1933) Reich lived in Scandinavia (1933–39) then he settled in America (1939). In his work *Character Analysis* (1933) he focused on character defenses which individuals used to resist the discovery of their underlying neurosis. In America he investigated "orgone energy", units of cosmic energy he believed to be found in the nervous system. The development and sale of "orgone boxes" to treat illness led to his arrest and a two-year sentence for contempt of court. Reich's theories were very influential during the 1960s.

Riefenstahl, Leni 1902–

German film director and actress. She learned basic film technique while starring in semi-documentary films which extolled the beauty of nature. She wrote, produced (and starred in) her first directorial credit, *The Blue Light*, in 1931. In 1934 Hitler asked her to film the "Nuremberg Party Convention", and she produced a powerful piece of propaganda, *Triumph of the Will*. *Olympia* (1936), a record of the 1936 Berlin Games, seems in reality to have been dedicated to the human body.

Robeson, Paul 1898–1976

US singer and actor. The son of a slave, he turned down a football career to read law. Unable to get work, he became an actor. He had a big hit in *Emperor Jones* (1924), but it was in the film version of *Show Boat* (1936) that he won world fame. His other greatest success was as *Othello* (1930 and 1943). Film credits include *Sanders of the River* (1935) and *King Solomon's Mines* (1937).

Robinson, Bill 1878–1949

US singer and dancer. A professional at eight, he became one of the world's greatest tap dancers and a star of vaudeville. He created the much-imitated stair tap-routine and had outstanding stage success in the revue *Blackbirds* (1927) and *The Hot Mikado* (1939). His cheerful personality earned him the nickname "Bojangles" and he reached a wider audience in films. Film credits include *The Little Colonel* (1935) and *Rebecca of Sunnybrook Farm* (1938).

Robinson, Joan 1903–83

British economist. Graduating from Girton College, Cambridge, in 1925, she lectured in economics at Cambridge, becoming a full professor in 1965 and retiring in 1971. A strong advocate of Keynesian economics, Robinson in her most famous work, *Economics of Imperfect Competition* (1933), analyzed the impact of advertising, consumer preference and product differentiation on the traditional theory of perfect competition. Her works on Keynes, *Introduction to the Theory of Employment* (1937), and on Marx, *An Essay on Marxian Economics* (1942), helped popularize these two areas of economic thought. After the war, Robinson's work was concentrated on a new Keynesian-type theory of long-run economic growth under capitalism. In her later career she moved increasingly away from the tenets of orthodox economic theory.

▲ Franklin Delano Roosevelt (center)

▲ Antonio de Oliviera Salazar

Rodgers, Richard 1902–79

US musical-comedy composer. His most successful collaborations were with Lorenz Hart and Oscar Hammerstein II. He met Hart at university and they put on the varsity show in 1920. Their first professional success was a revue, in 1925; their later, increasingly sophisticated musical comedies included *Babes in Arms* (1937), *The Boys from Syracuse* (1938) and *Pal Joey* (1940). After Hart's death, he worked with Hammerstein on eight musicals, including *Oklahoma!* (1945), *Carousel* (1945), *South Pacific* (1949), *The King and I* (1951) and *The Sound of Music* (1959).

Roosevelt, Franklin D. 1882–1945

32nd US president, who was elected for four successive terms. In 1910, Roosevelt entered the New York Senate as a Democrat. Stricken by paralysis in 1921, he maintained his political interest during his convalescence. In 1932 Roosevelt defeated Hoover in the presidential elections. His "New Deal" effected a partial economic recovery from the Depression. Government reorganized agriculture, industry and finance and undertook new labor legislation, welfare programs and public works using the then radical policy of deficit financing influenced by new Keynesian ideas. He made an unsuccessful attempt to reform the Supreme Court, after it had declared some of this legislation unconstitutional. This, together with another bout of recession in the late 1930s, lost him much popularity. In the 1930s he tried to avert war while maintaining neutrality. In 1940 he concluded the Destroyer Deal, thus supporting Britain. In 1941 the Lend Lease Act was passed, enabling the US to sell war supplies to the Allies on credit, and Roosevelt defined the Four Freedoms he saw as essential to world peace – freedom of speech and of worship, and freedom from want and fear. Later in 1941 he and Churchill drew up the Atlantic Charter, which defined any postwar settlement, and Roosevelt asked Congress to revise the Neutrality Act. In late 1941 the Japanese attacked Pearl Harbor, and the US entered World War II. Roosevelt became one of the three major Allied leaders, and in 1943 met with Churchill and Stalin in Tehran. They met again in Yalta in 1945 to plan the defeat of the Axis forces and postwar reconstruction.

Ross, Harold 1862–1951

US journalist. Founder of *The New Yorker* magazine, he was a major influence on reportage, humor and fiction in the USA. He edited the servicemen's newspaper in France during World War I before establishing his weekly in 1925. He aimed to encapsulate the contemporary scene in a light-hearted yet rigorous style, an approach which allowed satire and parody and attracted new writers and artists, like humorist James Thurber and cartoonists Helen Hoskinson and Mary Petty.

Roy, Jamini 1887–1974

Indian painter. After imbibing the Western academic artistic tradition at Calcutta Art School, Roy came under the influence of the Bengal School, which attempted to revive ancient art. His realization of the impossibility of doing this amounted to a spiritual crisis, and he proceeded to develop an individual style which drew on his beloved folk art. He used organic pigments. As Roy's sense of the importance of art in society grew, he abandoned "original" for "mass" art, to be generally accessible, and normally executed his work with his pupils.

Salazar, Antonio de Oliveira 1889–1970

Portuguese dictator. In 1921, Salazar, then a professor of economics, helped to found the Catholic Center party, and served briefly as a member of parliament. After a military coup in 1926, he was appointed finance minister, but resigned five days later. He was restored to the post in 1928, and proceeded to balance the national budget. Appointed premier in 1932, in 1933 he introduced a new constitution, concentrating power in himself. He later created a single-party state. He supported Franco in the Spanish Civil War, and was neutral during World War II. He obtained Portuguese membership of NATO in 1949, and of the UN in 1954. He showed great determination to maintain the Portuguese empire, but was unable to prevent the return of Goa to India in 1961. Later in the 1960s, his domestic program suffered from his substantial diversion of resources to suppress independence movements in the African colonies. He retired in 1968.

Sartre, Jean-Paul 1905–80

French novelist, philosopher and playwright. Sartre studied philosophy at the Sorbonne, where he met Simone de Beauvoir, his lifelong partner. He taught until 1945, and imbibed the phenomenology of Husserl and the existentialism of Nietzsche. *Nausea* (1938) is a diary-novel describing a neurotic repulsion from objects; *Being and Nothingness* (1943) further expounds Sartre's existentialism and theory of consciousness. Sartre believed that freedom included concern for society (engagement), and *The Roads to Freedom* trilogy (1945–49), is an ethical exposition in novel form. His excellent plays, like *The Flies* (1943) and *No Exit* (1944), dramatize the passionate hostility bred of human alienation. In 1948, with Beauvoir, he produced the review *Les Temps Modernes*; the entrenchment of his radical position as he embraced Maoism caused him to break with many friends, including (1952) Camus. His autobiography, *The Words* (1963), won him the Nobel Prize, which he declined. The later years of his life were spent writing a biography of Flaubert, on which he worked until he went blind.

Schiaparelli, Elsa 1896–1973

Italian-born couturier. Like Dior, she commercialized Parisian fashion. Settling in Paris in the late twenties, she toyed with writing and sculpture before opening a small salon. By 1935 she was a leader of fashion: in 1932 she introduced the padded shoulder. Her designs were simple yet eccentric and she used color flamboyantly, introducing shocking pink and ice blue and designing fur bedjackets and rhinestone-trimmed lingerie. After 1935 she expanded into jewelry, perfume, cosmetics and swimsuits and in 1949 opened a New York branch.

Schoenberg, Arnold 1874–1951

Austrian US composer. Schoenberg, took violin lessons from the age of eight and began composing in 1883. He was largely self-taught. His work until the *Second String Quartet* (1908) was an attempt at maintaining the tonal basis while exploring chromaticism, but eventually expressive needs drove him to atonality. From 1910 he taught at the Vienna Academy, where Berg and Webern were among his pupils. In 1911, in Berlin, he exhibited his paintings with the *Blaue Reiter* group. He achieved a degree of popularity with the remarkable *Pierrot Lunaire* (1912). With his *Piano Suite* (1923) he broke through into dodecaphony, the method he created to tame the chaos of atonality that laid the foundation for postwar serialism. In 1926 he directed the composition masterclass at the Prussian Academy of Arts. In 1933, under the threat of Nazism, he left the Academy, and Germany. Schoenberg returned to Judaism, which he had abandoned in 1898. He settled in the USA, worked as a teacher and, from 1936, university professor in Los Angeles, and was naturalized in 1941. Schoenberg felt that the problems of harmony and harmonic direction created by his entry into the non-tonal world had not been solved, and his theoretical writings explore this dilemma.

Seferis (Seferiades), George 1900–71

Greek poet. Seferis started writing after graduating in law; in 1931 his first collection won him acclaim as a major poet, the greatest in the Symbolist genre. *The Thrush* (1947), and some fine translations of English poetry, including *The Waste Land*, consolidated his reputation. "Helen" from *Logbook C* (1955), is probably the finest modern Greek poem. He was ambassador to the United Nations (1956–57), and from 1957 to 1962 he was Greek ambassador to the UK. In 1963 he won the Nobel Prize. He was harassed for his public denunciation, in 1969, of the junta. A friend of T. S. Eliot, Seferis drew on the classical Greek tradition, to confine passion in cool, lucid language; his work is suffused with compassion for Greece's tragic position in the modern world, its fall from grace.

▲ Elsa Schiaparelli

▲ Amrita Sher-Gil

▲ Joseph Stalin

Selznick, David O. 1902–65

US film producer. He set up his own company in 1936 and produced the immensely profitable *Gone With the Wind* in 1939, writing and directing parts of it: his involvement was always detailed and highly creative. Earlier he had worked on productions at MGM, Paramount and RKO, including *King Kong* and *Dinner at Eight* (both 1933) and *Anna Karenina* (1935). He brought Ingrid Bergman and Alfred Hitchcock to Hollywood, for *Intermezzo* (1939) and *Rebecca* (1940) respectively.

Shahn, Ben 1898–1969

Lithuanian-born US painter. Shahn's parents emigrated in 1906 to the USA, where he worked as an apprentice lithographer before (1919–22) studying art. Influenced by Rouault and Rivera, he was a Social Realist, painting in photographic detail; after visiting Europe, he adopted elements of the style of the early Italian masters. *The Passion of Sacco and Vanzetti* (1931–32) exemplifies the social protest which constantly fired his work, like that of Rivera, with whom he collaborated in 1933 on the Radio City murals. Other major works are the Bronx Post Office frescos (1938–39) and the Washington Social Security Building mural (1940–42). Shahn moved into poster production in the 1940s, with work like *Hunger* (1946) for the State Department.

Sher-Gil, Amrita 1913–41

Indian painter. Sher-Gil studied at the Paris École des Beaux-Arts, and was influenced initially by Cézanne and Gauguin, exhibiting in 1933. In 1934 she returned to India, and studied ancient art, notably the 2000-year-old Buddhist cave-paintings of Ajantá. She was led by this art and that of Gauguin to a strongly stylized idiom, without perspective, dealing with Indian life.

Shostakovich, Dmitri 1906–75

Soviet composer. Shostakovich attended the Petrograd Conservatory (1919–25), producing his First Symphony at his graduation, and winning acclaim as pianist and composer. In 1936 his opera *Lady Macbeth of the Mtsensk District*, was attacked in *Pravda*, as a warning against modernism. Shostakovich produced a *Fifth Symphony* which pleased the Party, and reestablished him as the leading Russian composer. His *Seventh Symphony* (*The Leningrad*), used to symbolize the fight against Fascism, was massively popular. The *Ninth Symphony*, a breezy, serene celebration of the war's end, was not well received and in 1948 a decree was issued denouncing "anti-democratic music". He confessed, and proceeded to compose accessible, non-formalistic music. At the same time he was producing, and withholding, "anti-democratic" pieces like the *First Violin Concerto*; these were released after Stalin's death. The *Thirteenth Symphony* (*Babi Yar*) was also attacked,

for its use of lyrics by the dissident poet Yevgeny Yevtushenko. Shostakovich was unique in the survival and triumph of his genius under the difficult and dictatorial conditions of the Communist regime.

Sieff, Israel M. 1889–1972

British industrialist. An economics graduate, Sieff joined the board of Marks and Spencer in 1915, becoming joint managing director, with his childhood friend Simon Marks, and vice-chairman, in 1926. He had a gift for securing high-quality, low-priced suppliers, bypassing wholesalers; and he was the creator of the exemplary human relations system for which the firm is famed. In 1931 Sieff was asked to join the newly founded Political and Economic Planning (PEP), a group formed to inform and assist government and industry. He contributed a practical emphasis, produced its first, brilliant, industrial report, and became PEP's chairman (1931–39) and vice-chairman (1939–64). In 1966 he was made a life peer.

Sikorsky, Igor Ivan 1889–1972

Russian-US aeronautical engineer. After graduating in engineering he immediately entered the newly fledged aircraft industry. In 1909 he built a helicopter, which was unsuccessful, but from 1914 had to devote himself to conventional aircraft, building for the Russian government the first four-engined bombers. After the war he emigrated to the USA and set up the Sikorsky Aero Engineering Corporation. This enabled him to resume his interest in helicopters in the 1930s but not until 1939 did he construct a model judged satisfactory: this was the VS30. During World War II he manufactured three variants of this for the US government, producing a total of 400 craft. After the war he designed a series of other helicopters.

Sirk, Douglas 1900–87

Danish-born director. A successful German-based theater director, he turned to films in 1933, becoming known for the visual power of his work. Still finding Nazi interference unacceptable, he left for Hollywood in 1937. Much of the material he was given was absurdly weak and his budgets minute. Nonetheless he contrived to create some memorable films, including *Magnificent Obsession* (1954), *All That Heaven Allows* (1955), *Tarnished Angels* (1957), *A Time to Live and a Time to Die* (1958) and *Imitation of Life* (1959).

Speer, Albert 1905–81

German architect and politician. A qualified architect, he undertook commissions for the Nazi party after joining it in 1931, and became Hitler's chief architect in 1934, when he was commissioned to build the Nuremberg stadium. He was given responsibility for the planned reconstruction of

Berlin, which was never achieved. From 1941 to 1945 he was a member of the Reichstag, representing Berlin, and in 1942 became minister of armaments and war production. Speer supervised the conversion of the German economy to capacity war production, greatly improving industrial performance and increasing armaments output three times (1942–44). Production of war materials was maintained by a supply of slave labor from the concentration camps, a system Speer expanded. Toward the end of the war he openly opposed Hitler and especially the Führer's wish to destroy German industry as the Allies advanced. The only Nazi leader to admit even token guilt for the regime's crimes at the Nuremberg trials, he served 20 years in Spandau prison. Released in 1966, Speer published two memoirs in the 1970s.

Stalin (Djugashvili), Joseph V. 1879–1953

Leader of the Soviet Union. In 1898 Stalin gave up studying for the priesthood, and soon after joined the Russian Social Democratic Labor party. In 1903 he joined the central committee of the Bolshevik wing. After the Bolsheviks seized power in the October Revolution, Stalin became Commissar for Nationalities (1917–23), Commissar for State Control (1919–23), and a political commissar during the civil war of 1918–20. After Lenin's death in 1924 Stalin, now Party general secretary, eliminated his political rivals and won control of the Comintern. Under a series of Five-Year Plans, he massively accelerated the industrialization of the Soviet Union, and collectivized agricultural production with brutal force, at the cost of many thousands of lives. In the 1930s he conducted a reign of terror, purging potential rivals. In 1939 Stalin and Hitler signed a nonaggression pact, whereby the Soviet Union occupied eastern Poland and the Baltic states. However, after Germany had attacked the Soviet Union without warning in 1941, Stalin appointed himself commander-in-chief and premier, and became one of the three major leaders of the Allies. When, by 1943, the Soviets, after suffering enormous losses, finally began to drive the Germans back, Stalin secured agreement for the opening of a second front in the west at a meeting with Roosevelt and Churchill in Tehran. He met with them again for postwar planning in 1945 at Yalta. During the late 1940s he increased his influence in eastern Europe, making most of the countries Soviet satellites, and conducted a cold war against the Western bloc countries headed by the United States. At home, he launched a fourth Five-Year Plan, increased political repression and tightened the hold of the Communist party. By his death in 1953, Stalin had produced a highly industrialized nation, second in output to the USA only. However, collectivization did not work and Soviet agricultural production remained inadequate.

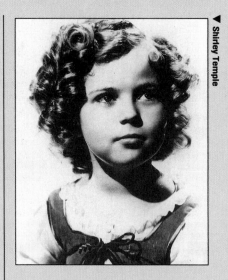

Shirley Temple

Fritz Thyssen

Shin'ichirō Tomonaga

Stanley, Wendell Meredith 1904–71

US biochemist. He graduated in chemistry in 1929, and joined the Rockefeller Institute in Princeton (1931). Learning that J.B. Sumner and J.H. Northrop had prepared enzymes in crystalline form, he sought to do the same thing with viruses. In 1935 he succeeded in crystallizing tobacco mosaic virus (TMV), introducing the concept that a living organism could also be a pure crystalline chemical. During World War II he worked on an influenza virus and prepared a vaccine against it. He shared the Nobel prize for chemistry in 1946 with Northrop and Sumner.

Tatum, Edward Lawrie 1909–75

US chemist, pioneer of biochemical genetics. After graduating he worked at Stanford before moving on to Yale, latterly as professor of microbiology (1946–48). He then returned to Stanford as professor of biology (1948–56) and biochemistry (1956–57), before joining the Rockefeller Institute. In 1946 he worked with J. Lederberg on bacterial mutants and refuted the then current belief that bacteria have no genes, and thus no sex. In fact, occasional individuals are produced by sexual conjugation. With Lederberg and G.W. Beadle he formulated the "one-gene-one-enzyme" concept, and demonstrated that enzyme action is controlled by genes. Tatum, Lederberg and Beadle shared a Nobel prize in 1958.

Temple, Shirley 1928–

US film actress. The most popular and most talented child star ever, she appeared in one-reelers before she was four. Fox put her under contract in 1934 and that year she won a special Academy award. Cute, dimpled and precocious, she could sing, dance and act. In 1938 she was the top box-office attraction and the focus of a thriving spin-off industry. By 1940 adolescence loomed and her career was almost over. In her forties she found a second career in public life, as an ambassador.

Theorell, Axel Hugo Teodor 1903–82

Swedish biochemist. In 1921 he enrolled at the Karolinska Institute, Stockholm to study medicine. On graduating in 1924 he went to Paris and worked briefly at the Pasteur Institute with the bacteriologist L.C.A. Calmette. Returning to Sweden he worked with the Medico-Chemical Institute and in 1936 was appointed director of the new Biochemical Department of the Nobel Medical Institute. His early research (1924–35) was on the constituents of blood – partly in association with The Svedberg, using the ultracentrifuge – but after spending two years with Otto Warburg in Berlin he devoted himself to oxidation enzymes. He succeeded in showing that the so-called "yellow enzyme" was in fact a mixture of a colorless protein moiety and a coenzyme, which proved to be a nucleotide. He received a Nobel prize in 1955.

Thyssen, Fritz 1873–1951

German industrialist. Son of the wealthy industrialist August Thyssen, Fritz became general director of the Thyssen foundries and in 1928 founded, with his father, the United Steel Works which became the world's largest mining and steel cartel. One of Hitler's first financial supporters, he was regarded as an economics expert and made director of an institute for research on the corporate state after Hitler became chancellor in 1933. He also became a deputy in the Reichstag but by 1935 had begun to doubt the Nazi regime. In 1938 he resigned from the Council of State in protest at Jewish persecution. Although rapid German rearmament was good for business, Thyssen spoke out in the Reichstag against the coming war. With the outbreak of war he fled Germany, forfeiting his nationality, and his property. Arrested in France in 1940, he spent the rest of the war in concentration camps; postwar, he settled in Argentina.

Tippett, Michael 1905–

British composer. Tippett, after attending the Royal College of Music (1923–28), and taking private lessons in composition, worked as a French teacher, conducted an orchestra for the unemployed (1935) and became (1940–51) music director of Morley College. He did not come to public notice until 1944, with the oratorio *A Child of Our Time*. His works of this period are neoclassical – the *Double Concerto* (1938–39) and *First Symphony* (1944–45). Thereafter, with six operas (and libretti), including *The Knot Garden* (1955), a superb Piano Concerto (1955), three more symphonies, and choral pieces like *The Mask of Time* (1984), he established and held his reputation as an innovative composer. He taught at the London College of Music from 1983. Tippett's humanitarian idealism showed in his life and his work; musically, he was eclectic, incorporating jazz and negro spiritual elements for example, in his opera *New Year* (1988).

Tomonaga, Shin'ichirō 1906–79

Japanese theoretical physicist. He graduated at Kyoto Imperial University in 1929. After postgraduate research in Japan he worked for two years (1937–39) with W. Heisenberg. During the war he did research on microwave systems. Afterward he returned to academic work in the Tokyo University of Education, of which he became president in 1963. His research was particularly concerned with quantum electrodynamics. This embraces the quantum mechanical laws governing the interaction of charged particles, particularly electrons, and the electromagnetic field. In the hands of Tomonaga and of J. Schwinger and R. Feynman – with whom he shared a Nobel prize in 1965 – it came to occupy a central position in atomic physics, giving very precise interpretation of events at the atomic level.

Toyoda, Kiichiro 1894–1952

Japanese automobile pioneer. In 1933 he established an automobile division within his father's loom business after visiting automobile factories in America. He produced his first prototype vehicle in 1935 and in 1937 the business was incorporated as the Toyota Motor Company, Ltd. Japan's lack of natural resources forced Toyoda to develop highly fuel-efficient engines. In 1940 the Toyoda Science Research Center and the Toyoda Steel Works were established and in 1941 the Toyoda Machine Works, Ltd. After the war, reconstruction led to recovery. Toyota avoided the US- and European- dominated market of large and medium-sized car production, concentrating on the smaller car, of which it produced its first prototype in 1947. However, in 1949, the Japanese economy was severely depressed and Toyoda faced financial and labor difficulties. The Toyota Motor Sales Company, Ltd., was established in 1950 to increase sales, the workforce was reduced to avoid bankruptcy and Toyoda (the president) and all his executive staff resigned. Toyoda died less than two years afterward.

Tudor, Anthony 1908–87

British/US choreographer. Tudor studied with Marie Rambert from 1927, then danced and choreographed for her. In 1938 he formed the London Ballet, leaving in 1939 to join the Ballet (later American Ballet) Theater. In 1950 he worked with the Metropolitan Opera Ballet, in 1952 began to teach at the Juilliard Academy; he was artistic director of the Royal Swedish Ballet (1963–64), in 1974 became Associate Director, and in 1980 Choreographer Emeritus, of the American Ballet. *The Lilac Garden* (1936) and *Knight Errant* (1968), are among the many penetrating pieces in which he has examined the deeper, darker reaches of the human psyche.

Van Doren, Harold 1895–1957

American industrial designer. After an artistic career in Paris which encompassed translation, novel-writing and even film-acting, he returned to the USA to become the director of the Minneapolis Institute of Arts, later resigning in the belief that design was a more effective means than art of contributing to the modern world. His first major design, for the Toledo Scale Company in 1934, initiated the use of large-scale lightweight plastic molding, and his designs were always geared to the development of new materials. An innovative but practical designer, his work ranged from Maytag washing-machines to Goodyear tires.

Vargas, Getúlio Dorneles 1883–1954

Brazilian political leader and social reformer. As president (1930–45, 1951–54), he enacted social and economic changes that helped to develop the modern Brazilian state. He introduced extensive

educational reforms, social security laws, measures
to improve working-class living standards,
including the establishment of a minimum wage
and labor organizations, and a program of rapid
industrialization. He took political power away
from the previously dominant rural landowners
and, despite his authoritarian rule, was viewed as
a "man of the people". Vargas came to power as
leader of a revolution that over threw the republic.
He was himself overthrown by a military coup in
1945 and went into semi-retirement before
returning to win the 1950 presidential elections.
Unable to satisfy his followers and facing
mounting opposition, Vargas eventually lost the
confidence of the armed forces and committed
suicide rather than accept forced resignation.

Voznesensky, Nicholas 1903–50
Russian economist and government official. Joined
the Communist party in 1919 and studied
economics at Svardlov Communist University and
the Economic Institute of Red Professorship, where
he lectured from 1931. In 1934 Voznesensky
became a member of the Soviet Control
Commission and after 1935 worked with Andrey
Zhdanov in Leningrad. In 1938 he became
chairman of Gosplan, the State Planning
Commission, which planned and coordinated
economic activities. He advanced to deputy prime
minister in 1939 and was chief economic planner
in the state defense committee during World War
II. From 1943 Voznesensky was a member of the
Committee for Economic Reconstruction in Former
German Occupied Areas. In 1947 he became a full
Politburo member. Early in 1949 he fell into
disfavor as a colleague of Zhdanov and lost his seat
in the Politburo. He was arrested for supposed
involvement in the Leningrad affair and shot. His
popular book *The War Economy of the USSR During
the Fatherland War* (1947) was declared "anti-
Marxist" by Stalin.

Watson-Watt, Robert Alexander 1892–1973
British pioneer of radar. After graduating in
engineering at Dundee he remained there until
joining the Meteorological Office in London in
1915. There he worked on the radio location of
thunderstorms: this was based on the detection,
with a directional aerial, of the "static" they
generate. Later (1921) he was appointed to the
government's Radio Research Station and then
to the radio division of the Natural Physical
Laboratory. In 1935 he put forward a proposal for
detecting enemy aircraft by means of pulsed radio
signals reflected back from them to a ground base.
Field trials quickly proved its feasibility and, with
war looming, the British government approved the
immediate establishment of a network of radar
stations to give early warning of attack. This
proved of critical importance during the Battle of
Britain in 1940.

Webb, Martha Beatrice & Sidney James (1858–1943 & 1859–1947)
British historians and pioneers of social and
economic reforms who did much to shape social
thought and institutions in England. Beatrice
helped her cousin Charles Booth research his study
The Life and Labour of the People of London and she
went on to publish *The Cooperative Movement in
Great Britain* (1891). Sidney, a civil servant, joined
the Socialist Fabian Society in 1885 and became a
leading member. They married in 1882 and
together published *The History of Trade Unionism*
(1894), *Industrial Democracy* (1897) and *English Local
Government* (9 vols. 1906–29). Sidney reorganized
the University of London and both he and Beatrice
played a leading role in the establishment of the
London School of Economics (1895), founded the
New Statesman (1913) and campaigned for the
reform of the Poor Law. Labour M.P. for Seaham
(1922–29), Sidney became president of the Board of
Trade (1924), Colonial Secretary (1929) and was was
created Lord Passfield (1924). After their retirement
they visited the USSR and subsequently wrote a
number of books on Soviet Communism.

Weissmuller, Johnny 1904–84
US swimmer and film actor. He totaled five gold
medals in the 1924 and 1928 Olympics and set
many freestyle world records. Film stardom came
with his custom-built role in MGM's *Tarzan* series.
Between 1932 and 1948 there were 12 films, starting
with *Tarzan the Ape Man*, and various co-stars
(Maureen O'Sullivan the most sultry pairing).

Welles, Orson 1915–85
US director, producer, screenwriter and actor. He
co-founded the Mercury Theatre in 1937, going on
air in 1938 and engineering a notorious panic with
his broadcast of *The War of the Worlds*. RKO gave
him artistic control for his Hollywood directing
debut: *Citizen Kane* (1941). Many of its startling
effects were not original but he clearly had a
brilliant organizing vision. Judged as bad
box-office, his later work was hampered by studio
interference or finance problems. Credits include
The Magnificent Ambersons (1942), *The Lady from
Shanghai* (1948), *Othello* (1952), *Touch of Evil* (1958),
Chimes at Midnight (1966) and *F for Fake* (1975).

West, Mae 1892–1981
US actress. An entertainer at five, she wrote,
produced and directed her first stage play, *Sex*, in
1926. Jailed for obscenity, she went on to direct
several more of her own plays before going to
Paramount. She was a shrewd woman with a
talent for innuendo and *double entendre*, and her
blowsy persona made her both a sex star and a
parody of that image. Her witticisms became
folklore, and in 1935 she was the highest-paid
woman in the USA. Her films include *She Done
Him Wrong* and *I'm No Angel* (both 1933).

Whittle, Sir Frank 1907–
British aeronautical engineer. As a Royal Air Force
apprentice mechanic he was sent to Cambridge
University where he graduated in mechanical
sciences, and was given a commission. He next
transferred to the RAF School of Aeronautical
Engineering, Henlow (1932–34). He did
postgraduate research in Cambridge (1934–37) and
realized that the future of highspeed flight lay with
the gas turbine. In 1935 Power Jets was set up to
allow him to develop his ideas and by 1937 he had
a prototype engine running. With war looming he
then got massive support from the Air Ministry.
The first British jet-propelled aircraft made its
debut in May 1941. It proved to be too late for such
aircraft to have a significant effect on the course of
the war, but jet propulsion dominated the
development of postwar aviation.

Wright, Frank Lloyd 1869–1959
US architect. Wright studied in Chicago under
Sullivan, the early skyscraper architect, and in 1895
founded Oak Park Studio. In 1904 he first used
reinforced concrete, for an Illinois church. He built
long, low, "prairie houses", like Robie House
(1909), in Chicago's suburbs. He designed Tokyo's
Imperial Hotel, many private houses, the 1938
Broadacre City Project, featuring dispersed
"organic" office buildings, the Johnson Watt Tower
(1950) and New York's Guggenheim Museum
(1957) using a center spiral. Influenced by Art
Nouveau and Japanese styles, Wright believed we
should live closer to nature, in scattered buildings,
and pursued individuality in architecture – houses
such as the *Falling Water* (1936) house bear this out.

Zanuck, Darryl F. 1902–79
US film executive, producer and screenwriter. He
joined Warner Bros as a screenwriter in 1923; by
1929 he was in charge of production and
responsible for the studio's successes in the early
thirties. With Joseph Schenck he formed 20th
Century Pictures in 1933, merging with Fox in
1934, to become a major force in Hollywood. In
1956 he went independent, having his only real
success with *The Longest Day* (1962). In 1962 he
went to the rescue of 20th Century-Fox after
Cleopatra, becoming president and later chairman
with his son also on the board. Both left during
1970–71, with his management style under attack.

Zworykin, Vladimir Kosma 1889–1982
Russian-US physicist. An engineering graduate of
the University of St Petersburg, he served during
World War I as a radio operator. In 1919 he
emigrated to the USA and joined the
Westinghouse Electric Corporation, moving on to
the Radio Corporation of America (RCA) in 1929,
but returning to Westinghouse later. He developed
(in 1923) the first practical storage camera tube
(valve), the iconoscope.

ACKNOWLEDGEMENTS

Picture credits

1 A Komsomol at the wheel, Balakhna, 1931 Arkady Shaikher
2-3 Immigrants from Oklahoma to California, 1937 LC
4-5 Busby Berkeley *Gold Diggers of 1933* APL
7 The Grand Coallee Dam LC
8-9 A school for brides, Germany SV
10-11 Nuremburg rally, FPG International, N.Y.
46-47 Abandoned farmstead after duststorm, 1937 Oklahoma HDC
82-83 A "Hooverville" on the outskirts of Seattle, USA Special Collections Division, University of Washington Library Photo: Lee
118-119 Finale of Broadway Melody, 1938 KC

15 PF **16-17** HDC **17t** Arthur Lockwood **17c** David Low **18** Alexander Meledin **19t** ICP Library of Photographers, N.Y. **19b, 20-21** ILON **20t** HDC **20b, 21t** IKON **21c** FSP **21b** CP **23** M/David Seymour **24tl** HDC **24tr** IKON **24br** IWM **25t** M/Rene Burri **25b** HDC **26** PF **26-27** M/Robert Capa **27tr** Centro Internacional de la Historia, Barcelona **27br** M/Robert Capa **29** Tom Benton **30** Museum of Modern Art, N.Y. **31** New School for Social Research, N.Y. Joseph Martin/Scala/Art Resource © DAC 1990 **32t** AA **32b** TPS **33** Bildarchiv Preussischer Kulturbesitz **34** Dr. Franz Stoedtner, Dusseldorf **35l** IWM **35r** Zeitgeschichtliche Bildarchive Heinrich Hoffmann, Munich **36** BFI Stills, Posters and Designs **36-37** Bridgeman Art Library/Museo del Prado, Madrid © DACS 1990 **37** The Library, University College London, George Orwell Archives **38t** Lee Miller Archives **38b** BFI Stills, Posters and Designs **39** M/Inge Morath **40** Lee Miller Archives **40-41** Wadsworth Atheneum, Hartford, The Ella Gallup Sumner and Mary Catlin Sumner Collection © DACS 1990 **41** Yad Vashem, Jerusalem **42** CPI **42-43** BFI Stills, Posters and Designs **44-45** Library and Museum of the Performing Arts, Lincoln Center, New York Public Library **45** BFI Stills, Posters and Designs **51** Fotomas Index **52-53** TPS **53t** HDG **53b** PF **54t** Mainichi Newspapers **54b** Newspaper Library **55, 56t** HDC **56b** TPS **57t** Ullstein Bilderdienst **57b** HDC **58-59** Arthur Rothstein/Dover Pictorial Archive Series **59t** LC **59b** Glenbow Archives **61** Brown Brothers **62t** PF **62b** HDC **63** Canadian High Commission **64tl** MEPL **64-65** HDC **65** CPI **66** PF **67** Aramco **68-69** Robert Hunt Library **68** MEPL **69t** PF **69c** SPL/US Department of Defense **69b** CP **71** Lenin Library, Moscow **72** Consolidated Edison Company of New York Inc. **73t, 73b** AA **74t** Texaco **74b** British Petroleum Co Ltd. **74-75** Millbrook House Collection **75** U.S. Army **76t** SV **76b** AA **77** Willard R. Culver **77 inset** Hagley Museum and Library **78** Institut Curie Archives **79l** SPL **79r** Cavendish Laboratory, Cambridge **80t** Arkady Sajaket **80b** John Hillelson/Marc Riboud **80-81** Fotomas Index **81tl** Ivan Sajin **81bl** PF **81r** Bettmann Newsphotos **87** LC **88** AA **88-89** LC **90** PF **91t** Weimar Archive **91c** Robert Hunt Library **91b** Edimedia **92t** Bodleian Library **92b** RV **93** M/H. Cartier Bresson **94l** RV **94r** Collection of Beryl Williams, University of Sussex **95** MEPL **96, 97** PF **98** SV **98-99** Roman Vishniac **99t** FSP **99c** Juhan Kuus **99b** Richard and Sally Greenhill **101** LC **102** AA **103t** Beryl Williams **103b** RV **104t** AA **104b** SV **105** MEPL **106-107** M/Robert Capa **107** HDC **108t** The Robert Opie Collection **108b** Courtesy of Mitchell Beazley **108-109** CPI **109t** FSP **109c** M/Raghu Rai **109b** M/Eve Arnold **110-111** RV **111** AA **112** LC **113t** CP **113b** AA **114-115** The British Library **115t** M/H. Cartier Bresson **115b** HDC **116** Deutsche-Afrika Linien **116-117** HDC **117** PF **123t** AA **123b** Chicago Historical Society **124** CP **1125** Metropolitan Museum of Art, N.Y. **126** APL **127t** FP **126-127b** SV **128l** TPS **128r** RV **129** Freemans Ltd. **130-131** John Smallwood/FP **130bl,br,bc** AA **131t** CP **131c** KC **131b** AA **133** CP **134** PF **135tl, 135 tr** CP **135b** HDC **137** SV **138, 139, 140-141b** KC **140** CP **141t** APL **142t** Wisconsin Center for Film and Theater Research **142b** BFI Stills, Posters and Designs **143t, 143b** KC **144** APL **145l** KC **145r** BFI, Stills, Posters and Designs **146-147, 146bl, 147tl, 147ttr, 147br** Rex

Features **148-149** Adler Planetarium, Chicago **148t** KC **148bl** Donald K. Yeomans, California Institute of Technology **148br** MEPL **149t** KC **149b** Boeing Aerospace Company **151** HDC **152** Saturday Evening Post **152l** MEPL **152-153** PF **153t** SV **154l** AA **154c** CP **154r, 155l** PF **155c** AA **155r, 156l** HDC **156c** PF **156r** IKON **157l** HDC **157c** KC **158l** FPG International **158c** Val Wilmer **158r** PF **159l** AA **159c** PF **159r** Barbara Morgan **160l** Lucien Aigner **160c** KC **160r** Ida Karr Archives **161l** PF **161c, 161r** HDC **152l** M/Robert Capa **162c** Novosti **162r** APL **163l** HDC **163c, 163r** PF **164l** TPS **164r** BFI Stills, Posters and Designs **165l, 165c** PF **165r** CP **166l** SV **166c** PF **166r** HDC **167l** Novosti **167c** PF **167r** HDC **168l** Arthur Lockwood **168r** PF **169l** HDC **169c** AA **169r, 170l, 170c** PF **170r** AA **171l** HDC **171r** KC

Abbreviations

AAZ	Andromeda Archive
APL	Aquarius Pictuure Library, E. Sussex, UK
BFI	British Film Institute, London
CP	Camera Press, London
CPI	Culver Pictures Inc, New York
FP	Futile Press, Brighton
FSP	Frank Spooner Pictures, London
HDC	Hulton Deutsch Collection, London
IWM	Imperial War Museum, London
KC	Kobal Collection, London
LC	Library of Congress, Washington DC
M	Magnum Photos, London
MEPL	Mary Evans Picture Library, London
PF	Popperfoto, Northampton, UK
RV	Roger Viollet, Paris
SPL	Science Photo Library, London
SV	Suddeutscher Verlag, Munich
TPS	Topham Picture Source, Kent, UK

t = top, tl = top left, tr = top right, c = center, b = bottom etc.

Editorial and Research Assistance
Steven Chapman, Mary Davies, Jackie Gaff, Jane Higgins, John Horgan, Louise Jones, Nick Law, Andy Overs, Mike Pinchcombe, Maria Quantrill, Graham Speake, Michelle von Ahn

Artists
Alan Hollingberry, Ayala Kingsley, Kevin Maddison, Colin Salmon

Design Assistance
Cyndy Gossert, Nicholas Rous, Dave Smith, Del Tolton

Photographs
Shirley Jamieson, David Pratt

Typesetting
Brian Blackmore, Catherine Boyd, Anita Wright

Production
Stephen Elliott, Clive Sparling

Cartography
Maps drafted by Euromap, Pangbourne; Alan Mais (Hornchurch); Sarah Rhodes

Color origination
J. Film Process, Bangkok; Scantrans, Singapore

INDEX

Page numbers in *italics* refer to illustrations or their captions and to datafile captions. **Bold** numbers refer to special or ancillary text features.